Animals in American Literature

Animals
in American
Literature

MARY ALLEN

UNIVERSITY OF ILLINOIS PRESS

Urbana Chicago London

© 1983 by the Board of Trustees of the University of Illinois
Manufactured in the United States of America

This book is printed on acid-free paper.

Library of Congress Cataloging in Publication Data

Allen, Mary, 1939-
    Animals in American literature.

    Includes index.
    1. American literature—History and criticism.
    2. Animals in literature.   I. Title.
    PS169.A54A44   1983   810'.9'36   82–17369
    ISBN 0-252-00975-4

For
Ralph
and
Fozdick

Contents

Animals in American Literature

Introduction

Animals[1] have served literature well. They have stood as allegorical figures to represent human nature and as a rich body of metaphors for the inanimate as well as the animate. Beyond their figurative uses, animals have been man's servants, his companions, the objects of his hunt, and the food on his table. And sometimes they have been allowed to play their own parts.

Before man could write he drew pictures of animals on the walls of caves in paint made of their blood, figures that transcend time in their immediacy.[2] Man looked to the heavens and saw animals sketched in the stars. The spirit that could make the corn grow was envisioned as a bull, a wolf, or even a dog. Animal properties were imagined to be magically transferred to man: he thought if he stepped on a tortoise, his feet would be made hard.[3] The totem animal, taken as the tribal ancestor of a clan, was looked to as its tutelary spirit and protector. Whether as the earliest subjects of art and worship or as the later symbolic images of a culture, animal figures tell of a people's values. The Egyptians bowed to the bull. And the Christians gave us the lamb.

Animals remain a source of awe. Their means of locomotion, self-defense—the way they *look*—are incredible. But man's relationship with them is complex, often paradoxical. He would have their powers but would not be called an animal. Primitive man drank a beast's blood for vitality, then apologized for slaying it. Modern man reveres what is free and must possess it.

Beyond man's language, animals appeal to the symbol-making mind. They were initially established and still are usually seen as representative images in literature. It was in the sixth century B.C. that the legendary Aesop is said to have composed his fables. The collection of tales from which the medieval bestiaries derived, the *Physiologus,* came in the second century, giving a mystic meaning to each of fifty legends of animals and natural objects. Animals were epitomized by a single characteristic—the industry of the ant, the cunning of the fox, the majesty of the lion. Such stereotyping served a definite moral end. Yet it also reflects cultural and aesthetic biases. In the East, the placid cow is revered—in the motion-loving West, the horse.

As the beast fable and the bestiary gave way to the humanism of the Renaissance and the metaphorical language that centered on man, the basic symbolic values of the earlier period were retained. The animal simile became so prevalent during the late fifteenth and sixteenth centuries that natural history was "ransacked" for material to illustrate everyday experiences.[4] Caroline Spurgeon finds in her study of Shakespeare's imagery, based on the premise that analogy holds the spirit of the universe, that the second largest category of Shakespearean metaphors (after references to the human body) is birds—not for their form or their song but for their flight. It was the life of things which most enchanted Shakespeare,[5] and that life in his work is unimaginable without the allusions to animals, over 4,000 of them.[6]

The power of Shakespeare's animal metaphors is felt through realistic detail and a keen compassion for suffering creatures. Yet as Elizabethan drama assumes a metaphorical view of the universe around man, most of Shakespeare's references to animals are figurative. The sharpness of the serpent's tooth is of interest as it illustrates human ingratitude. *King Lear* needs no real snakes. Even Richard III's "My kingdom for a horse!"—indeed, a call for an actual horse—is rather a revelation of the man's desperation than a focus on the animal.

As the age of satire presented a diminished version of man, the animal metaphor served a specific message of disdain. Swift's human race is equated to "odious vermin." But he also satirizes the happy beast tradition of seventeenth-century France, in which animals were considered equal or superior to man because of their naturalness. The Houyhnhnms, who have only the bodies of horses and not their other characteristics, excel not as animals but as beings with extraordinary powers of reason.

The eighteenth century also saw the development of the non-human narrator in the novel, based on the rationale of the fifth-century B.C. philosophy of metempsychosis, the transmigration of souls. The use of the animal's point of view became the target of satire in France, most vividly with the minuscule creatures who could see all, a satire reaching the epitome of coarseness in such a work as *Memoirs and Adventures of a Flea.*[7] The humanitarian movement to prevent cruelty to animals of this period, however, led to a more sympathetic version of their point of view. By the nineteenth century a literature for children had developed that presents the animal's own account of his suffering. Black Beauty draws tears for the abused cab horse. Such a sympathetic rendering of the animal has become a standard feature of juvenile fiction (as well as a temptation to those who would present animals realistically but with compassion).

The romantic literature of the late eighteenth and early nineteenth centuries, with its intent to free man physically as well as spiritually, epitomizes the spirit of the new freedom in the symbolic bird. While suggested as an actual bird, this romantic figure is distant, impalpable, even static. The nightingale lives primarily in the imagination. In a study of the modern bestiary Christopher Nash points out that when actual animals are referred to by the romantics, even in their more vivid roles, Blake's tiger and Coleridge's albatross, for example, they are not alive. For the romantic, the more "terrestrial" the creature, "the less worthy of the poet's song it is."[8]

The realism that superseded romanticism focused for the most part on social man, an increasingly urban man, a context in which animals play little part. While realism follows no particular style, the tendency is away from symbolism, in some cases away from metaphor altogether; thus the figurative animal occurs less frequently than before. With naturalism, the metaphor of man *as* beast in an urban jungle is a standard feature—Frank Norris's brute McTeague and O'Neill's hairy ape. Yet the animals themselves are rarely featured.

As science, psychology, art, and new kinds of mass communication have reestablished the worship of symbols in the twentieth century, the earlier symbology of animals is revived. Joyce's Dedalus, based on the Greek artisan ordered to design an elaborate cage for the Cretan Minotaur, confronts the labyrinth of the unconscious as "a human structure fabricated to contain and withhold an animal core."[9] Reverting to the fable, Kafka creates his unforgettable image of modern man—Gregor Samsa as a beetle swept into the trash.

The metaphorical far outnumber the literal animals in literature. But actual ones do appear from time to time in their own right. If they also serve a symbolic function, the power of the symbol depends on how vivid the actual animal is. While some types of literature, the fable, for one, preclude the development of realistic animals, no genre or literary movement has made particular use of them. They are invited in rather at the inclination of the individual author, whether he be classic or romantic, poet or novelist. Poetry has most often featured the bird, while fiction's favorite is the pet dog—*the* loyal, obedient companion, who offers a satisfaction untainted by the complexities of human relationships. Thomas Mann's "A Man and His Dog," for example, centers on the "dumb paean of joy"[10] the dog Bashan brings his master. The source of this happy connection is attributed to the patriarchal instinct of the dog to honor the man as his absolute master.

One of the most moving accounts of an animal in all literature is the scene in *The Odyssey* when Odysseus comes home. His son thinks he is a beggar in town, and his wife requires proof of identity. Only the dog knows him: "Here lay the dog, this Argos, full of fleas. Yet even now, seeing Odysseus near, he wagged his tail and dropped both ears, but toward his master he had not strength to move. Odysseus turned aside and wiped away a tear." Argos does not represent anything but himself, nor would we wish him to. He acts as a dog acts, and that is enough.

While the animal simile is far more prevalent than the literal animal in Greek poetry, regard for the physical world is reflected in a view that is not primarily metaphorical. In a study of Homer's perception of reality Paolo Vivante makes the case that the function of the Homeric simile is to stress the essential nature of the subject, not to suggest other possibilities. If warriors are said to move like scared fawns, it is simply their common response to fear which the simile presents. For Homer things exist in their own right, "with nothing to sustain them but their solitary power and the earth upon which they stand."[11] This process works in the reverse of the symbolic approach in which the tangible is a sign of a superior spiritual realm. The Greek passion for this world is suggestive of the spirit with which many actual animals are portrayed in modern literature. The brilliantly intellectual art of our time rarely offers such feeling. But where animals are, so is emotion. It is worth reading about them for that refreshment alone.

It was to the actual animals that Aristotle turned in the classification which was the beginning of natural science, *The History of Animals*. Although much factual information was available, it is probable that many accounts of remote species came through the limited descriptions of explorers. In fact, by the thirteenth century Europeans still knew of the rhinoceros only through Marco Polo's description of "lion-horns."[12] To illustrate fables of exotic animals, the miniaturists used the familiar bodies of dogs and horses and added a fabulous version of teeth or tails.[13] In this way many fantastic creatures came into being. Still, man's creations did not outdo the uncanny subjects in nature.

The commencement of modern zoology in the sixteenth century heightened the artist's interest but at the same time enhanced many a zoological fable. Sir Thomas Browne continued in the belief that mice were generated by wheat, and Milton reaffirmed that creation is a process rising up miraculously from slime and mud. Investigations by the newly established Royal Society set forth ideas such as parthenogenesis, which led to the belief that as the creator of art forms his work, so are animals brought into mysterious being. In *Hudibras* Butler supports the notion that the baby bear is created as the mother licks lumps of matter into shape.[14] As scientific fact did take hold, the literary artist became more precise, although rather with the approach of the naturalist, who sees the creature whole in his habitat, than the scientist, who dissects.

As the old hierarchy of the kingdoms toppled with Charles Darwin, and the belief in human dominion over the animal lost its force, the creatures consequently loomed into a new place. Darwin's intent was not to reduce man; only one line in *On the Origin of Species* even suggests that light might be shed on human origins. He intended rather to "ennoble and humanize animals." Stanley Edgar Hyman describes *Origin* as a scientific argument that reads like a dramatic poem in which animals are the actors.[15] It is one of the ironic twists of history that an appreciative view of animals was reversed in the image of man as ape. But if Darwin's ideas were received in a spirit contrary to his own, he did succeed in raising animals to a more important place than they had occupied for centuries.

Man's ambivalent relationship with animals has raised many an intriguing issue. If man and beast commit the same vicious deeds, are they not similarly responsible? This line of reasoning led to the bizarre practice of criminal prosecution and capital punishment of animals, dating from the ninth century. Sentences were inflicted by secular tribunals on pigs, cows, and horses for the crime of homicide; judicial proceedings of ecclesiastical courts against rats, mice, locusts, and weevils resulted in exorcisms and excommunication. It was believed that if domestic animals were not punished for homicide, devils would take possession of them and their masters. In the sixteenth century a French jurist made his reputation as a counsel for rats charged with eating a barley crop, successfully arguing that the rats summoned to appear were prevented by serious perils, "owing to the unwearied vigilance of their mortal enemies, the cats." As late as 1906 in Switzerland two men and a dog were convicted of murder. The men were sentenced to life imprisonment, and the dog was condemned to death.[16]

If primitive man was mystified as to his kinship with animals, the Bible of his literate descendants did little to eliminate the confusion. The distinction between man and the other creatures in Genesis as the creation evolves from whale to man is not a moral one, a fact not lost on Darwinists. While all creatures are said to be good, as God's creations, some are worthier than others. The animal in man, on the other hand, is vile. Man is commanded to be master over the other creatures (although he is commanded otherwise not to kill), and yet elaborate Levitical laws must be followed in using animals for subsistence (e.g., only true ruminants, animals with four-chambered stomachs, were considered clean enough to eat). The practice of animal sacrifice is a more difficult concept still, presenting the idea of a father's sacrifice of his son, the killing of a God.

The revolutionary doctrine of Christianity is impressively captured in the image of the lamb, in sharp contrast to the representatives of power and fertility held by many cultures. For the nomadic Hebrews, sheep were an economic necessity, used for meat, milk, and wool. The choice of this domestic animal rather than an exotic one is both natural and appropriate to the modesty of Christ's image and message. Sheep are good followers. As the worthiest creatures in the Bible, lambs and sheep are mentioned oftener than any other, 742 times.[17] Frequency of mention, then, is evidently an important indication of worth. But does this mean that the one familiar animal missing in God's creation is so despicable as not to be mentioned even once in a work where the pygarg, chamois, and wanderoo are given a place? In the Bible there is not a single cat![18]

If the gentle lamb is first in value to illustrate the New Testament ethic, creatures as they are arranged by power and beauty on the chain of being also operate as symbolic figures in both the Old and the New Testaments. Leviathan's enormity is cause alone for respect, despite his destructiveness. The lion is used to represent both the Lord and Satan. The paradox Blake poses in bringing tiger and lamb together is never rationalized in the Bible. Not only is the power ethic of the Old Testament never fully reconciled with the code of humility in the New, but animals are placed in striking aesthetic and traditional patterns as well as didactic ones. The moral sense attributed to animals, and it is impossible to take them amorally in a work whose every line is instructive, is never clear.

Although the Bible raises many confusing issues regarding animals, it unquestionably places humankind above the other creatures in the hierarchy of being. Man's deposition from that place as a result of the Darwinian revolution, with its inescapable impact on literary characters, has received substantial critical attention. But little has been said of how that shift affects the place of animals in literature—not so much that their nature is revised as that their position in regard to man is vastly altered. Nash makes the case from examples of prominent animals in the twentieth-century novel that man is no longer the supreme animal. The Great Chain of Being is reversed so that the realm of the beast lies above that of man, a realm of the "super-natural" that may be attained only through nature, not, as formerly supposed, through culture.[19]

It was during the Darwinian awakening that the first great blossoming of American literature took place. No evolutionist himself, Melville wrote rather in reaction to the developing argument that man was to be deposed. But he did use Darwin's account of species in the Galapagos Islands as a source for "The Encantadas" and was much influenced by the revolutionary theories of Lyell and Chambers as well. It is no coincidence that, eight years before *On the Origin of Species* appeared, the biggest creature on earth should become a major character—pursued by angry, shrinking man—in the mightiest American novel of the century. However supreme Moby Dick became as a symbol, he rides first as an actual whale.

The fact that Moby Dick looms at the center of American fiction in mid-nineteenth century America, while Dickens was writing of the working conditions of the poor, illustrates the diverse national concerns. The commonplace that Americans write of the individual, freedom, and violence while the British deal with society, domesticity, and manners is dramatized by the presence of *wild* animals in American literature, a phenomenon that has scarcely been noted.

An astonishing number of actual animals play impressive roles in American literature. No other national literature makes them so important. Those discussed in this book were selected from among the most prominent examples in works by major authors. As the animals are referred to in the literature most often by the personal pronoun (almost always male), so are they designated here. (In those cases where the impersonal pronoun is used, the author's intention to objectify will usually be evident.) The focus on literal animals here is meant to raise issue with the literary assumption that they must stand for something else. And they are, emphatically, distinct from mineral and plant aspects of *nature,* a term that for too long has been used in literary criticism as a general reference to the out-of-doors, as if there were no difference between a bird and the branch he sits on—between active and passive. These animals are alive.

The pastoral convention tended to make all aspects of nature similarly serene and harmonious: no storms, no mosquitoes, no violence. The out-of-doors is a place more for contemplation than for action. The complete angler goes fishing for peace, not for struggle. In the poetry of British romantics nature is usually something seen from inside the house so that features are indistinct. Even inside Wordsworth's woods the atmosphere is as calm as that of a well-ordered living room. It is not disturbed by the movements of animals, certainly nothing savage.

Such a tradition is followed in America by such poets as Freneau and Bryant. Whitman is as much at home in his poetry with the wild animal as the tame, yet his harmonious approach to nature links him to the pastoral tradition as well. The "peaceable kingdom" predominates for animals in American art, according to a study by Mary Haverstock, although the "howling wilderness" does offer a strong countertradition.[20]

The overwhelming appeal in the literature, however, is for the tangibility and ferocity of the new land. As Henry Nash Smith has pointed out, firsthand reports of the frontier did much to dispel the myth of an edenic garden.[21] The retreat is to the wilderness, but not for peace—for challenge and profit. Cooper's hero is a hunter, not a singer of love songs. And when Hemingway's characters take their "pastoral retreat," it is to duel with an animal. The challenge of nature is epitomized through confrontations with bold creatures who stand out as distinctly from tree and lake as man himself. The animals come close enough to show their delicate coloring, their texture, to look man in the eye. Close enough to grab.

These animals have lives of their own. In one of the few examinations of different ways animals appear in literature, W. H. Auden lists the figurative uses (fable, simile, and allegory); the romantic encounter, in which animals provide a stimulus to man but have no feelings and are not realistically described; and the animal as the object of human interest and affection.[22] But he notes no category in which the animal's own dramatic role operates as the instigator of man's actions or where they are equals. Yet the animal has emerged as a powerful actor in the drama, bringing about significant responses from man. This view is in direct opposition to the commonly held notion that nineteenth-century romanticism was the last great occurrence of nature in literature. In both the nineteenth and twentieth centuries American authors classified as transcendentalist, realist, determinist, imagist, and existentialist, as well as those who fall in no category, have developed important realistic animals. The realism with which these animals are depicted by writers as unlike as Jack London and Marianne Moore has little to do with the term *literary realism,* which suggests a time period or even a sordid view of man. But it does contain a sense of wonder for the actual.

These realistic animals are wild, terrestrial beings. Many are big and violent, though their spirit is more important than their force. They are usually disciplined, clean, and utilitarian. They are celibate males, free or fighting to be free. And they are markedly independent. The favorites are the big fish (including the mammal, the whale), the bird on the ground, the untamed dog, animals with tough hides, and the horse. Of these only the horse has been a favorite traditional subject for the artist. Kenneth Clark states that for the painter the horse is "without question the most satisfying piece of formal relationship in nature." Because the painter who was required to flatter people in his painting was not under the obligation to do so with animals, "the realism of animals came as a pleasant change from the monotonous idealism of Hellenistic figure sculpture."[23] The horse as a central literary subject, however, came much later, after the time when it was most important in society. Except for myths and legends, few stories with the horse as a central figure existed before the opening of the West in frontier America.[24]

America's affair with the frontier is clearly behind the appeal of untamed animals. And surely the dramatic possibilities of conquering the beast surpass those of a battle with the elements alone. One may survive a storm, but he can look his prey in the eye. Conquest of another creature and economic gain were brought together in the whaling industry of the 1850s and in the fur trade, which took men to the western horizon and to the top of the world before they ever went for gold. For the lover of frontiers, whether he be abroad or at home, the untamed is salubrious, a "tonic of wildness," as Thoreau put it. He sensed a "strange thrill of savage delight" when a woodchuck crossed his path and was "tempted to seize and devour him raw." As unlike Hemingway in tone as Thoreau is, he finds the same purifying effects in the conquest of the wild animal. In contrast to Emerson's cool symbolic nature, Thoreau's flesh-and-blood version is savagely alive. He speaks for others who write of animals when he says, "I love the wild not less than the good."[25]

If to be wild is good, to become domesticated is to sell out to a master. Pets are a rarity, and those who do live under a human's roof may yet exhibit their wildness—the cat in a deliciously fierce attack. Examples from juvenile literature illustrate this point as well. The beasts of Tarzan's jungle are extravagantly ferocious (while those of Kipling, Burroughs's British counterpart, are civilized). If Lassie had been an American creation, instead of a Yorkshire dog who wants nothing more than to find her way back to an English hearth, the story might be *Lassie Leaves Home*. The primeval Buck in *Call of the Wild* is rather the hero in American fiction. And *The Black Stallion,* a classic fantasy of boy and horse on a deserted island, shows the ideal companion to be the "wildest of all wild animals," whose nature is "to kill or be killed."[26] Back at a New York race track, the horse is as ferocious as ever, attacking another horse at the starting gate. The black stallion makes Black Beauty look like a pussy cat.

Where the untamed reigns, the cultivation of the mind is suspect. The anti-intellectual strain in American literature, which makes books anathema and learning the work of the devil—Hawthorne's evil scientists, Melville's rigidly bookish Captain Vere—perpetuates the notion that one should be wary of the brain. The savagery of animals is pure in contrast to the convolutions of man's mind. One of the most appreciated qualities of animals is that they are beyond language. That they feel but do not require conversation is a great relief to most people. Language cannot be trusted, even by those who use it most carefully. When Hemingway's Frederick Henry renounces abstractions as a form of falsehood, he speaks not as a disbeliever in matters of the spirit but as one who distrusts the articulation of them. Animals do not lie.

In American literature animals offer a type of purity that rarely conflicts with violence but does require chastity. Their most peculiar characteristic is the avoidance of sexual activity—even the absence of desire. Virility is assumed in most cases, but mating is as much to be avoided by the animal as by the human character. Even Moby Dick, for all his Freudian critics, is not a participant. When a whale's organ is described, it is that of a dead whale. The great white whale rides alone, with a whole sea to put between himself and the lady whales. His mating activities are properly behind him. Animals are generally beyond sexual activity, by age or makeup or because of other interests. Emily Dickinson's robins are gentlemen singers; Mark Twain likes the mule; Jack London's dogs would rather eat; Marianne Moore's animals are too well covered; and John Steinbeck's turtle must travel. Richard Wright's creatures are driven beyond the privilege of mating. And just as William Faulkner's racehorse lives to run, not mate, Ernest Hemingway's bulls reserve their energy for the fight.

A comparison of these animals with those of D. H. Lawrence emphasizes the antisexual quality in the American works. Lawrence's creatures ooze sensuality, either as sexual participants or as phallic symbols. His whales roll together lusciously in an open sea, in hedonistic contrast to the sober celibacy of Moby Dick. Lawrence's horses are quite obviously representatives of the healthy sexual life he offers as the cure of modern man's ills. The major British writer of the modern period, perhaps ever, who makes greatest use of literal animals, Lawrence gained his interest in horses when he became a horseman in New Mexico. Only after that period did he raise the horse to apocalyptic proportions, a development which could not have been suspected in his philosophical writings before that time.[27] In reading Lawrence one returns to the traditional suggestion of potency assumed with so much iconography of animals. By one definition, *animal* means carnal. That so many significant male animals exist in American literature with so little sexual suggestion, except to the reader who will find it every-where, is the strangest fact about them.

With animals, the American writer might have released Puritan inhibition and shown lust without guilt. But that did not happen. Perhaps the notion that sex is nasty goes too deep. More important, since the sexual encounter has traditionally been connected with the idea of family and responsibility to a remarkable degree in America, the absence or avoidance of mating is necessary for the greater value of *freedom*. As the American hero (created by such settled married men as Cooper and Twain) is not only free of marriage but free of sex urges—Natty Bumppo escapes the woman and Huckleberry Finn isn't interested—so is the animal. The compelling reason for avoiding mating is that freedom is preferred above all else. In the American myth there is no greater threat to liberty than a mate. Not even animals can have both.

Animals are enviably free in their motion. How fine it would be to swim far and deep through endless seas. To run with the thunder of wild horses. To fly. Even to buzz off. Locomotion is close to the heart of energy-loving America. But perhaps even more critical is what animals are free *from*. As Lawrence has observed, the concern with freedom in American literature is likely to take the form of retreat. Animals are free from social connections, free from words. And they are free from the guilt of the hero who may willingly have chosen his liberty but who feels damned for doing so. The freedom of animals holds no ambivalence; they will fight for it against hook, harness, and cage. "The muskrat will gnaw his third leg off to be free."[28]

The animal's integrity rests in his stoic independence. Without excuses, without complaints, he is. Alone he maintains his place in the universe and follows his personal course. Where he is restrained, he rebels. The massive animal asserts himself most dramatically—a whale overturning a whaler, a bear hurling off a pack of dogs, a lion with a bullet in him rising to charge. But the smaller animals define their place with the same tough integrity. Dickinson's bee has as much sense of himself as Moby Dick. A mule hangs tight to a mountainside, against all admonition to move on. And a single turtle heads west. The gesture may be offensive or defensive, but it is willed by an individual being facing the perils and refreshments of this earth. Free of family and culture, such American creations are these. They have no masters.

Notes

1. The term *animal* in this study refers to any member of the animal kingdom as distinguished from man.

2. Hugh Kenner maintains in *The Pound Era* (Berkeley and Los Angeles: University of California Press, 1971), p. 29, that interest in cave paintings of animals "may one day seem the seminal force in modern art history."

3. Sir James George Frazer, *The New Golden Bough,* ed. Theodor H. Gaster (New York: Criterion Books, 1959), p. 56.

4. Percy Ansell Robin, *Animal Lore in English Literature,* 2d ed. (Norwood, Pa.: Norwood Editions, 1975), p. 19.

5. Caroline Frances Eleanor Spurgeon, *Shakespeare's Imagery and What It Tells Us* (Cambridge: Cambridge University Press, 1935), pp. 48, 50.

6. Robert Martin Moore, "Toward a Definition of Man and a Clarification of the Paradox of the Happy Beast: An Analysis of the Animal Imagery and Man-Animal Analogy in *Gulliver's Travels"* (Dissertation, Kent State University, 1971), p. 44.

7. Richard Kilburn Meeker, "Experiments in Point of View: Animal, Vegetable, and Mineral Narrators in the Eighteenth-Century English Novel" (Dissertation, University of Pennsylvania, 1955), pp. 16, 61.

8. Christopher Weston Nash, "A Modern Bestiary: Representative Animal Motifs in the Encounter between Nature and Culture in the English, American, French and Italian Novel, 1900–1950" (Dissertation, New York University, 1970), p. 17.

9. Lars Charles Mazzola, "Labyrinthos: The Animal as Generative Center in the Life and Work of James Joyce" (Dissertation, University of Minnesota, 1975), p. 8.

10. "A Man and His Dog," in *Death in Venice and Seven Other Stories,* trans. H. T. Lowe-Porter (New York: Alfred A. Knopf, 1936), p. 272.

11. Paolo Vivante, *The Homeric Imagination: A Study of Homer's*

Poetic Perception of Reality (Bloomington: Indiana University Press, 1970), p. 79.

12. Ronald Albert Marchant, *Beasts of Fact and Fable* (New York: Roy Publishers, 1962), p. 59.

13. Francis J. Carmody, trans., *Physiologus* (San Francisco: Book Club of California, 1953), p. 7.

14. Robin, pp. 19–20, 29.

15. Stanley Edgar Hyman, *The Tangled Bank: Darwin, Marx, Frazer and Freud As Imaginative Writers* (New York: Atheneum, 1962), pp. 16, 36.

16. Edward Payson Evans, *The Criminal Prosecution and Capital Punishment of Animals* (London: William Heinemann, 1906), pp. 2, 6, 334.

17. Lulu Ramsey Wiley, *Bible Animals* (New York: Vantage Press, 1957), p. 370.

18. Ibid., p. 187. Speculation is that the onus against the cat was based on the Egyptians' worship of it.

19. Nash, p. 328.

20. Mary Sayre Haverstock, *An American Bestiary* (New York: Harry N. Abrams, 1979), p. 33.

21. Henry Nash Smith, *Virgin Land: The American West As Symbol and Myth* (Cambridge, Mass.: Harvard University Press, 1950).

22. *The Dyer's Hand and Other Essays* (New York: Random House, 1962), pp. 300–302.

23. Kenneth Clark, *Animals and Men* (New York: William Morrow, 1977), pp. 36, 26.

24. Ned E. Hoopes, *The Wonderful World of Horses* (New York: Dell, 1966), p. 12.

25. Henry David Thoreau, *Walden and Other Writings of Henry David Thoreau,* ed. Brooks Atkinson (New York: Random House, 1937), p. 189.

26. Walter Farley, *The Black Stallion* (New York: Random House, 1941), p. 24.

27. Kenneth B. Inniss, "D. H. Lawrence's Bestiary: A Study of His Use of Animal Trope and Symbol" (Dissertation, University of Kansas, 1965), pp. 93, 168.

28. Thoreau, p. 59.

CHAPTER 1

"God created great whales, and
. . . saw that it was good."
—Genesis

The Incredible
Whale:
Herman Melville

The burden of proof in *Moby-Dick* (1851) lies not with the persuasion that a whale may represent inscrutable nature, evil, God, or whatever else comes to the human mind. This remote giant has always been a subject for the imagination. Because the whale is more often the source of rumor than observation, and so fantastic when encountered, the more strenuous task is to make the world's largest creature believable. Melville seeks to establish "in all respects the reasonableness of the whole story of the White Whale, more especially the catastrophe. For this is one of those disheartening instances where truth requires full as much bolstering as error. So ignorant are most landsmen of some of the plainest and most palpable wonders of the world, that without some hints touching the plain facts, historical and otherwise, of the fishery, they might scout at Moby Dick as a monstrous fable, or still worse and more detestable, a hideous and intolerable allegory."[1]

The idealistic view of nature that was Melville's literary inheritance spawned a placid, nostalgic version of the sea such as the popular "The Sea! The Sea! the open Sea! / The blue, the fresh, the ever free!"[2] Having lived the harsh life of a seaman and possessing an uncommon appreciation for factual truth, Melville grants us a keener vision in *Moby-Dick,* whose power rises from the concrete evidence that was lacking in his earlier works. One of the realistic accounts before him was Dana's *Two Years before the Mast* (1840), which Melville applauds because it "impairs the relish with which we read Byron's spiritual 'Address to the Ocean.' "[3] In *Moby-Dick,* along with supernatural interrogations, Melville sets out to give the physical world its due and to accept its amoral law. Ahab's contortion of a whale into a symbol of universal malice not only bends the man with hate but constrains the fullness of this world. That his life hinges on vengeance to the creature is a backhanded tribute. But Ishmael's openness to the phenomenon of the whale, the I-thou connection that allows for the integrity of the other, brings the greater truth.

Melville's ambition to make the seemingly ubiquitous whale reasonable is accommodated by his extraordinary open-mindedness to various kinds of evidence. Going beyond tales of whales, he turns to dictionaries, histories, ships' logs, speeches, newspaper accounts, Darwin's journals, and scientific classifications. If his undertaking to unite dissociated sensibilities, in a time when the splits were widening, does not produce a smooth novel, it yields a work rich with the complications of truth. Comparing the unfolding of his chapters to the growth of branches on a tree makes a useful analogy for a better understanding of the makeup of this strangely fashioned work. But rather than following the smooth and inevitable development that usually occurs in the organism, this structure fuses the flawed materials of intellect and imagination. God created his whale easily in a day. The author shows us the wrenching difficulty of the task.

To introduce the whale is the word's etymology, an initial strike for objectivity through denotation. By naming *whale* in thirteen tongues, Melville establishes not only that the animal is a world citizen but that definitions from far-removed lands note a similar quality: the whale's tendency "to roll" (1). If a story about the pursuit of whales most brilliantly dramatizes their violent defense, a return to this gentle verb should balance that view with what is more regularly the case, the whale at his ease, undisturbed by human pursuers.

Melville gradually builds his literal whale alongside the myths of whales, later showing the view from the outside working back in.

First comes the skeleton, the whale's jawbone jutting from the beams of the Spouter-Inn. This version of creation not only allows for comic potential but raises epistemological issues: when is an organism itself? Does the bone or flank count? Is the whole body the self when the life of it is gone? Because the whale is sought after for its parts in the whaling industry, and the diverse materials are all of value—the blubber and sperm oil, for illumination; the spermaceti, for candles; the bone, as a structural material (a man's leg!); the teeth, as ornamentation and fortification; the flesh (and brain), as provision for man; and even the waste product created in the whale's intestine, the costly ambergris, as a fixative in perfume— any one part might be thought of as whale. With a pragmatic respect for the value of the whale cut into matter, Melville nevertheless considers the essential reality of the whale to exist only when he is whole and live, in his own element.

That it may be simpler to comprehend the part than the whole of a living being is evidenced in the visibility of the whale's jaw in the Spouter-Inn compared to the murkiness of the black mass in the picture there, a hint of the ineffable whale. The mock entering into the whale's cavernous insides makes a nervous joke for those in the business of whaling, but it also calls for an understanding of the actual dangers of the occupation. Starbuck wants no man in his boat who is not afraid of a whale. The warning is continued more seriously in the chapel where those who came to death in the business of whaling are memorialized. This unnerving note is linked to the sermon on Jonah, a story which, if its conclusion is mythicized, illustrates the fact that a whale is easily capable of swallowing a man whole.

Next Melville turns to the flesh. The chowder at the Try Pots, made of "small juicy clams, scarcely bigger than hazel nuts, . . . and salted pork cut up into little flakes" (65), introduces another part of the organism, however it may be transformed. One may wish to repress the thought of what his dinner once was, but Melville will not allow the subject to be ignored. Flesh is flesh, whether it be that of animal or man; and all who indulge in it, not just Queequeg, join in the cannibalism of this world. As Stubb eats his steak by the light produced from whale oil, the fact that his supper is the whale who was alive that afternoon hangs over the ghoulish meal.

Melville exhibits this cannibalism not with the outrage that Darwinism elicited in a later period but with the dark humor that comes from his realism, as he transforms the classic celebration of the feast to the stark devouring of one being by another. Ishmael's meal at the Try Pots could not be more innocent, but it is juxtaposed to the jarring information he hears soon after—that Ahab's leg was "devoured, chewed up, crunched" (69) by a whale.

In his creation of an actual whale Melville is the exceptional artist who gives science its due. The chapter on "Cetology," which was at first considered extraneous, has since been defended as an integral part of *Moby-Dick*.[4] The seeker of truth must be open to this information, just as Ishmael considers it part of his homework, "a matter almost indispensable to a thorough appreciative understanding of the more special leviathanic revelations" (116). Accurate data on whales were limited in Melville's time, although even Aristotle had correctly distinguished the whale from the fishes in the first classification of animals. According to Beale's *Natural History of the Sperm Whale,* a main source for *Moby-Dick,* in 1829 the condition of knowledge on the subject was "utter confusion." Melville finds only this and one other book, also by a whale-ship's surgeon, "which at all pretend to put the living sperm whale before you" (117–18) and succeed in the remotest degree. The inclusion of popular terms in "Cetology" not so much discounts the scientific approach as it indicates science's human origins and the desire shared by scientist and artist to organize material. Melville's definition of the whale as a "spouting fish with a horizontal tail" (119) is a rational explanation simply in opposition to Linnaeus's determination that whales are not fish because of their lungs and warm blood. "Cetology" contains much useful information, as Melville draws on zoological data and a method of organizing at the same time that he recognizes the limitations of both science and art. "The sperm whale, scientific or poetic, lives not complete in any literature" (118).

Melville's occasional speculations as to the whale's sensations are also based on factual evidence. He theorizes that the whale is exhausted not as a result of battle with human attackers, as a more egocentric artist might have told the story, but as the whale withstands the immense amount of water above him, "bearing on his back a column of two hundred fathoms of ocean!" (299). And the author's empathy for the bleeding whale is based on his knowledge of the nonvalvular structure of the whale's blood vessels and his thin skin, which result in hours of bleeding if he is pierced by even a small point.

The acceptance of the unique physical makeup of this other mammal calls for a release of egocentric anthropomorphic standards. The man of ego is threatened; the explorer is enchanted. The whale's eyes look in opposite directions. He has no nose. His ear is only about one-fifth of an inch in diameter,[5] so small that "into the hole itself you can hardly insert a quill, so wondrously minute is it" (280). Yet this ear is one of the most intricate in nature. The huge forehead, which to the whale hunter is the bank of oil for lighting his lamps, is for the whale a radar screen for echo-location of squid[6] at the pitch depths where man cannot travel. Melville's burlesque of these attributes—what need of olfactories, "No roses, no violets, no Cologne-water in the sea" (312)—is the high-spirited form of praise for the ingenuity of creation.

The facts themselves speak for an incredible whale. And although we learn of him through the poetic sensibility of Ishmael, the narrator excels rather in the communication of his subject than its invention. With the poetic license of speaking as men do not speak, Melville's characters, like Shakespeare's, nevertheless do represent a station in life. Ishmael is a simple sailor. His point of view is that which any man might have if he would be sensitive to the same phenomena. The "ungodly, god-like" (76) Ahab looks only to a plane of possibility beyond the ordinary. But in perceiving the physical world as nothing but a mask, he misses what commoner men may see.

Of all the renditions of whales, Melville finds the painter's work the least faithful. In the chapter entitled "Of the Monstrous Pictures of Whales," *monstrous* refers to the delusions of the artists who show the whale's spouts as any hot or cold bubbling spring or the whole whale as a squash. Those who copy stranded whales are little more accurate, only as correct as one would be in drawing a ship by observing the wrecked vessel. The skeleton of the whale, so impressive as to be proof of God to some landlubbers, carries limited significance in that it fails to hint at the whale's living form.

The carved models on the forecastles of ships are more accurate than portraits of the whale, "that one creature in the world which must remain unpainted to the last" (228).

The first dead whale to be found in America was washed to the beach of Nantucket, yet to Melville this stranded body was never a fair sight of a whale. Critics have suggested that the whale in *Moby-Dick* serves the function of death.[7] But the opposite is true—Moby Dick is evidence of life. And whales are not man-killers, a fact Starbuck tries to impress upon Ahab at the last: " '*See!* Moby Dick seeks thee not' " (465). It is Ahab who brings death, and if the whale did not exist, the captain would destroy himself trying to control something else. The vast corpse of a whale is a blunt reminder of death, but the bounty of animals in *Moby-Dick* are alive.

Ahab's obsession with the extinction of Moby Dick may be judged evil only because of the destruction it brings to men, not because there is anything wrong with the business of killing whales. But in differentiating between the motives of the *Pequod*'s crew, Melville raises the most disturbing issue related to animals in American literature: the morality of the hunt. Few hunters in modern times kill sheerly for survival, although most still maintain that the slain animal must be used. Motives range from a rationalized necessity to unapologetic love of the kill, but not without moral discomfort. Justification is given by purifying the motive; the hunter may prove his courage in the kill. And only certain animals of stature are to be considered as worthy opponents. Melville, too, requires stature in his subject, but he does not side with the hunter. *He lets the whale get away.*

Ahab's use of whaling for a personal vendetta is not the only ambition in question. There is something chilling in Starbuck's thought that "I am here in this critical ocean to kill whales for my living" (103). Queequeg is more innocent of the kill than the others only because he has not been taught Christian ways. And if the idea of killing animals could be justified by the Bible in an earlier time, it does strike the thinking man of the mid-nineteenth century in a new way. Even the least sensitive whaler in Melville's seas knows that to kill *the* Moby Dick would be to do away with a unique being. When he was a whaleman, Melville no doubt wanted to get his whale. Perhaps his art allows for complexities that a vocation may not permit. Or he may have had a change of heart in behalf of the whale. By making Ishmael the appreciative narrator, the caretaker of the knowledge of whales, as well as the least active participant in the killing of them, the author as much as appoints him to be Moby Dick's protector.

Ishmael protesteth much in defense of whaling. As one who goes to sea strictly for pay, not leisure, he establishes the work ethic as the moral base for his involvement in the business of whaling. Christ himself honors the fisherman (although how far Peter's unvisualized fish are from the living Moby Dick). But "Butchers we are, that is true" (98), Ishmael admits. At a loss for a defense of moral purity, he protests that the whale ship is "at least among the cleanliest things of this tidy earth" (98). Whaling was an imperial occupation and the whale a royal fish by the old English statutory law. Thus, he reasons, the hunter of the royal fish must be noble, too. But the *Pequod* is a thoroughly American boat, and its band of men are far from being subjects of a crown. The will of a single man drives them in a quest that is far from noble.

Melville's vision of man, which is bound to a belief in human fellowship, calls also for a new understanding of the life of all creatures. It may not be possible to kill a whale nobly. As man seeks power, and the dream of brotherhood dies, *Moby-Dick* is the darkest of tragedies. In his characterization of the whale, however, Melville is freed of the awesome moral responsibilities he sees for man. With the animal he may indulge in amoral, tangible reality both because it offers a level of truth and because he enjoys the material for its own sake. Such a wealth about an animal (in a book whose other name is The Whale) is not given simply to prove a point about man. But in developing his whale—and Moby Dick is, for the most part, an accurate whale—Melville allows certain "amoral" qualities to become an alternative *moral* standard. In so doing he dramatically sanctions his other American hero, Moby Dick.

Going to meet that whale provides a classic frontier experience, the very thought of which brings life to Ishmael on that deathlike November day. Chief among his motives for going to sea is the "overwhelming idea of the great whale himself" (16). The eternally motivating journey is combined here with the challenge of battle against the world's biggest, most lucrative creature, literally at the "outer edge of the wave," as Frederick Jackson Turner defines the frontier.[8] Moby Dick's mighty bulk is given in frontier terms, extending in the westerly direction of America's frontier: the whale's stomach is the Kentucky Mammoth Cave, the windpipe the Erie Canal.[9] The spirit of the frontier affirms life, and Moby Dick not only represents but is an essential part of the frontier. Ahab, on the other hand, has no frontier in him, chained as he is to his single motive. With his whale, too, Melville injects the tonic of wildness that was missing in the conventionally serene land of the Typees into his new frontier. *Moby-Dick* unleashes the primeval energies that have come to characterize nature in American literature and that are most vividly embodied in its animals.

An essential quality that allows so many animals to be important characters in this literature is its anti-intellectual bias. Like his master Hawthorne, Melville fears the mind's sway over the heart. As he centers his most important work on a huge animal, it would at first appear that brawn is pre-eminent; Moby Dick is referred to more than once as a "dumb brute." But the term is not convincing. Starbuck fails to persuade Ahab that the object of his life's pursuit is but a mere animal. The evidence builds rather to create an undefinable entity, cause of an understandable anxiety for insecure man. One may curse the whale, but he cannot be reduced to brute force. In fact, Melville has ingeniously put before us one of the most intelligent creatures in existence: the sperm whale has the largest brain on earth, perhaps even the most highly developed one.[10] The classic view of the sperm whale is the squared head that makes up one-third of his body. As the form of the whale would illustrate, his sensibilities are not split, as there is no dividing line between head and tail. That man's head and heart are at war, with his mind most often the destructive agent, brings Melville not so much to an anti-intellectual position with the whale as to a questioning of the definition of intelligence itself.

The "genius" of the whale is to remain in "pyramidical silence" (292). He has no vocal cords. As anti-intellectuality extends to a suspicion of words themselves, a premium falls on silence, even for those whose medium is language. The eloquent Ishmael proclaims, "Seldom have I known any profound being that had anything to say to this world" (312). The richest impressions remain locked in the consciousness. Moby Dick's size and silence conjoin to suggest an enormity of interior life. The blatancy of his size belies the subtlety of his form generally, as his organs are smoothed away. He goes deep—in that marvelous act of sounding—and keeps stoically silent even when wounded (with no tear ducts). Melville disclaims a report that a whale roared when struck by a harpoon.[11] Rather, the harpoon is quietly buried, leaving no prominence where the flesh heals around it. Only in the post-mortem are the historical markers discovered.

Like other classic frontier heroes, Moby Dick is a single male. His frontier is a man's world, and the ideal state is that of the bachelor. In fact, the male sperm whale does travel significantly farther both north and south than the female. Like other whales, most sperm whales are among the most highly developed social creatures on earth: a whale cub is cared for by "aunts" as well as the mother, and even when an adult is wounded, the others gather to defend him. Young males travel in herds, while the older males usually circulate with a harem. But there is an old bull who lives as a hermit, whom biologists doubt has any social connections with his kind. Moby Dick is such an "unaccompanied" (155) whale. That a whale would be alone in the vastness of the sea might seem the usual case, but the caravan the *Pequod* encounters is more the rule. When it is suggested, however, that Moby Dick might be hidden in such a caravan, the thought is disappointing. How could the great Moby Dick be lost in a crowd?

The animal makes a more successful loner than the human hero, who might have the drive to be by himself but not the stoicism, and who feels guilty for wanting freedom more than he wants a mate. Natty Bumppo desires no wife and yet proposes marriage. Luckily he is refused but is spared isolation through the comfortable companionship of an inferior. The urge to be free and its accompanying unease make for one of the darkest confusions in American literature. Ahab suffers in the thought of the family he left behind not because he cares to be with them but because he has not cared enough. His majestic struggle to assert his place in the universe may be expressed in terms suggestive of Lear, but their goals are antithetical. Not only is there no incongruity in the ideas of heroism and love for Lear, but his deeper majesty is reflected in his capacity to love. On the other hand, the American hero finds love a barrier to his free will. With Ahab, Melville was torn by this dilemma, but in the creation of Moby Dick, he develops the isolate hero without restraint. Despite a conscious commitment to brotherhood, with this second character the author reveals as much relish as any American for the blessed state of being alone.

Not only is Moby Dick a mighty bachelor, but as a sperm whale he is one of the better-looking fish in the sea, at least compared to the hare-lipped right whale. This free male animal by all rights might be expected to be distinguished by uninhibited sexual behavior. Unlike some whales, the sperm whale is not monogamous. And yet our hero has no interest in breeding. In fact, according to Melville, such old whales go about "warning each young Leviathan from his amorous errors" (330). What such errors does a whale commit? Do the young lady whale's parents call for a preacher? Family responsibility and sexual activity are inextricably linked, in that order: "my Lord Whale has no taste for the nursery, however much for the bower" (329). Even though the male does not stay with the young, the threat of offspring prefaces the cloaked reference to mating, which is relegated to the past. Melville's proud, mature whale is beyond all that. Not only does the sexual connection create the burden of family, but it requires that the male fight off every competing Lothario aiming for his bed. "As ashore, the ladies often cause the most terrible duels among their rival admirers; just so with the whales, who sometimes come to deadly battle, and all for love" (329). Deadly battle is exactly what Moby Dick does best, but not for love. More important, he establishes his individual supremacy.

In his otherwise bold book Melville squeamishly skirts the topic of mating. The single firsthand description of the love life of whales is given in one sentence: "We saw young Leviathan amours in the deep" (326). This incident occurs in the seemingly peaceful "The Grand Armada," a domestic pause between episodes of the main action. But even here, destruction comes of connection, by means of the "long coils of the umbilical cord of Madame Leviathan, by which the young cub seemed still tethered to its dam.

Not seldom in the rapid vicissitudes of the chase, this natural line, with the maternal end loose, becomes entangled with the hempen one, so that the cub is thereby trapped" (326). The sentence about amours concludes this paragraph, as Melville again reverses chronology so that a warning of consequences prefaces the reference to breeding.

The most rudimentary biological treatise on the whale highlights the playfulness of the mating habits. D. H. Lawrence, for one, rejoices that "the great bull lies up against his bride / in the blue deep of the sea / as mountain pressing on mountain, in the zest of life."[12] That the whale mates at any time of the year makes him a splendid specimen of uninhibited physical activity for Lawrence. That same fact allows Melville to minimize the subject. The censorship requirements of his time did not keep the topic from a deliciously oblique treatment by the author who enjoyed the subject. But Melville is puritanically severe. He who dares question God himself strains with delicacy when it comes to sex.

In keeping with a complete account of the physical parts of the whale, Melville describes the phallus in "The Cassock." Referred to as an "enigmatical object" (350),[13] it is euphemized and deanimated at once. In "Cetology" this part of the anatomy is translated into Latin. (Interestingly, the unaroused whale is suited to Melville's own fastidiousness, as the genitals are folded away into a pocket.) In "The Cassock" the phallus is revealed in the post-mortem: this is the organ of a *dead* whale. Elsewhere it is emphasized that a dead whale is not a representative whale—and a lifeless phallus is considerably less authentic than other remnants of the whale, such as jawbone or ambergris. The description of the whale's organ pays regard to size, but then size is the impressive factor in an account of the whale generally: this "unaccountable cone" is "longer than a Kentuckian is tall, nigh a foot in diameter at the base, and jet-black as Yojo, the ebony idol of Queequeg" (351). The pagan Queequeg is made superior in fellow feeling, but here by showing a pagan custom to be debased, the author disposes of an awkward subject, moving to an incident in Christian history where a queen is deposed for the sin of worshipping the phallic idol, which is consequently burnt "for an abomination" (351).

Moby Dick's lack of interest in mating might be explained as the result of impotence. Biologists speculate that this may be the case with the old hermit whales. Melville's account is that "the ardor of youth declines," as the whale becomes like the sated Turk whose "love of ease and virtue supplants the love for maidens." Like the Ottoman, the whale enters upon the "impotent, repentant, admonitory stage of life, forswears, disbands the harem" (329–30). Moby Dick a lover of *ease*? Hardly. He is the embodiment of energy. And nowhere is leisure approved. But to make celibacy a virtue, even in an animal, is classically American. How ironic that Melville's animal would be called the sperm whale, an erroneous designation given by early whale hunters who mistook the oil in his head for sperm cells. If Moby Dick is impotent, he makes an incongruous subject for the symbol makers for whom he offers phallic suggestion. A more convincing case is that when it comes to having a sexual relationship, Moby Dick just prefers not to.

The mature sperm whale's immunity from sexual need ensures his liberty. And he makes as exquisite a concrete manifestation of freedom as we find in a literature preoccupied with the subject— his buoyance, the streamlined, smooth-skinned body sliding through vast seas, occasionally leaping into the air for sport as he momentarily approximates the flight of a bird. But his plunge to the ocean's depths returns him to an even more liberating medium, as water aids locomotion, provides a rich supply of food, and serves as a bed. He is cleansed in that sea. At peace, a whale will go at a leisurely three to five miles per hour, but during the chase he may accelerate to twenty miles per hour.[14] Starbuck meditates with envy: "the hated whale has the round watery world to swim in" (148).

The harpoon line that would tow him in makes one of the most graphic images in literature to visualize the struggle for freedom. The gun, harness, and cage do not allow for the possibility of equality found in the fisherman's gear, as control shifts from one end of the taut line to the other. Cleverness and endurance, as well as power, determine the winner in the rugged contest which may go on for days. That Ahab would be strangled by his own line is a fitting fate not only because he determines his own doom but because the image is so specifically related to freedom. "Fast-Fish and

Loose Fish" takes the fishing line as the underlying image for the more general issue of the right to possess. "Often possession is the whole of the law" (333) in the doings of men, as well as in the amoral life of the sea. But the issue of freedom is a passionately moral one for Melville as it is for most Americans, no matter what being's freedom is at stake or how violently he defends it. Because violence often carries its own overwhelming aesthetic appeal, many a writer who would bless peace does so by showing destruction— Milton, for example, whose Satan outshines his Christ. But there is no question that Satan will be damned. And Ahab is damned. Yet the ferocious Moby Dick is saved—not simply as a result of Ahab's folly, or as the amoral survival of the fittest, but because he must be free. Maybe this is why Melville says he wrote "a wicked book" but felt "spotless as the lamb."[15]

Moby Dick's other seemingly amoral qualities are given a more open moral sanction. As to the whale's most stunning feature, size, which is referred to oftener than any other, Melville leads us causally with the report that Moby Dick is the " 'noblest and biggest' " (365). A mighty theme for a mighty book, he says, claiming that no great volume can ever be written on the flea, a statement which not only reflects the aesthetic limitations of such a subject but argues that the fall of the sparrow is not as valid as the death of a larger animal. The equation of size and value works remarkably well with the whale, for he happens to be not only the biggest but the most commercially valuable creature, as well as one who is richly gifted with intelligence and highly developed mechanisms of survival.

Melville mistakenly claims that the sperm whale is the largest inhabitant of the globe.[16] But his estimation of length at 85–90 feet, while not an average measure (60 feet), approximates the maximum length now on record for a sperm whale: 83½ feet.[17] Such an animal weighs between 80 and 90 tons. And the sperm whale is the largest of the toothed whales. The male, as Melville accurately notes, is nearly double the size of the female, a fact appropriate to the characterization of the supreme male, Moby Dick. Analogies need not exaggerate the animal's hugeness; he is not compared to an island—he *is* an island under a ship. Likening the masthead to legs on stilts big enough for the hugest monsters to pass through fantasizes the size of a man, but there is no need to increase the proportions of the whale. Reports of his "two-fold enormousness" (178) are simply thought facetious. His size alone is so terrifying to all fish, sharks included, that they often dash themselves in fright before his "pre-eminent tremendousness" (157).

That the whale's tail provides the power for his massive body serves Melville in a humorous deflation of a romantic ideal with a physical reality. As the antithesis of the weightless bird of the spirit, this mountain of a creature must work with his lower parts. And, says Ishmael, "less celestial, I celebrate a tail" (314). It operates five different ways: as a fin, as a mace, and for sweeping, lobtailing, and peaking the flukes. His jaws make for good drama, but they are not the most sophisticated or regular demonstrations of the whale's power. The sperm whale rarely uses his teeth. The more remarkable and subtle manifestation of his immense power is not even destructive—his capacity to sustain himself at depths of over 3,000 feet, holding his breath for more than an hour.

Beyond brutal force, the whale has "real strength," which "never impairs beauty or harmony, but it often bestows it" (315). Such strength rests with his secure role as king of the seas. More fortunate than any human ruler, he does not know the fear of an enemy: he has none, except man. It is hypothesized that the reason why whales allow whalers to approach and capture them (especially when the hunt was conducted from rowboats) is because they do not comprehend the danger human beings represent.

The secure hermit whale is thus the most independent of beings. Moby Dick's whiteness makes him a strikingly individual figure, as do his particular wrinkled brow and his crooked jaw, features that are all found among actual sperm whales, though uniquely joined in him. And as whalemen did entitle particular whales, Moby Dick is further distinguished by a name. Although Melville never refers to Mocha Dick, that notorious white whale was described in the kinds of records he used. The artist who begins with the symbol might have created his own whiteness in a whale to illustrate the manifold functions of that hue so unforgettably discussed in "The Whiteness of the Whale." But Melville begins with the albino whale in existence. He knows, too, of the way a whale's skin folds in wrinkles on the head, for Moby Dick's scowl, and the way a sperm whale's jaw may be broken with little impairment to his effectiveness.

The whale's striking appearance is matched by internal features of individuality: this is the creature with a "magnitude" of backbone. His ability to maintain his temperature in extreme conditions shows the "rare virtue of thick walls, and the rare virtue of interior spaciousness. Oh, man! admire and model thyself after the whale! Do thou, too, remain warm among ice. Do thou, too, live in this world without being of it. Be cool at the equator; keep thy blood fluid at the Pole. . . . retain, O man! in all seasons a temperature of thine own" (261). As if the two words were made of the same piece, the *whale* is *whole*.

When we are finally granted the sight of Moby Dick, Melville exceeds an almost unmatchable anticipation with an even more exquisite actuality. As "reality outran apprehension" (109) when the notorious Ahab first appeared, even more unmistakably does Moby Dick outdo the dream. The stage was carefully set for Ahab. The whale rises as naturally as a wave crashing out of the sea.

The literal animal reveals himself to be handsomer than the imagined one. First to be distinctly visible is his "high sparkling hump"; the battering-ram head is a "broad milky forehead" (446–47). The most frightening feature, the jaw, imagined when it is fully hidden as "wrenched hideousness," opens within six inches of Ahab's head to show the "bluish pearl-white of the inside" (448–49). Before the chase begins, "a gentle joyousness—a mighty mildness of repose in swiftness, invested the gliding whale. Not the white bull Jupiter . . . not Jove, not that great majesty Supreme! did surpass the glorified White Whale as he so divinely swam" (447). It was the Greek gods who envied the mortals, and thus it is to the Greeks that the author turns here for the terms of heaven to honor an inhabitant of earth.

All allusions to deity are dropped when the whole whale finally appears:

Moby Dick bodily burst into view! For not by any calm and indolent spoutings; not by the peaceable gush of that mystic fountain in his head, did the White Whale now reveal his vicinity; but by the far more wondrous phenomenon of breaching. Rising with his utmost velocity from the furthest depths, the Sperm Whale thus booms his entire bulk into the pure element of air, and piling up a mountain of dazzling foam, shows his place to the distance of seven miles and more. In those moments, the torn, enraged waves he shakes off, seem his mane; in some cases, this breaching is his act of defiance. (455)

In his entirety Moby Dick is matter and energy in living form, expressed through terms of measurement for physical phenomena—velocity, depth, distance—and the incendiary verbs—burst, breach, boom, pile, and shake. He represents nothing but himself as he slams his head into the boat, toppling metaphysician and pragmatist alike. Water may be wedded to meditation, but a live whale crashing into your boat is not. Despite Moby Dick's terrifying proximity, however, his distinct features are regarded apart from the danger they impose. "The wide tiers of welded tendons overspreading his broad white forehead, beneath the transparent skin, looked knitted together; as head on, he came churning his tail among the boats" (464). The detail here reflects not the inventiveness of a single narrator but the clear-eyed perception of any person who might look closely at this amazing animal he had never seen before. Even during the catastrophe, the human ability not only to see but to accept the existence of the other is made the last of the satisfactions of being alive.

It is the climactic "defiance" that ultimately earns heroic stature for Moby Dick. Turning on his pursuers, the harpoon lines, seemingly the whole ambitious world of men, he defies death itself. "Bedraggled with trailing ropes, and harpoons, and lances" (464), his vast form shoots lengthwise intact. When a final harpoon strikes its place, he writhes but spasmodically *rolls*, resuming his essential gesture even in distress. Then, snapping the "treacherous line" (466), he goes free. Ahab has come to death. Ishmael, the man to say that "in many of its aspects this visible world seems formed in love" (169) (and the invisible spheres in fright), is spared. And Moby Dick triumphs.

It was Melville's genius to have made the whale his subject. Not only does he inspire a wealth of metaphysical possibilities, but as a literal animal the sperm whale is so composed as to make an extraordinary but distinctly American character. And he is so breathtakingly alive one cannot meet him without new wonder for this watery earth—and a yearning to see such a mighty living creature as this.

Notes

1. Herman Melville, *Moby-Dick: An Authoritative Text, Reviews and Letters by Melville, Analogues and Sources, Criticism,* ed. Harrison Hayford and Hershel Parker (New York: W. W. Norton, 1967), p. 177. Subsequent references to this edition of *Moby-Dick* will appear in the text.

2. Quoted in F. O. Matthiessen, *American Renaissance: Art and Expression in the Age of Emerson and Whitman* (New York: Oxford University Press, 1941), p. 388.

3. Herman Melville, review of *Etchings of a Whaling Cruise* by J. Ross Browne, in *Moby-Dick: An Authoritative Text,* p. 529.

4. See, for example, J. A. Ward, "The Function of the Cetological Chapters in *Moby-Dick,*" *American Literature,* 28, no. 2 (May, 1956), 164–83.

5. Karl-Erik Fichtelius and Sverre Sjölander, *Smarter Than Man?: Intelligence in Whales, Dolphins, and Humans,* trans. Thomas Teal (New York: Random House, 1972), p. 101.

6. David J. Coffey, *Dolphins, Whales and Porpoises: An Encyclopedia of Sea Mammals* (New York: Macmillan, 1977), p. 19.

7. See, for example, Charles Olson, *Call Me Ishmael* (New York: Reynal & Hitchcock, 1947).

8. Frederick Jackson Turner, *The Frontier in American History* (New York: Holt Rinehart and Winston, 1962), p. 3.

9. Edwin Fussell, *Frontier: American Literature and the American West* (Princeton, N.J.: Princeton University Press, 1965), p. 273.

10. Fichtelius and Sjölander.

11. Melville, review of *Etchings of a Whaling Cruise,* p. 530.

12. "Whales Weep Not!" *Selected Poems* (New York: Viking Press, 1961), p. 134.

13. Identified by the editors' note, *Moby-Dick: An Authoritative Text,* p. 350.

14. Richard Mark Martin, *Mammals of the Oceans* (New York: G. P. Putnam's Sons, 1977), p. 54.

15. Herman Melville to Nathaniel Hawthorne, Nov. 17, 1851, *Moby-Dick: An Authoritative Text,* p. 566.

16. The blue whale is the largest species on earth.

17. Fichtelius and Sjölander, p. 94.

CHAPTER 2

"All the breath and the bloom of the year in the bag of one bee . . ."
—Robert Browning

Concise Creatures: Emily Dickinson

Immensity and power are not what count in Emily Dickinson's world of animals. "The Gnat's supremacy is large as Thine—" (583).[1] Not that she rejects status: she reallocates it to the little creatures. In over 300 poems featuring animals (compared to very few about people), most are no bigger than a robin. The focus on the minute is not Emersonian; although a tiny being may be complete, he is not a microcosmic model. His identity is shaped by his position of relative obscurity on a traditional chain of being. Neither are Dickinson's animals remote or symbolic. In the American tradition, they are not domesticated. Her finest subjects are those characters she meets in the garden or meadow, where the poet's chilling magic puts them before our eyes so that what is familiar becomes new. Because she shows no intent to capture or kill, the animal is not forced to fight for his freedom. It is assumed. And Dickinson's fascination with death rarely applies to her creatures, who exemplify continuing life through economy, independence, and good works. In a world of human dread a song rises "From Miniature Creatures / Accompanying the Sun—" (606).

Dickinson's affinity for small animals is that of one unacclaimed artist for another. They are outsiders together, beyond the ranking system of man and God. Their mutual deprivation stimulates and purifies their art and expands the freedom of their lives. But that this poet, whose New England soul is grounded in the inevitability of the individual, is not one with nature does not make it alien to her, as Charles Anderson, for one, suggests.[2] It is in the human world where union is expected but tragically fails that the poet is most alone. Dickinson does not go into the garden—and she goes there often—anticipating solace from a butterfly but to enjoy it. Her best subjects are the most distinctly *other* beings she meets. The world of animals *is* a retreat from the hazards of human connections—the emotions and the words that kill. It is an alternative to religion. But it is not an escape from the artist's responsibility; it is, rather, a buoyant affirmation of it. Not only does the arrival of animals literally mark the season of growth, but they are shown as regularly performing artists who, without the influence of praise, maintain an artistic integrity. And their precise form is more thrilling to this poet than the expansive, just as a word is more potent than a sentence. Conciseness holds not only the excitement of condensation but worthiness itself.

Dickinson's few experiments with larger exotic animals fail to produce the hair-raising immediacy of her dramatic small creatures. The distant character becomes a vehicle for a sympathetic view of the outcast, a concept unconvincing with jungle beasts: the leopard, because of her bold and unchanging gown, is spurned by civilization; the tiger fasts on a "Crumb of Blood" (872), Dickinson's favorite measure, exact in describing the meal of a bird but awkward as a unit for blood. At best, the image of survival on the crumb makes for resilience and independence. But it becomes sentimental when used to evoke pity. The overly sympathetic plights of leopard and tiger fail to reorder the conventions of status in the animal kingdom, a reversal that comes about through the active presence of the talented members on the small end of the scale.

Animals in groups are uninteresting. Cattle make no vital impression but are the dissolving image found in a sunset, even there reflecting Dickinson's uncompromising sense of the individual in the "Single Herd" (628). Horses are too closely associated with people to be of interest as subjects with their own lives. The passenger may comment to those drawing her buggy, but she does not honor them by a description. A horse tied in front of a house operates only as a sign that his owner is inside. That one who "scents the living Grass" will be "retaken with a shot / If he is caught at all—" (1535) assumes a desire for freedom. But the struggle for it is not Dickinson's concern. The animal owned or connected to man does not captivate her.

Dickinson's dog Carlo appears occasionally as a companion to the poet. But he is never the subject of a poem. Perhaps he is too familiar. "Tell Carlo— / He'll tell *me*!" (186). This named being, official resident of the house, does not evoke the mystery of the animals on the outside. The poet *takes, rejoins,* or more often *leaves* her dog, but she never describes him. The other domestic animal, the unowned cat, is the exception by being the subject of three poems (the best of which takes place outdoors), in each case a power figure to be thwarted. A single stroke reduces God and cat: "Papa above? / Regard a Mouse / O'erpowered by the Cat!" (61). The cat as malevolent authority not only murders the mouse but does so "by degrees—" (726), offering first the reprieve that punishes worse than death.

A better poem about the cat dramatizes rather than articulates an anti-authority theme: "She flattens—then she crawls— / She runs without the look of feet— / Her eyes increase to Balls— / Her Jaws stir—twitching—hungry— / Her Teeth can hardly stand— / She leaps, but Robin leaped the first—" (507). With verbs such as *flattens* and *crawls* Dickinson characteristically brings her animal thrillingly close to the ground, close to us. The traditionally female cat, whose gender is stressed as the first word of the first seven lines of the poem, comes as the only female authority in Dickinson's poetry, where in the few cases in which animals are female, they are generally associated with clothing, frivolity, or meekness. But in female or male, such power is monstrous and almost never prevails in the few poems where it is treated. And the joyful thrust of "She flattens—then she crawls" comes with the smaller animal's escape. The bird gets away. Physical violence is not only an unappealing and unfruitful topic for Dickinson, but it would mean the demise of her small animals, whose strength is not in physical force. And rarely does she show them facing destruction. They prove themselves not in the death struggle but in the normal manifestations of their lives.

Dickinson's chief animal characters, who defy many of the standards of power and authority, are not genuine rebels. They do not attack those of a more powerful order or usually even concern themselves with mightier characters. They destroy nothing. And they show no inclination to rule, for that is the very thing the poet despises. The small and often "undesirable" creatures instead exhibit the virtues of economy and productivity on their own terms. The rat, for example, is the "concisest Tenant. / He pays no Rent. / Repudiates the Obligation— / On Schemes intent / . . . Hate cannot harm / A Foe so reticent— / Neither Decree prohibit him— / Lawful as Equilibrium" (1356). His outlawed state grants him a privilege, but it does not turn him into a destroyer. His lawfulness reflects the conservative strain of the natural world rather than its brutalities. More important, he resides within the law by right of his existence. When trapped, the rat *surrenders* "A brief career of Cheer / And Fraud and Fear" (1340), the verb indicating his choice in the matter as well as the martyr's capacity to benefit through acquiescence, not resistance. The most telling item, however, in terms of Dickinson's favored animals generally, is the rat's *career,* the ultimately dignifying attribute assigned to many an unlikely animal character.

The most brilliant animals shock through the unorthodoxy of their very existence as seen by anthropomorphic man. Their appearance jars against conventional harmonies—and exhilarates this extraordinary poet. Unlike the arrival of the human subject, which tears into the soul, the encounter with nature's people brings only a momentary undoing of the emotions. Dickinson's unorthodox rhyme, cryptic stanza, and epigrammatic wit are well suited to present the animal's electric arrival-departure. That charisma is not to be found in duration is never more dramatically illustrated than with that "narrow Fellow in the Grass." Myths are unnecessary as referents here; it is what we *see* that counts, the real snake, so scary as to knock his name right out of the voice box. This poem that can take the breath away with every reading proceeds on terms that would appear to do just the opposite by making the visitor familiar, unimpressive. His narrowness is a form of the concise set for limitation, not influence; that he "Occasionally rides—" makes him as polite as a proper gentleman on a train. And he is not impolite. But to extend the human privilege of riding to the snake brings him terrifyingly close, as it also allows for him a destination all the more unnerving because it is undetermined. The even more familiar comb is perhaps most offensively associated with him: not only is he without the appendage for holding such an implement—he has no hair. (Yet how accurately the poet shows the grass to part.) Only the "Whip lash / unbraiding in the Sun" suggests violence, yet the image is used for speed, not punishment.

The snake does no evil. It is human subjectivity reacting against the form and manner so unlike our own that ostracizes him from other of nature's fellows. His only crime is to inspire "Zero at the Bone—" (986), a sensation usually paraphrased as pure terror. But unlike that bone marrow fear of the more ambiguous poems of dread, this is a stimulating voyeuristic fright brought on by something exterior to man—something that does go away. Compared to the horror of death, devastation from love, and the numbness after pain, the sight of a snake is a stunning spectacle, the kind that sends a child dashing home to relate what he's seen. Even this most disturbing creature has nothing of death about him. "As a little Girl, I was told that the Snake would bite me, . . . but I went along and met no one but Angels, who were far shyer of me, than I could be of them."[3]

Many of Dickinson's most intriguing poems feature the "undesirables" of the animal kingdom, among them the night people: cricket, lightning bug, beetle, bat, and spider. All exist in opposition to accepted standards of pre-eminence: where grandeur is equated with size, they are minute; where godliness is associated with light, they live in the devil's night; on a scale topped by gold, they are of dusky hue. But they are not opposers of those qualities of day. They are merely forced to do their work in the dark.

The cricket who ushers in the night, as he also announces the end of summer, "September's Baccalaureate" (1271), is the one specimen Dickinson associates primarily with death, the "utmost / Of elegy to me" (1775). He is, nevertheless, a respected harbinger of the dark, who performs as nature's "gentle Clock." For all Dickinson's love of surprise, she ranks regularity high (especially the annual return of birds). It is the dying of the light marked by the cricket, with his "pathetic Pendulum," a monotony of sound so out of keeping with the poet's best effects, that saddens. Marking that "esoteric Time" (1276) beyond man's comprehension, the cricket ticks off the seconds that add up to death. In offering his "timid prayer" (790) to nature, like any being in a subservient posture (Dickinson claims she never learned to pray), the cricket loses not only authenticity but force. Still, seen in the dignity of their earthly labors, the minor nation of crickets move the mightiest star in the heavens with their art: "The Crickets sang / And set the Sun" (1104), an act of further significance as it brings workmen home from their jobs. The causal fallacy takes us to the primitive's sense of nature, although Dickinson, whose refreshing vision makes her similar, differs in an important way: it is the conscious talent at work in her creatures that produces effects. Not only does the cricket's song close off the day, but his lyrics mark the end of summer when he "drops a sable line" (1635).

The night ushered in by the cricket comes on conventionally deathlike. But this poet sets it alive with small creatures at work. One miraculously becomes a "winged spark," the "speck of Rapture" (1468) that is the lightning bug. The joke that he is taken for lightning, posing minute against cosmic, in Dickinson's scheme reverses the usual priorities. Violent power is not the greater marvel; more extraordinary is that a living being, especially one so small, can make his own light.

Dickinson's night is a time of special freedom: "These are the Nights that Beetles love— / From Eminence remote." Being apart from authority brings the giddy delight that comes with the boss's day off, except that freedom is more likely to be used for labor than for play. The beetle "hoists" himself to walls where his unique skill is to drive "perpendicular . . . Depositing his Thunder." The effect of this act is an "improving thing—" as "It keeps the nerves progressive—," just as the snake's whiplash performance undeniably does. The beetle as "Bomb upon the Ceiling" (1128) shatters the monotony of the blank wall, the too serene night. In hanging upside down, he demonstrates a skill unknown to men, an act that earns him a place in the Dickinson poem. He takes no idealistic flight from the earth with his firm wings, but he does gain command of it.

To show the explosive reaction resulting from the minute source is not a device for mock heroic humor alone, although mighty effects created by the little people bring out Dickinson's express delight. She is not a poet of exaggeration. The beetle that terrorizes the child and draws merriment from men is for her the source of both responses and more. The limits of her life, which had the effect of condensing emotions to scale—the sound of a footstep, a single drop of rain—allow for a thunderous reaction to one bug on the ceiling. In this case fright and amusement, both superior to peace, are deliciously bound. Thus this small citizen of the ceiling shows his clout over bigger, more "important" souls below—men, children, the poet herself. And his reputation follows him in the animal kingdom: the bird who bites an angleworm in half hops to the wall to let the beetle pass.

The antithesis of the day's romantic bird, who escapes towards the ultimate light, is the dun-colored bat, "with wrinkled Wings— / Like fallow Article—." No less capable than the bird whose feath-erly flight is the subject of dreamers, the bat owns more substantial wings, his "small Umbrella" the utilitarian equipment of one pre-pared for the life of earth where rain falls, where night comes. Yet there is no sign of gloom about him. His "quaintly halved" wings reflect the artistry of precision in one who is considered abhorrent not because he is destructive but because he is different. Not only is the bat able to fly in a dark closed place, but the poet allows him the possible attribute of song, her word for an animal's individual sound: "not a song pervade his Lips— / Or none perceptible." So set on the bat's worth is Dickinson that her last stanza errs in too explicit praise: "Beneficent, believe me, / His Eccentricities—" (1575), following a tendency to argument on behalf of the obscure being after he has been presented dramatically.

The super artist of the nocturnals is the spider, who "sewed at Night / Without a Light / Upon an Arc of White. . . . His Strat-egy / Was Physiognomy" (1138). This artist's sense of form is in-trinsic, though no mere animal instinct drives him. It is a creator's plan, charmingly turned to logic, a strategy. Anderson's excellent explication of this poem is useful in this context. He finds the triple rhyme-scheme lines to be an incantation for casting a spell on the spider to give up the secret of his web, which might be either a fine collar or a shroud. But that secret cannot be named. The creator's physiognomy is revealed not as the mystical claim would have it, that outward appearances furnish a true method of divining the inner self, but to the extent that some part of the being is inexplicably transmuted into his art.[4]

The spider, creating a most complex and unappreciated art under the meagerest of conditions, epitomizes the case of the over-looked artist. A comparison with Dickinson is unavoidable: "The Spider holds a Silver Ball / In unperceived Hands— / And dancing softly to Himself / His Yarn of Pearl—unwinds— / He plies from Nought to Nought—In unsubstantial Trade—. . ." (605). Animal artist is given the human hand, rejoicing only to himself, as this poet who affirms creation undoubtedly did. Like the "Spider as an Artist," who has "never been employed—" (1275), she continues her "Trade" (605), weaving fragile words into the off-rhymed hymn stanzas, queer as a spider's weave. In his economy, however, the spider who founds "the fairest Home" with a flower "in an Hour" (1423) is the superior artist. The temporal quality of the flower may set a condition necessary for speed, but its brief life, calling for a carpe diem philosophy, has little in common with the spider's competence. In her appreciation for this "Neglected Son of Genius," Dickinson directs an edge of blasphemy at that other Son before whom the world bows and who presumably would assist the un-heralded of the earth.

Should the Dickinson persona be too closely likened to the spider artist, one fact clearly halts the analogy: the spider, like her other animal artists, is male. That he unwinds yarn and sews a delicate thread does not contradict her concept of the male. But it is apparently antithetical for her to associate a career with the female. She who dares rattle the seat of Deity is unquestionably bold enough to have created a revolutionary female. Whether she wished to revamp the idea of the male artist, adding delicacy and removing muscle, or whether she automatically made her artists male, is a matter of speculation. Dickinson's own achievement is undeniable feminist evidence of one who broke the mold. But her thinking is often antifeminist as she belittles much that is associated with women.

In his insightful conclusion that the establishment of rank and status are a major theme in Dickinson's work, Richard Chase lists "queen," "wife," "woman," and "poet" on a par,[5] apparently missing the hostility and irony she brings to the womanly roles. Poet far outranks the others. While Clark Griffith's theory of a tragically neurotic recluse who turned from the normal (presumably happier) life of a woman to her art shows little understanding of the satisfactions of that choice, a perspective Richard Sewall's biography[6] wisely revises. Griffith's point that Dickinson sees man as the possessor of everything she craves[7] is not inaccurate. While she scorns male authority—God as burglar, banker, even Father—what she values most also belongs to the male—a career. Her spider might easily have been female, but he is not. And woman's functions are antithetical to his: the housewife casually destroys the splendid creation of the spider in both poems about his web. Every "Broom and Bridget / Throughout a Christian Land" certify his "surpassing Merit" (1275), as the obtuse female, following her Christian-ordained menial role, wipes out the art she never even recognizes.

With even more meager reputations than the night people are worm, fly, and gnat. The worm is Dickinson's only victim for whom she shows no sympathy. He is a piece of meat, cut in half. Even the poet, in the name of science, "slew a worm the other day—" (70). But if she fails to develop the worm as a being worthy of life, her slaying of him does call for an explanation. It is not like her to kill anything. The worm's association with the corpse might be reason for discounting him, only he is merely alluded to in that connection, never dramatized (and if he were, this poet would make something of the fact that he was the living party).

One strange poem, which has become fertile ground for a psychoanalytical reading, does put the worm directly at the center: "In Winter in my Room / I came upon a Worm— / Pink, lank and warm—" (1670). This uncharacteristic verse turns out to be the account of a dream, where the worm is superseded by a snake, both undeniably erotic symbols. Yet the worm is introduced with literal detail, not metaphor, the way most of the animal poems begin. Either this is a translation from a more phallic representation to a form from nature the poet was comfortable with, or she saw a worm. If Dickinson did recognize the symbolism in the dream, where her persona ties the worm with string, Griffith's interpretation that she does so to punish the male[8] might be a clue as to why, of all nature's people, only the worm is allowed an unsympathetic destruction.

In granting purpose and rank to the disreputable small creatures, Dickinson most ingeniously addresses "the Charter of the least Fly—" (570). The freedom of movement available to the beetle is considerably quickened in the fly, who with the liberty of wings nevertheless makes the house his home, through the facility denied bulkier beings. The amusing comparison of flies to cattle finds the fly superior in every respect. "Those Cattle smaller than a Bee . . . Whose tillage is the passing Crumb—" show subsistence to be simpler for them, their motion is more fluid than the heavy tread of cattle, and, inhabiting "Extemporaneous stalls / They found to our objection—On eligible walls—" (1388), they locate lodging more easily. Because the scheme of creation provides no special home for flies, their freedom is ironically expanded as they take the wall for their continent, breaking the monotony of it as the beetle does. Facility, but noticeably not vulnerability, is the significant attribute of these flies. After all, here they are in the presence only of the poet-observer. And that persona does not swat flies.

Dickinson's touch with beetle and fly is necessarily light; to move gravely with these minute subjects of disdain would be to invite ridicule. And the further her offbeat characters take her from the ponderousness and sentimentality that come with her creatures closest to God, the more pleasingly detached the artist is. Flies are humorously granted weight (although great weight is not of value) as they "suddenly descend / And gallop on the Furniture / Or odiouser offend—." In the creation of the comparative from odious, the Dickinson wit undercuts the offensiveness of her harmless insect. The fly bothers people, but he does no real harm. He is a mere trespasser, as are other small beings relegated to positions of pettiness that lack even the dignity of being terrible. Dickinson's featuring of the disdained and the small not only refreshes the stale subject of nature but revolutionizes a system that places all value in the grandiose. Thus the fly's offense is for her a charmed moment. His aptitude as irritant to the more powerful is, then, a "peculiar calling" (1388).

This insect opens one of Dickinson's most awesome poems about death.

> I heard a Fly buzz—when I died—
> The Stillness in the Room
> Was like the Stillness in the Air—
> Between the Heaves of Storm—
>
> The Eyes around—had wrung them dry—
> And Breaths were gathering firm
> For that last Onset—when the King
> Be witnessed—in the Room—
>
> I willed my Keepsakes—Signed away
> What portion of me be
> Assignable—and then it was
> There interposed a Fly—
>
> With Blue—uncertain stumbling Buzz—
> Between the light—and me—
> And then the Windows failed—and then
> I could not see to see—   (465)

As the immediate life before the fading eyes of the dying, the fly functions as the image upon which that person's failing senses are measured. This last rite radically revises a version of the soul's flight to heaven at death—especially if one regards the fly as nothing more than the filthy insect that feeds on carrion. But while death (or dying) is the first subject of this poem, with the fly as agent, there is a further subject: the fly himself. In this room where human life recedes—the mourners, too, are emptied—where the King (death? savior?) might but does not appear, only the fly lives. Displayed against this backdrop of death, he is unmistakably potent, first in holding the poem together as a reflector of weaker forms of life and then in his independent journey outward, leaving death behind. Nor is the synesthetic "Blue uncertain stumbling buzz" an inaccurate description of a fly seen by the healthy eye. At close range the blue-green tint of the fly is visible. Following an indirect course, he makes a noticeably interrupted buzz. And in one so small these effects do blur.

This is an unquestionably palpable, living fly, as introduced in the clear-headed first line. The fly is more than comic or Gothic relief, / of "homely inconsequence," as John Crowe Ransom asserts, although the insect does indeed lighten the tone.[9] The fly exists, however, not merely for the enhancement of the human characters in the poem. His life has its own direction, and under the circumstances this life is a miracle—even if it seems so only by a relative measure. To that person about to die, the significance of the merest form of life might well be intensified just as sensations shift. The superiority of human being to insect is overturned here by nothing less than the reduction of the human in death, the extreme measure necessary for a fly to be given his prominence. He lives.

In Griffith's approach to the tragic Dickinson, he arrives at the question of what to do with this fly he discovers is the only representative of life in the poem. His conclusion is that the poet must be reducing life to an ugly irritation from which the dying might well escape.[10] His assumption is understandable given any conventional response to a fly. But the basis for disgust does not derive from the poem any more than it is to be found in those featuring other "distasteful" characters—rat, bat, and spider. Dickinson does not select her subjects for the gratuitous task of dramatizing despicability of those already of low reputation. Hers is a contrary and unconventional spirit. This strange lady likes flies, often mentioning them favorably in her letters. "I enjoy much with a precious fly, during sister's absence, not one of your blue monsters, but a timid creature, that hops from pane to pane of her white house, so very cheerfully, and hums and thrums, a sort of speck piano."[11]

With conciseness at a premium, the gnat ranks as winner in the wee class. Though he with "minutest Fan" may be more easily extinguished than any in the kingdom, his superlative accessibility makes him "sufficient to obliterate / A Tract of Citizen—" (422). The weighty word for the near weightless is not only a technique of irony but a questioning of conventional usage, here with pertinence to the poet's view of creation: what is sufficient? Paradoxically, "Size circumscribes—it has no room / For petty furniture—/

The Giant tolerates no Gnat—." Those of "intrinsic size" (641) are blinded to the possibilities of the tiny, while they are cognizant of their "superiors." When the fingers of morning light arrive, it is the gnat who is wise enough to hold up "His Cup for Light" (1000).

Dickinson's superb touch with obscure animals comes not only with her affinity for the peculiar artist but with an eye for beauty in animal forms considered ugly. Yet, in her commitment to artistic activity, she is not a poet to turn away from the light. With day come the birds—many birds, generally, and those of particular families: lark, sparrow, bluejay, oriole, crow, bobolink, robin, hummingbird, and others. As birds are traditionally represented, hers are free-spirited creatures of song. But they are not symbolic of the heavens. Most of them are on the ground or not far from it. They are punctual performers whose talent is not for escape.

The arrival of the birds signaling the end of the long Amherst winter, which Dickinson laments from girlhood, is the single most important idea associated with them: "The Orchard, when the Sun is on— / The Triumph of the Birds" (575). In that "magical frontier," "Between the March and April line—" (1764), the traveled male bird brings news of the world beyond. His talented song as announcement of spring is of another order from that of the organic unfolding of plants. The bird inexplicably musters the spirit for new life, qualifying him as the implied metaphor of the distinctive definition poem, " 'Hope' is the thing with feathers— / That perches in the soul—" (254).

The first principle of the bird's art is punctuality, the one element associated with productivity that Dickinson attributes to the female. Although the unannounced arrival of the male animal makes for her most thrilling poems, this poet for whom anxiety is the rule finds cause for gratitude and rejoicing in the "confirmed perpetual" (973) of the seasonal creatures. The punctual beginning of the birds' workday reflects both the discipline of the artist and the early rising of those who do what they love. "The Birds begun at Four o'clock— / Their period for Dawn—" (783). Like Thoreau in her economies, Dickinson is never closer to him in spirit than with this act of improving the quality of the day, as the birds' genius brings them alive at dawn. But their art follows careful, measured stages: "At

Half past Three, a single Bird / Unto a silent Sky / Propounded but a single term / Of cautious melody. / At Half past Four, Experiment / Had subjugated test / And lo, Her silver Principle / Supplanted all the rest" (1083). Formal terminology applied to the creative experience supports a view that creation is not an unconscious act. But neither is it a tortured one: "What respite from her thrilling toil / Did Beauty ever take— / But Work might be electric Rest / To those that Magic make—" (1585). The modern notion that the artist's work is agony would be a lie for one who thinks New Englandly, for whom "thrilling toil" and "electric Rest" are not paradoxical.

The animal subject of romantic literature, the bird, is not the favorite in American literature, where so many animals are substantial citizens of this world. And Dickinson's birds are unconventional in their immediacy, making those of romantic renown blur by comparison. "A Bird came down the Walk— / He did not know I saw— / He bit an Angleworm in halves / And ate the fellow raw . . ." (328). The characteristic straightforward introduction, offering no metaphor and not even a particularizing verb, creates its drama simply because the bird is there, on the ground coming toward the poet, when he might be flying away. That he is not given a specific designation is also a mark of immediacy in the Dickinson poem, where some of the most brilliant characters are not named at all, as if to do so is to take a formal step away from the immediately present animal. That the bird is not thoroughly individualized also allows his double to reappear each spring, as if proving immunity to death. But he is otherwise not representative of the immortal. Rather, to love birds, Dickinson writes, is "economical. . . . It saves going to Heaven."[12]

That Dickinson's bird coolly devours the angleworm has been used as evidence, along with climatic destruction, in an argument for naturalism or a similarly hostile view of "nature." The tone of the first stanza is that of the amoral workings of a natural world where power is all (although it is precision which marks the account). But this predatory situation, especially where the living victim plays no active role, is the exception. And the stanzas that follow the bird's cool kill do not hold with a deterministic philosophy. The bird moves aside for a smaller, less powerful creature, and his eyes become "frightened Beads" (328), revealing him not as an insensible agent of nature but one who is vulnerable to an intrusive rather than a destructive force. His partaking of a singular dew reveals him as citizen of a sophisticated miniature world beyond the reach of bigger beings rather than a coldly materialistic one. Even if this bird were portrayed as a thoroughgoing deterministic agent, to lump animal behavior with the frost's destruction of a flower and a thunderstorm's splitting of a tree (the storm which sends animals as well as people to cover) is not only to miss a crucial distinction in Dickinson's natural world but to make the error of literary criticism generally which heaps animal, plant, and elements into a single theory.

This bird *came* down the walk, *bit, ate, drank, hopped, glanced, hurried,* and *stirred*—all verbs indicative of earthly motion. Even in his leave-taking, he "unrolled his feathers / And rowed him softer home—" (328), the exquisite rendering of flight that connects the bird with water rather than air, a precisely accurate image of the motion of birds' wings, too, as high-speed photographs have since shown.[13] Not only for the sake of the unorthodox word but because her birds are more attached to earth than sky, Dickinson rarely uses the word *fly.* The verb of being is at times enough for an electric appeal, as after winter, "the *birds* were here!" (97). They come, stand, and sit with charm. One rides as a man on horseback: "Upon his Saddle sprung a Bird / And crossed a thousand Trees / Before a Fence without a Fare" (1600) thrillingly close to earth, the trees his challenge. When the bird does leave the ground, it is with the effort necessary to lift weight. A bird "hoists" (514) up to a tree. Another "trod upon the trees," then "situated . . . Upon a pile of wind" (1723). The gravitational pull is not a grim tug away from heaven but the realistic draw to the place of life. While much of her poetry addresses the immortal, Dickinson's animals provide the antidote to the merely speculative. Even financial terminology—"Fare" and "squandered" (1600)—is more than sardonic comment on the absence of praise for the birds' song; it adds a worldly toughness.

It is the bird's will to sing that above all endears him to this poet. Beyond reason, he (and male birds do most of the singing) delivers a song of joy. "The most triumphant Bird I ever knew or met / . . . sang for nothing scrutable / But intimate Delight" (1265); "Nor was it for applause— / That I could ascertain— / But independent Ecstasy / Of Deity and Men—" (783)—*ecstasy*—a term practically archaic to the modern mind. This song, like the bird's flight, requires effort—that of lifting the throat to sing. The unusually violent "Split the Lark—and you'll find the Music—" (861) not only conveys the energy involved in producing music, but it makes the song so nearly inseparable from the lark as to suggest the force unifying the atom, the cohesion that exists only with the most concise. Unlike the romantic bird, Dickinson's, though a life-bringer, is not oblivious to death: at the burial gate he stoically "trilled, and quivered, and shook his throat" (1761)—therapy for despair. To dread "that first Robin so" (348) is to turn from the life of creation. To live it fully requires "An Aptitude for Bird—" (1046).

With some birds who exist on a crumb, Dickinson maintains, if not the joy of creation, the keenness of the hunger associated with it, known only to those "outside Windows" that, "Entering— takes away—" (579). But it is also with this image of impoverishment that she degenerates from pity to self-pity: "God gave a Loaf to every Bird— / But just a Crumb—to Me—" (791). The ironic result of God's "Oath to Sparrows—" is that they "know how to starve—"; to continue her point, Dickinson would have the eagle strangling on his "Golden Breakfast" (690). In his inevitable biblical connection the martyr-sparrow makes a hopelessly sentimental subject. Whenever God enters the poem, the poet's attempt to rank the least creature either collapses or strains in argument. The Father is not denied as creator. But if the animals are His creations, they are nevertheless individuals operating apart from Him. Their talents are clearly their own.

Dickinson's favorite bird is the robin, "that Bird of mine" (5), her "Criterion for tune" (285). At best, the focus is on the wonderfully minute detail of the bird's attire, not on the poet's impulses. Her eye for the fashionable line reflects an intrinsically aesthetic outfit for the robin, whose grooming also indicates the esteem of one who dresses for self. The robin's incredible lightness, so delicate as not to offend the earth by placing pressure on it—"The

smallest Gamboge Hand / With Fingers—where the Toes should
be— / Would more affront the Sand— / Than this Quaint Creature's Boot—" (634)—combines with the sturdiness produced by
boot, vest, jacket, and cap, tight-fitting to resist the New England
winds. The shades are warm and tasteful: the bright yellow (gamboge) in moderation—the color nature "rarer uses . . . Than another Hue" (1045)—coordinating with the brown and orange vest.
Velvet and wool are bettered in the robin, whose garment does not
fray or go out of style, and whose fit cannot be matched by man.
Its superior tailoring eliminates button, hat brim, seam.

At worst, the Dickinson robin, her most familiar animal subject—"I grow—where Robins do—" (285)—becomes the most
clichéd of birds. This victim of smallness, used for the humanitarian
message that drains her animals of their own lives, serves as the
unfortunate subject of one of this great poet's tritest poems: "If I
can stop one Heart from breaking / I shall not live in vain / . . . Or
help one fainting Robin / Unto his Nest again . . ." (919).

Sparrow and robin, the meek of the earth, are excelled by the
rarer and spunkier birds. The "executive" jay, "Bold as a Bailiff's
Hymn—" (1177), summons the poet's more rigorous spirit. The
crow, as close to genuine outlaw as any, with "sweet derision"
(1669) defies the conventional color and season for birds, scorning
the deceptive crumbs of fame's "fickle food" with his "ironic caw"
(1659). Another favorite "outlaw" is the "Prodigal" oriole, so generously awarded by Midas that he appears (like others, gravitation-
ally) as an "alighting Mine—." This "Epicure—a Thief" is yet
"Betimes an Oratorio— . . . a Pageant" (1466), whose only crimes
are handsomeness and talent, the mock decadence Dickinson plays
with. The oriole's cheer defies Puritan severity—he whose continuous song is a surer sign of the final retreat of winter than that of
robin or bluebird. And the "seditious" bobolink, guilty of "Heresies of Transport" (1279), is no more decadent than the oriole. The
great heresy is the exhibition of a joyful talent. No idler, the bobolink, whose song is the sweetest in all nature, is employed as the
poet's own "Chorister" (324) in the orchard where they keep the
sabbath at home.

The concisest bird, whose song is no more than a hum of
wings, surpasses all others.

A Route of Evanescence
With a revolving Wheel—
A Resonance of Emerald—
A Rush of Cochineal—
And every Blossom on the Bush
Adjusts its tumbled Head—
The mail from Tunis, probably,
An easy Morning's Ride—   (1463)

The hummingbird combines the most exciting aspects of Dickinson's animals generally: ecstasy of performance is in inverse proportion to duration; motion, particularly flight, is congruent with a solid connection to earth; impressiveness of form and color is in inverse proportion to size; the local citizen is also an exotic traveled male; and the animal is a worker. To condense these qualities into eight short lines is Dickinson's supreme achievement with the concise. The coalescence of senses (seen as the result of human deterioration in "I heard a fly buzz") into the synesthetic "Resonance of Emerald" is now practically unavoidable, as the bird's performance ends almost as it begins. In eliminating verbs altogether in the first four lines, the poet erases the distinction between present and past, allowing the hummingbird's coming-going and the impression that remains to occur as if simultaneously. Action words become nouns—*Rush* and *Ride*. *Route, Wheel, Blossom, Head,* and *mail* could be turned into verbs. *Adjusts,* the single, appropriately present tense verb, is ironically the motion of stationary blossom. And to have that emblem of the transitory remain as the enduring figure ingeniously highlights the speed of the bird's passage. Also in contrast to the vanquished flower that remains to die, the hummingbird lives on. He *is*.

Incredibly in motion, this apparition made of wings is yet associated with earth, moving on a horizontal plane as a wheel, in an earlier poem, as a "Fairy gig" (500). The colors varying with the slant of light in the hummingbird paradoxically carry the solidity of gemstone, the permanence of pigment (cochineal), in the incredibly small proportions that thrill as a larger splash of color does not. The exoticism rising from immense condensation is matched by speed and rarity of appearance. Though a native of New England, this ruby-throated species migrates (if not to Tunis) to Central America. And for Dickinson, this frontiersman brings word of land more exciting than skies. As purely aesthetic as this hummingbird is, he is also given the role of common laborer—a mailman following his route, and completing that appointed task with breathtaking efficiency. His delivery pollinates. Dickinson could not have found a more exquisite model in nature for so much that she values. Smaller than the female, this three-and-one-quarter-inch male is a phenomenon of beauty and economy. Only he wears a ruby throat. And this energy-efficient marvel, seeming in perpetual motion, rides 500 miles without stopping for rest or fuel.

As certainly beyond the "eyelids of the Sepulchre" as the bird, "Color's Revelations break— / And blaze—the Butterflies!" (496). Lighter than the hummingbird, and with perhaps too great a splash of color, the butterfly lacks the hummingbird's paradoxical stability. Like others with an "Aptitude to fly" (1099), butterflies travel as those on earth—they *step* "through the firmament" (533). But their wing movement is too slow to be exciting. With the freedom of nature's other people, that spirit in the butterfly is one rather of insecurity. Although this is said to be "Joy's insuring quality" (1434), the butterfly's unnerving tendency is to "shut its spotted Fan" and "panting on a Clover lean / As if it were undone" (1387). It must *rest* "on a Beam—" (533), having, of all nature's people, the least energy. Easily "defrauded" (730), the butterfly does not even "know its Name" (1521). It is either that rare neuter animal or it is frivolously female. Its dress is all, spangled but excessive, like the word *butterfly* itself. Even in its aptitude to waltz, it does so with the unevenness of the pattern of threes, not the smoothness of a dance. The butterfly does little but attempt to entertain itself. And this lack of meaningful labor is the crucial flaw. This "dreamy" creature "Fritters itself away!" (64), an "Audience of Idleness" compared to the "Bee—that worked." As one without career, the distinctly female butterfly emerges from her door "Without Design—. . . On Miscellaneous Enterprise," going in "purposeless Circumference—." Her "pretty Parasol be seen / Contracting in a Field / Where Men made Hay—" (354). Never is Dickinson more antifeminist than in this unmistakable version of the vapidity of the model female.

One of the more fascinating aspects of the butterfly is its mysterious origin, the cocoon's secret, "perched in ecstasy" (129). The caterpillar, who *is* intent upon a career, arrives as a versatile "fuzzy fellow, without feet, / Yet doth exceeding run! . . . Sometime, he dwelleth in the grass! / Sometime, upon a bough." The light-hearted treatment of this purposeful larva does not undercut his achievement. Successful creation brings gaiety—it can afford understatement. The caterpillar need not exhibit his tiny legs for them to do their work. He is confident enough even to model the costume of a lady and outdo her at that. "He taketh *Damask* Residence— / And struts in sewing silk! / Then, finer than a Lady, / Emerges in the spring! / A Feather on each shoulder!" (173). This clever technique of allowing the caterpillar to maintain his male identity, in female form, explains the mysterious shift in gender from male caterpillar to neuter or female butterfly. Dickinson's immense compliment to her male animals is not only in granting them practically sole rights to the nobility of work and art but in replacing masculine strength with the delicacy usually considered feminine. And as a final triumph, as in nature where males are the better dressers, hers are at least as elegant in attire as the females.

The acknowledgment "I know the Butterfly" is a key to its weakness. But "The Bee is not afraid of me" (111). While he appears oftener in Dickinson's poetry than any other animal, he is most distinctly an *other;* although the bee is a swarming creature, hers is clearly a single male other. Of all her concise creatures, he is the most complete. This is, after all, the insect with two sets of wings that fold so he may enter the precise honeycomb or flower; he is also the insect with five eyes. Exemplar of the joyous life of noon's moment, Dickinson's bees nevertheless do not "despise the tune— / Their Forefathers have hummed—" (342). The bee's sturdy black body is complemented by "Gilt" (the favored color) "Surcingles" (1405)—a word meaning either the girth that secures a horse's saddle or the girdle of a cassock; thus he is ingeniously bestowed with both worldly and ecclesiastical powers. Prepared in helmet of matching gold, he is one of the few characters allowed a military aspect without the pejorative associations of power. Solid as "a Single Onyx," the gem that is one piece contains layers of various colors, still his feet are "shod with Gauze—" (916), allowing for the imperative light touch of the Dickinson artist. Armored and dense as a gem, he may yet balance on a blade of grass.

The bee's name could not be more perfectly suited to his concise form, just as it so deliciously reflects his song—a confident hum. With her ultimately onomatopoeic creature, Dickinson exercises a variety of alliterative patterns: "the Bee be booming" (1381); "Baronial Bees—" (64); "Bees are Black . . . Buccaneers of Buzz" (1405). His "song" is more distinctly represented than that of birds; though a hum that disturbs, it is a reliable sound at that, "Like Trains of Cars on Tracks of Plush / I hear the level Bee—" (1224). Connected most definitely to earth for his benefits, the shrewd bee is not defrauded by the "sophistries of June—" (130). Worldliest of creatures, he is that animal practically nonexistent in American literature—one who is both sexy and free. Quick to the flower, he also propounds "Continual Divorce" (896). Known for his "abashless play" (1738), this reveler, seducer, blasphemer, drunkard is yet the most solidly established worker in the animal kingdom, supreme as a model of the healthy, creative life.

That Dickinson's bee is one of the few erotic animals in American literature says more for the absence of sexuality than it makes a case for a super lover in the insect who seduces and abandons nothing more than the flowers. He is no drone who sacrifices himself for the queen. The contrived role of lover is set in the Valentine's day poem that opens the variorum edition of the complete poems, an uncharacteristic long verse in rhymed couplets (never again were pairs to match so tidily), where among pairings—bride-bridegroom, sun-moon, Adam-Eve—are bee who "doth court the flower, the flower his suit receives" (I). Although this atypical verse is to be superseded by a devastating view of romantic love, the image of bee and flower, establishing the dichotomy of male activity and female passivity, is consistent throughout Dickinson's work. A "profound / Responsibility—" of the stationary flower is to "Escape the prowling Bee" (1058), although no means of escape is evident.

That the passionate Emily Dickinson allows female sensuality, in a literature which has obscured it, to surface in nature through blossom rather than through living animal is quaint certification of the repressive convention. The flower's "Velvet Masonry / Withstands until the sweet Assault / Their Chivalry consumes— / While He, victorious tilts away / To vanquish other Blooms" (1224); the bee drives his "burnished Carriage . . . boldly to a Rose— / . . . Their Moment consummated— / Remained for him—to flee— / Remained for her—of rapture / But the humility" (1339). In each case the female flower is drained of life and character while the productive bee is enhanced by the encounter. This painful, traditional image of the woman's situation allows superiority to the male on every count, not the least of which is mobility. Envy of the bee is not so much for his sexual role as for his energy and for that endearing American cause, his freedom: "Could I but ride indefinite / As doth the Meadow Bee / . . . And dwell a little everywhere / Or better run away. . . ." (661).

The bee, free from reprisal by the love object, is beyond all authority. Mocking deity, "An aged Bee addressed us— / . . . In the name of the Bee— / And of the Butterfly— / And of the Breeze— Amen!" (18). He buzzes the pompous into obscurity. With powers of witchcraft and "oriental heresies" he fills the air with "gay apostasy" (1526). The heady Dickinson shows poet and bee as drinking companions—"We—Bee and I—live by the quaffing—" (230). The "connoisseur in Liquors" (1628) pledges "in minute flagons," as bachelor (the title she used for herself) artists celebrate beyond that other celebration, the marriage feast. "He and I—revel—," "*I*— never wed" (230). Far from an erotic association with the bee here, the poet is his equal. And both only play at revelry: they are intoxicated through natural juices, more particularly, their own creative powers: "Of juleps, part are in the Jug / And more are in the joy—" (1628). Better than sex, power, or liquor is their creative high.

In his seeming decadence the bee is actually producing all along. The cliché of industrious bee is not reduced by Dickinson, even in a play on the words—"Bees as bustling go—" (54). Far from mocking his industry-art, it is that which she values above all else. The more completely one's career may be followed, the more triumphant, even lighthearted the creator may be. One need not work in the dark. And the daytime bee is the ultimate success: he produces the sweetest, most valued commodity, which, unlike the spider's web, does last. American creature that he is, he is responsible for it

himself. "The Pedigree of Honey / Does not concern the Bee—"
(1627).

While some citizens are pathetic with their meager sustenance,
bees add their "Amber Crumb" to "Loaves of Honey" (1160).
Though the future and death are not the bee's concern, he is stoic
rather than oblivious to destruction. When "A single Clover Plank"
is all that saves him from sinking to the "Firmament below" (the
earth that is better than heaven), the "harrowing event" (harrowing
at least to the poet) does "not so much as wring from him / A
wandering 'Alas' " (1343). He is too busy to mourn. The "loaded
bee" is a full jar riding the meadow he would not replace with sky.
So complete, so competent is he that he heads the list of "The most
important population . . . bumble-bees and other nations" (1746).
No wonder all it takes "To make a prairie" is "a clover and one
bee" (1755). And contrary to the poet's aesthetic notion, even she
probably could not do it without the bee.

He does not sting. It is enough that he might. Such violation,
instead, is metaphor for the anticipated arrival of the human guest,
whose approach undoes the nerves for good. The concise creatures
offer a more invigorating emotional awakening in their coming, in
a world the poet turns over to them.

Notes

1. Emily Dickinson, *The Complete Poems of Emily Dickinson,*
ed. Thomas H. Johnson (Boston: Little, Brown, 1960). Subsequent
references to the poetry will be from this edition and will appear in
the text.

2. Charles R. Anderson, *Emily Dickinson's Poetry: Stairway of
Surprise* (Garden City, N.Y.: Doubleday, 1960), pp. 133–36.

3. Emily Dickinson "To T. W. Higginson," 1862, *The Letters
of Emily Dickinson,* ed. Thomas H. Johnson (Cambridge, Mass.:
Belknap Press of Harvard University Press, 1958), II, 415.

4. Anderson, pp. 141–44.

5. Richard Chase, *Emily Dickinson* (New York: Sloane, 1951),
pp. 121–22.

6. Richard B. Sewall, *The Life of Emily Dickinson* (New York:
Farrar, Strauss and Giroux, 1974), 2 vols.

7. Clark Griffith, *The Long Shadow: Emily Dickinson's Tragic Poetry* (Princeton, N.J.: Princeton University Press, 1964), p. 182.

8. Ibid.

9. John Crowe Ransom, "Emily Dickinson: A Poet Restored," in *Emily Dickinson: A Collection of Critical Essays,* ed. Richard B. Sewall (Englewood Cliffs, N.J.: Prentice-Hall, 1963), p. 90.

10. Griffith, p. 137.

11. Dickinson "To Louise Norcross," 1859, *Letters,* II, 354.

12. Dickinson "To Eugenia Hall," 1876, *Letters,* II, 500.

13. Charles R. Metzger, "Emily Dickinson's Sly Bird," *Emerson Society Quarterly,* 44 (3d Quarter, 1966), 22.

CHAPTER 3

"If a frog had wings, he wouldn't bump his ass so much."
—John McCabe

Lowbrow Animals: Mark Twain

A Twain mule thinks straighter than a man. Son of the frontier, iconoclast, America's king of the lowbrow fled the European museum to go to the zoo. Twain's outspoken view of animals is the most startling in American letters, and if his critters don't get center stage, they do persistently bring relief from the damned human race. Twain halts a travelogue to tell of an animal any time. And even in the tall tale, the creature gets to be himself, mostly. For the creator of the quintessentially free Huckleberry Finn, an animal's freedom is as essential as that of the classic Ameican boy. Among the favorites—and inspirers of Twain's comic genius—are cur, coyote, and Mexican plug. They are low, they are cowardly, and they are ugly. But nobody lords it over them.

Under the comedy stirs the compassion. Twain's mother, a champion of the "other animals," taught her son well. Notorious for her interest in animal welfare, she ordered a cartman to stop beating his horse and to never do it again. Nineteen cats lived with the family at one time, but no caged pet was ever allowed. Twain claims that not even a rat would have been deprived of his liberty. As a boy, he took the usual delight of his time in the coon hunt. Everybody enjoyed it, he recalls—everybody except the coon.[1]

Twain's calling for hunting ended when he saw the bird's neck twist in the sky before the victim dropped dead at his feet. His mother's admonition not to kill was then enforced upon his life forever.[2]

One may be forced to kill for survival, as Huck is when he slaughters the hog as a decoy to protect himself from pap. But this gory task is no sport and would be better avoided. The hunt is rather the satiric subject, beginning with the self-parody of the supremely inept hunter. As a boy with a shotgun "not much heavier than a broom . . . I was not able to hit anything, . . . but I liked to try." While the bigger boys kill hawks and wild geese, the Twain persona is harmless. An "ostensible lame turkey" leads the youth "over a considerable part of the United States one morning" because he "believed in her and could not think she would deceive a mere boy, and one who was trusting her and considering her honest."[3] When he finally catches up, the turkey flies away. Success at fishing also eludes the bungling savior of the species, who need not look for the ideal fishing hole, as "one place is just as good as another, for the reason that the fish do not bite anywhere, and so there is no use in your walking five miles to fish, when you can depend on being just as unsuccessful nearer home."[4]

The hunter as hero is a favorite target. Twain recalls visiting a General Sickles, minus one leg, who reclined in a two-room suite spread thick with "lion skins, tiger skins, leopard skins, elephant skins. . . . You couldn't walk across that floor without stumbling over the hard heads of lions and things. . . . it was as if a menagerie had undressed in the place" (340–41 *A*). The reality of Twain's animals is impressed by physical contact. One may ram or caress them, but they have a right to their place. And the general's animal skins and heads have more life than their dismembered owner. They don't give off an odor, though the general's disinfectant stinks up the room.

As war hero is made defunct hunter, Twain's satire rises to level the president of the United States himself, Theodore Roosevelt. The chief of state à la shotgun comes within three miles of his prey when the bear bursts, and half the Rough Riders gallop off— to find the president. "Why don't they stop hunting the bear altogether and hunt the President?" White House domestics claim he did find an authentic bear, but Twain figures it was probably only a cow.[5]

A key doctrine in Twain's view of animals comes from the teachings of a man named Macfarlane, who fifteen years before Darwin's *The Descent of Man* explained that animal life was developed in the course of aeons of time on an ascending scale until the ultimate perfection was achieved with man. According to Macfarlane, however, the progressive scheme came to wreck and ruin, as only man developed envy, vindictiveness, hatred (146 *A*). Similarly, after studying the traits of the "lower animals," Twain concludes in "The Damned Human Race" (*Letters from the Earth*, 1974) that he must renounce his "allegiance to the Darwinian theory of the Ascent of Man from the Lower Animals; since it now seems plain to me that that theory ought to be vacated in favor of a new and truer one, . . . the *D*escent of Man from the Higher Animals." His proof, sin by sin, shows man as the only cruel or obscene animal, the only animal who goes to war, the only religious animal. His overall defect is his Moral Sense.[6]

Twain's attack on the Bible reviles Christians for their invention of malicious and masochistic doctrines. And yet he speaks as one who believes the biblical God is no invention—He is there to scorn. This vicious creator formed animals (including man) incapable of counteracting their temperaments, a concept illustrated "In the Animals' Court." Here the rabbit, for one, is found to be a coward and hanged because military law forbids desertion, although he had no choice but to follow the " 'law of God, which denies courage to the rabbit' " (170 *LE*). The lion, on the other hand, is rewarded with a dukedom for the strength and endurance granted to him. Within the limits of their natures, men are responsible for moral choice. But the other animals remain innocent.

Above all, the creatures are a life force set against the deadliness of religion. The church in Twain's hometown was perched on logs two or three feet from the ground, where he was relieved during the services by the sound of hogs snorting under the floorboards. An attraction in his next home, Hannibal, was the limestone cave with its bats, which he made famous in *The Adventures of Tom Sawyer* (1876). As one who deplumes the ethereal bird, Twain maintains that the bat is "as friendly a bird as there is. . . . I do not know any creature that is pleasanter to the touch or is more grateful for caressings, if offered in the right spirit" (104 *A*). Twain brings us into certain physical contact with animals, yet he was a man noted for *not* touching people. According to his friend William Dean Howells, "he had the fine instinct . . . of never putting his hands on you."[7] Justin Kaplan puts it this way: the man "detested pawing or touching other people."[8] Yet as a boy he carried a bat or a snake in his pocket to pet. Learning early that rattlers and puff adders were dangerous, he also admits that black snakes were so scary he "fled without shame." But the house snakes or garters were tame enough to carry home and put in his aunt's work basket (103–4 *A*).

The Mississippi River taught the young Twain critical lessons in the physical realities. A riverboat pilot had to know where the reef in the river was or he would slam into it. Animals, too, were obstacles. Marquette had run into catfish on that river. The novice Twain is told that alligators rammed the boats or ran them aground— the characteristic obstinate, palpable beasts who spoil men's plans. The story goes that alligators also tricked the pilots—"the damned things shift around so—."[9] The only way to convince an alligator was to dredge him.

Along the banks of the Mississippi lurk the beasts Twain most loves to hate—*dogs*. "Six or eight base-born and spiritless yellow curs, attached to the family by strings," are dragged onto a landing cabin, "all four feet braced and sliding along the stage, head likely to be pulled off" (187 *LM*). The horror of attachment is as keen for a dog as it is for a man. And a string—a pun on apron string, strings attached—is as devastating as a chain.

The benign dog-master relationship is virtually nonexistent in Twain's work. It's hard to imagine Huck with a pet dog. The hounds he meets up with are barking monsters, admirably defiant. A funeral is brought to life by the commotion of a dog catching a rat in the cellar. And on one deathlike Sunday Huck is resurrected by a mob of hounds "a-barking and howling . . . sailing over fences and around corners from everywhere."[10] Hounds break into Jim's room and *bulge* under the bed, piling into the place so a man can't get his breath. But if these "devils" invade the house, they are safely beyond domestication.

Twain's passion for freedom is matched by a bitterness against the destructive exploitation of animals. In *Life on the Mississippi* (1883) he walks out on a cockfight when a big, spur-equipped black cock bloodies a small gray one. (A victory is scored for the gray underdog, however, as the black cock dies.) A better southern sport is the mule race, easily superior to the conventional horse race. Why, the mule that Twain bets on "would have won if the procession had been reversed" (263 *LM*).

Twain's talent for relating the animal contest resulted in his first publishing success, "The Notorious Jumping Frog of Calaveras County" (1865). Maxwell Geismar maintains that Twain's prose is "at its peak in the descriptions of animals. . . . They are marvelously entertaining; but they are *themselves* always, too,"[11] a truth well illustrated in this favorite tall tale. Said to date back to Greece, it could not have suited Twain better as he shows vain man dependent on the "lower" animals. "If there was a horse-race, you'd find him [Jim Smiley] flush or you'd find him busted at the end of it; if there was a dog-fight, he'd bet on it; if there was a cat-fight, he'd bet on it; if there was a chicken-fight, he'd bet on it; why, if there was two birds setting on a fence, he would bet you which one would fly first."[12] Consistent with Twain's view of the evolutionary hierarchy, the passage climaxes with the "lower" species.

Smiley's horse, dubbed the "fifteen-minute nag" by observers, is everything a classic racehorse is not—sickly, awkward, out of control. But she wins. "Always at the fag end of a race she'd get excited and desperate like and come cavorting and straddling up, and scattering her legs around limber, sometimes in the air, and sometimes out to one side among the fences, and kicking up m-o-r-e dust and raising m-o-r-e racket with her coughing and sneezing and blowing her nose—and always fetch up at the stand just about a neck ahead, as near as you could cipher it down" (2 "JF"). Far from being disadvantages, imbalance and desperation are the very factors that lead to success.

The animal heroes in this tale—a bull pup named Andrew Jackson and a frog dubbed Daniel Webster—usually triumph, but by losing they score an ironic victory in their smug owner's defeat. The pup is beaten in a fight with a dog whose hind legs were cut off by a circular saw and are thus not there to grab. And the frog, stuffed with quail shot by Smiley's opponent, falls in his jumping contest. The dog dies after defeat, but the frog is above the anguish of competition, that affliction brought on by man. This talented jumper is content to flop to the floor "solid as a gob of mud," where he falls to "scratching the side of his head . . . as indifferent as if he hadn't no idea he'd been doin' any more'n any frog might do. You never see a frog so modest and straightfor'ard as he was, for all he was so gifted" (4 "JF").

The animals of "Jumping Frog" perform naturally, with the imposition of human traits carrying the satiric thrust. The "scattering" of the horse's legs and the jumping and scratching of the frog give an actual picture. The comical extensions of human attributes, modesty and indifference, are at the same time accurate terms: the frog is without vanity and beyond the motivation of the contest. Besides entertaining the community through feats of jumping, racing, and fighting, the animals surpass man in being free from those emotions that reduce him to a miserable fool—competitiveness, greed, ego.

The American West, where the tall tale flourished, is Twain's richest animal turf. The first things the narrator of *Roughing It* (1871) looks forward to seeing out there are "buffaloes and Indians, and prairie dogs, and antelopes."[13] If what he finds doesn't reflect his ideal, it is far from disappointing. Only the *lack* of wildlife is distressing—California's Mono Lake with "no fish, . . . no frogs, no snakes, no polliwogs—nothing, in fact, that goes to make life desirable" (202 *RI*). As if created for satire, the desert calls for the mocking exaggeration of the little that is there. Imagination is a must for the same reason as it is in *Don Quixote*. But where Cervantes' hero transforms ugliness to beauty, the Twain persona relishes the unsightly, seeks it out.

The embodiment of the deliciously homely is the western animal, that source of intrigue generally in the West. A tale is likely to begin, "Did you hear the one about the . . . ?" Such is the anticipation created for Jim Blaine's story of his grandfather's ram, which he finally tells one candlelit night to a crowd gathered in his cabin. "There never was a more bullier old ram than what he was" (288 *RI*), he begins. But the fraudulent narrator never gets back to that ram once.

The trip across America reflects a fool ambition and the victimization of animals. The Mormon pioneers are a group of "tired men and women" who have in tow "many a disgusted sheep and cow" (87 *RI*) that would no doubt have elected to stay home in the pasture. The alkali desert is a graveyard for beasts of burden: never are we allowed to forget that the West could not have been developed without them.

The first version of animal killer is a woman ensconced in Twain's coach. She would fasten her eyes on a mosquito "rooting into her arm" and then "launch a slap at him that would have jolted a cow; and after that she would sit and contemplate the corpse with tranquil satisfaction—for she never missed her mosquito; she was a dead shot at short range." In this manner she would kill thirty or forty mosquitoes, leaving the carcasses out for bait. A word from the other travelers sends this formerly Sphinx-like executioner into unstoppable chatter—"How we suffered, suffered, suffered!" (34 *RI*)—as the mock heroic attack levels both the woman traveler in the West and the pompous display of power over an insect.

The down-to-earth animals of the West are its color—gray. They are disproportionate, tough, and free. First is the jackass rabbit, a "long gray form" with "longer legs in proportion to his size" and "the most preposterous ears that ever were mounted on any creature *but* a jackass" (37–38 *RI*). The passive construction directs the responsibility for this peculiarity to the rabbit's Creator. Delight in disproportion rather than a focus on Deity, however, keeps the picture light. While the animal tale may issue a moral point about man, the chance encounter brings passages or even pages of pure description. A surface mockery cloaks a satisfaction with the surprise appearance of the scroungy beast, who is also sensible enough to run away from people. At the snap of a twig the jackass rabbit takes off, allowing that excellent, *rear* view. "Frightened clear through . . . he lays his long ears down on his back, straightens himself out like a yardstick every spring he makes, and scatters miles behind him with an easy indifference that is enchanting" (38 *RI*). The lifelike account needs no exaggeration. It does, rather, follow a denigrating process. The rabbit is a *jackass* rabbit; he is not white but gray; and no heroic advances for him—he retreats. Yet, outsmarting the man with the gun, he scores such wonderfully erratic leaps over the sagebrush as to be the envy of any potential escapee.

The meager life of the desert, and Twain's episodic style employing the short tale or description, are a perfect fit for those characters who randomly appear and abruptly depart. Many of *Roughing It*'s brief chapters are shaped around a single animal and perhaps others called to mind. The rabbit vanishes, leaving only the sagebrush he feeds on, which leads to an account of a camel in Syria who purportedly ate a Twain manuscript and died of it.

Generally in *Roughing It* Twain need not depart the West for animals who fit his requirements of disharmony and lack of sophistication. Mules, the worthiest of beasts, are available to replace horses. While the author has proclaimed an abhorrence of any kind of work—"from the beginning of my sojourn in this world there was a persistent vacancy in me where the industry ought to be"[14]— he respects the unpretentious labor of mules. Lest there be any eroticism, the substitution of mule for horse secures the neuter gender for the chaste Mr. Twain (whose male and female also seem neuter). Most important, the lowbrow triumphs. "Frantic mules" beat horses at their own trade as they "lay their ears back and scamper faster" (49 *RI*).

The supremely ugly, gray western lowbrow is the coyote. One rich chapter is devoted to this beast who lives in the desert with lizard, jackass rabbit, and raven, surviving on "windfalls of carrion, and occasional legacies of offal bequeathed to him by white men."

> . . . he was not a pretty creature or respectable either, for I got well acquainted with his race afterward, and can speak with confidence. The coyote is a long, slim, sick and sorry-looking skeleton, with a gray wolfskin stretched over it, a tolerably bushy tail that forever sags down with a despairing expression of forsakenness and misery, a furtive and evil eye, and a long, sharp face, with slightly lifted lip and exposed teeth. He has a general slinking expression all over. The coyote is a living, breathing allegory of Want. He is *always* hungry. He is always poor, out of luck, and friendless. The meanest creatures despise him, and even the fleas would desert him for a velocipede. He is so spiritless and cowardly that even while his exposed teeth

are pretending a threat, the rest of his face is apologizing for it.
And he is *so* homely! (49–50 *RI*)

This is simply, and wonderfully, an actual coyote. The insertion of
"allegory of Want" comes only after the literal is established, and it
emphasizes how far from traditional allegorical figures this one is.
    Outrunning the swift-footed town dog who thinks well of
himself, the coyote leaves that stuffy character "alone in the midst
of a vast solitude!" (51 *RI*). Lowbrow defeats highbrow on the
highbrow's terms. (The coyote's own more sensible use of speed is
to escape.) Far from a casualty of solitude, he maximizes the desert
as a place of liberty. In Henry Nash Smith's identification of the
coyote as the western veteran who triumphs over the eastern ten-
derfoot, he maintains that Twain's kinship with the unsophisticated
survivor is summed up in this coyote, who epitomizes what the
narrator calls " 'the gladness and the wild sense of freedom that
used to make the blood dance.' "[15]
    The inadequacy of man against beast is comically revealed in a
reversal of the hunt. A buffalo bull chases a man who claims the
bull went up a tree after him. The threat of violence is not necessary, however, to terrify Twain's puny men. A gang of the gover-
nor's alleged "paid assassins," who have become land surveyors for
something to do, fill their time by collecting a "great store of
prodigious hairy spiders—tarantulas" (130 *RI*), which they im-
prison in covered tumblers. When the deliciously hideous creatures
break free, not a one of the desperadoes goes back to bed. Paralysis
is scant punishment for that atrocity next only to the hunt,
imprisonment.
    The simple act of escape that marks the Twain animal makes
for the legend of Tom Quartz, the cat, the most admired of species
for being the only one not susceptible to the whip. Tom is known
to have "more hard, natchral sense than any man in the camp—'n-
a *power* of dignity—he wouldn't let the Gov'ner of Californy be
familiar with him. He never ketched a rat in his life—'peared to be
above it" (327 *RI*). Indeed, the "higher" animals are not predators.
Like others whose color derives from the desert, Tom is gray. But
as if he were not mangy enough to qualify for the Twain menagerie, a mine blast transforms him into "p'raps the orneriest-lookin'

beast you ever see. One ear was sot back on his neck, 'n' his tail was tove up, 'n' his eye-winkers was swinged off, 'n' he was all blacked up with powder an' smoke, an' all sloppy with mud 'n' slush f'm one end to the other." But like the other survivors of the abusive West, he is superior to men, to the miners who sweat for the sake of silver. He sniffs at their pans of ore on his way to nap on a dirt pile. Tom has learned to get out of the way the minute a fuse starts to sizzle. For this he is thought to have an understanding deeper than "sagacity." Why, " 'Twas inspiration' " (329 *RI*).

The pony express makes one of the handsomest sights in Twain's West. The industrious horse, delivering letters 1,900 miles in eight days, elicits pure admiration. But the description of the pony does not proliferate as do those of coyote or cat. He is a "fresh, impatient steed" seen as a "black speck" (63–64 *RI*) that moves at the edge of a dead-level prairie. The thrilling spectacle of that dot's becoming a horse gives immense energy to the picture. But the harmonious horse flashes by too fast to see. Either that, or Twain has neither words nor inspiration for the elegant animal.

The horse that lives is the genuine Mexican plug. What the coyote does for the dog, he does for the riding horse. The American esteem of the remote is mocked as Twain goes foreign—Mexican; adjective as well as noun declasses the favorite of all animals. The triumph of lowbrow beast over aspiring hero, through blunt physical contact, climaxes in this splendid episode where the classic image of man on horseback is scrapped. The naive persona (who has by now learned to tell a horse from a cow) can't bargain for a horse and he can't ride one. (Nor does the desperado Slade master his horse, for he can't get the beast to drink wine.) The Mexican plug has the simple sense not to want a man on his back, and all his energies go into making that decision clear.

The time-honored sight of man and horse, gliding as one, implants a passion for ownership that can't be denied. Just as the novice resolves he will have a horse, an auctioneer fortuitously arrives in the plaza on a beast that has "as many humps and corners on him as a dromedary, and was necessarily uncomely." The lust for ownership is matched by an ardor to beat out the other bidders. Our hero is lost. Though he claims to have no idea what a genuine Mexican plug is, he will own one "or die." For twenty-seven dollars, safely above the previous bid of twenty-two, the plug is his; with the help of several citizens he is about to mount. But when they let go, the beast placed "all his feet in a bunch together, lowered his back, and then suddenly arched it upward, and shot me straight into the air a matter of three or four feet!" This process is repeated until someone thwacks the horse with a leather strap and "when I arrived again the Genuine Mexican Plug was not there." All other comers meet the ground, too. The notion that a man may enhance himself by the use of an animal—literally be taller—is soundly revoked. The lower animal, man, is dumped to the ground where he belongs. Through his fall Twain learns "the poverty of the human machinery" (142–43 *RI*), particularly in comparison with the bony might of the plug. When he gets to Honolulu Twain requests a "safe horse . . . a horse with no spirit whatever—a lame one . . ." (343 *RI*).

The West provides the animal characters and the situations for them to dethrone man. In Twain's travels abroad animals are unfortunately not so available. The pleasure cruise to Europe and the Holy Land that provided the material for *The Innocents Abroad* (1869) offers animals or stories about them only as a luxury escape from obligatory sights. But the unforgettable Twain animals crop up to make his engagement with them all the more evident.

The trip on the *Quaker City* was not counted a success generally. Twain's report to the *New York Herald* calls it a "funeral excursion without a corpse." Dewey Ganzel's study of the trip, which focuses on the passengers, points to one reason for the author's disenchantment: he "*really* didn't care for most of his fellow pilgrims."[16] In *The Innocents Abroad* Twain ignores them when he can. Just as he had looked forward to the animals in the West, on this cruise his initial thought is of the "jellyfish and the nautilus over the side, and the shark, the whale, and other strange monsters of the deep."[17] One can envision the man with his back to the other passengers, gazing raptly at a fish. The truth is, much about foreign travel bores him: he is not awed by a single old master. But he does cheer up when he sees a dog.

Twain's taste for the unsightly animal continues on the continent, and if anything his appreciation is more explicit. He leaves a cemetery in Marseilles for the Zoological Gardens and finds a perfectly awful bird, built to specification: a "gray-bodied, dark-winged, bald-headed, and preposterously uncomely bird! He was so ungainly, so pimply about the head, so scaly about the legs, yet so serene, so unspeakably satisfied! . . . a godsend to us, and I should be an ingrate if I forgot to make honorable mention of him in these pages" (75 *IA*). The wretched bird makes the tourists laugh at last.

Of all edifices to distress the innocent abroad, Constantinople's St. Sophia, its "chief lion," tops the rest. If one religion is bad, another plastered on top of it is deadlier still. The dirt of St. Sophia is "more wonderful" (260 *IA*) than its historic dome. The celebrated curs of Constantinople are its truly outstanding sight, but in contrast to the reputedly ferocious dogs, the actual ones are the most "utterly wretched, starving, sad-visaged, broken-hearted looking curs" of the author's experience. Their abject laziness saves the account from being overly pitying, although these are among his most sympathetically treated hounds. Twain finds his way by noting the sleeping curs, who use the side streets rather than the Grand Rue, where they must be on the lookout for carriages. The dogs are "my compass, my guide."

Indeed, they are a *refuge* for fleas. "The hairless patches on a scalded dog are preferred by the fleas of Constantinople to a wider range on a healthier dog, and the exposed places suit the fleas exactly" (265–66 *IA*). They also suit Mark Twain just fine. With what gusto he heaps abuse on these dogs! As with other unexpected encounters with animals, the curs of Constantinople call for no moralizing. They are extracurricular to the tour—life-giving after the sights of the city and beyond the author's job as moralist. A mock defense of them carries a warmth rarely found in Twain's satire of people and never in his attack on God. Their distastefulness saves them from the sentimentality he shows in such a story as "Sailor Dog," where a beautiful St. Bernard is taken as a pet by sailors. The noble dog alerts them to a fire on the ship, but he must be abandoned by the crew, who escape in lifeboats but look back to weep.

Although it is the familiar animals who put Twain at home, he is fascinated with foreign species, particularly those of unusual proportions. The elephant's bulk qualifies him for the Twain menagerie, a size enjoyed in the account of a cat who napped on an elephant in the Zoological Gardens. A story is devoted to a stolen white elephant whose specifications are filled in on a missing person form, facts that don't need stretching for the sake of comedy. The elephant's footprint "resembles the mark left when one upends a barrel in the snow; color of the elephant, a dull white; has a hole the size of a plate in each ear for the insertion of jewelry, and possesses the habit in a remarkable degree of squirting water upon spectators and of maltreating with his trunk not only such persons as he is acquainted with, but even entire strangers."[18] Avoiding the violence animals might inflict, Twain shows instead a variety of ways they irritate and humiliate man.

A Tramp Abroad (1880) tells of Twain's more tedious second trip to Europe—and relies more heavily than The Innocents Abroad on tales of animals. The tedium is comically reinforced by the pest. A single bright interruption to the interminable German opera comes when a girl in the audience announces that she has fleas. And one entire night Twain is tormented by the sound of a mouse gnawing the woodwork, grinding away like a "nutmeg-grater" (96 TA). Throughout the night, stumbling in the dark, the miserable tourist can't touch the mouse, in one of the most memorable of "European" adventures—and one more instance of a creature's triumph over man.

Unusually sensitive to noise, Twain abhorred barking and squawking (thus viewing the nonbarking Australian dingo as the most precious dog in the world).[19] But the cacophonous bird is the very irritant to break the stultifying effect of culture—and nature: just as the tourist is ready to enjoy the "charm of legends and fairy tales" in Heidelberg, the supernatural mood of the woods is ruptured by a raven. Mocking the death symbolism of this suggestive bird, Twain's rude raven presumptuously exudes life. Eyeing the man, he croaks an insulting expression to a friend. Yet, the author notes, "they were nothing but ravens—I knew that—what they thought about me could be a matter of no consequence—."[20]

The frequent application of the word *thought* to animals comically suggests that whatever process they follow is superior to the human venture of thinking, which as Twain sees it leads to fool and often cruel ambitions. Animals are also used for an attack on man's egocentric view of language—"Animals talk to each other, . . . but I suppose there are very few people who can understand them" (16 *TA*)—the premise for "Jim Baker's Blue-Jay Yarn," which unwinds in *A Tramp Abroad*. Baker presumes to translate the remarks of birds, but while his observations run to the fantastic, the behavior of the bird in his tale is credible: a jay drops one acorn after another through a hole in the roof of a house. Baker concludes from this that the bird is trying to fill up the hole. An explanation of the cat's speech does cleverly illustrate the racket made in a cat fight: "You may say a cat uses good grammar. Well, a cat does—but you let a cat get excited once, you let a cat get to pulling fur with another cat on a shed, nights, and you'll hear grammar that will give you the lockjaw" (17 *TA*).

The satiric attack on things European relies heavily on animals in *A Tramp Abroad*. Charlemagne, for one, is reduced in a story of how he was lost in a fog and saved only when a deer led him and his troops across the ford in the river. Even the Alps, the "throne of God" (211 *TA*), are not exempt. This tourist sees only gigantic crags of dreary rock with not a vestige of plant life or a "glimpse of any creature that had life" (200 *TA*). The absurdity of climbing the Alps is sensed not by the other tourists but by the mules that carry them. Not one to illuminate harmonies in the natural world, Twain shows rock and mule in certain opposition. But the mule hangs skillfully to the edge of a trail which threatens to crumble under him—as his passenger turns white.

Horses climb too, but not as stoically. The most frightened is a "led horse that overtook us. Poor fellow, he had been born and reared in the grassy levels . . . and had never seen anything like this hideous place before. . . . he quaked from head to heel as with a palsy" (225–26 *TA*). Dependency on mules and horses leads to a tale of how the tourists attempt to get off the mountain by lashing themselves in a single file to a mule. He leads them in circles all day, and when they finally close in, at the end of the rope is an old black ram. Twain claims he made the stand between infuriated tourists and the ram, who butts him out of their way. Thus the "grace which eloquence had failed to work in those men's hearts had been wrought by a laugh" (251 *TA*), that special grace offered by the Twain animal.

One of the few fellow travelers Twain enjoys is a naturalist from New Zealand because "when he talked about animals it was a pleasure to listen to him" (729 *FE*). And again it is the triumph of animal over man that delights—the description of the extinct great moa, a bird thirteen feet high who could "step over an ordinary man's head or kick his hat off" (730 *FE*). Bizarre sizes and features are always a source of humor, but not the cruel tricks of nature: a lignified caterpillar with a plant growing out of his neck; a fish whose eyes are caked with parasites so he cannot avoid his enemies or find food. Twain does not dwell on the suffering of animals, but he painfully makes a note of it.

Bringing him back to good humor is one more wonderfully disproportionate character, "a long, low dog, with very short, strange legs—legs that curved inboard, something like parentheses turned the wrong way"—and with the dog's sagging back, it might be better if he had more legs. His owner brags as though he were responsible for his pet's assets. But Twain deftly, and characteristically, reverses the praise: "If I were built like that I could take prizes myself" (913–14 *FE*).

India was for Twain the most extraordinary land on earth, the only one he wanted to see again—significantly, a land where the lives of animals are sacred. Their reign is admittedly dangerous: government statistics show that tigers, for example, kill 800 people a year (992 *FE*). But Twain's subject is not the destructiveness of animals. He would rather bring a smile with such sights as that swaying conveyance, an elephant, who could be preferred "to any other vehicle, partly because of the immunity from collisions" (1014 *FE*). And the author is "infatuated" by the incorrigible Indian crow, "the hardest lot that wears feathers" (874 *FE*), who initiates pandemonium at dawn.

An ironic climax to the Indian trip comes with a visit to the high place of the dead known as the Towers of Silence, where the *quiet* vultures wait motionless on the rim of the tower. The funeral pyre is brought in, followed by a dog who directs the spirit. After the service the corpse is taken into the tower where the vultures swoop down to their dinner. This rite of purification keeps even the elements of fire and water free from the body. Only the vulture is foul enough to do the job—all to the satisfaction of an artist who rejoices in the creature of least repute. How fitting, then, that Twain's last trip took him to the land of belief in reincarnation, where members of the animal kingdom might rightfully be reordered. The Hindoo should not mind reappearing as an ass, the author maintains. Yet, "One could properly expect an ass to have an aversion to being turned into a Hindoo" (961 *FE*).

Twain's delight in the triumph of his lowly, higher animals, and his brilliance with the insult, make for an unforgettable menagerie of scroungy beasts: the Mexican plug that will tolerate no man, the indestructible pest, scavengers who live where no bird of paradise may be found. But it is not only as an iconoclast that Twain prefers ungainly lowbrows. Their very loathsomeness and disrepute earn a freedom that more "desirable" subjects may not know—that proud man may not attain.

Notes

1. Mark Twain, *Mark Twain's Autobiography* (New York: Harper & Brothers, 1924), I, 114–19. Subsequent references to this edition will appear in the text abbreviated as *A*.

2. Janet Smith, *Mark Twain on Man and Beast* (New York: Lawrence Hill, 1972), p. 151.

3. Mark Twain, "Hunting the Deceitful Turkey," *The Complete Short Stories of Mark Twain,* ed. Charles Neider (New York: Bantam Books, 1957), pp. 564–65.

4. Mark Twain, "A Day at Niagara," *Complete Short Stories,* p. 16.

5. Mark Twain, *Mark Twain in Eruption,* ed. Bernard DeVoto (New York: Harper & Brothers, 1922), pp. 8–10.

6. Mark Twain, *Letters from the Earth,* ed. Bernard DeVoto (New York: Harper & Row, 1974), pp. 176–81. Subsequent references to this edition will appear in the text abbreviated as *LE*.

7. William Dean Howells, *My Mark Twain* (New York: Harper & Brothers, 1910), p. 34.

8. Justin Kaplan, *Mark Twain and His World* (New York: Simon and Schuster, 1974), p. 16.

9. Mark Twain, *Life on the Mississippi* (New York: New American Library, 1961), p. 151. Subsequent references to this edition will appear in the text abbreviated as *LM*.

10. Mark Twain, *The Adventures of Huckleberry Finn* (New York: New American Library, 1959), p. 215.

11. Maxwell Geismar, ed., *The Higher Animals: A Mark Twain Bestiary* (New York: Thomas Y. Crowell, 1976).

12. Mark Twain, "The Notorious Jumping Frog of Calaverous County," *Complete Short Stories,* p. 2. Subsequent references to this edition of "The Notorious Jumping Frog . . ." will appear in the text abbreviated as "JF."

13. Mark Twain, *Roughing It* (New York: New American Library, 1962), p. 29. Subsequent references to this edition will appear in the text abbreviated as *RI.*

14. Twain, *Mark Twain in Eruption,* p. 143.

15. Henry Nash Smith, *The Development of a Writer* (Cambridge, Mass.: Belknap Press of Harvard University Press, 1962), p. 55.

16. Dewey Ganzel, *Mark Twain Abroad: The Cruise of the "Quaker City"* (Chicago: University of Chicago Press, 1968), pp. 296–97.

17. Mark Twain, *The Innocents Abroad* (New York: New American Library, 1966), p. 17. Subsequent references to this edition will appear in the text abbreviated as *IA.*

18. Mark Twain, "The Stolen White Elephant," *Complete Short Stories,* p. 201.

19. Mark Twain, *Following the Equator,* in *The Complete Travel Books of Mark Twain,* ed. Charles Neider (New York: Doubleday, 1967), II, 779. Subsequent references to this edition will appear in the text abbreviated as *FE.*

20. Mark Twain, *A Tramp Abroad,* ed. Charles Neider (New York: Harper & Row, 1977), p. 16. Subsequent references to this edition will appear in the text abbreviated as *TA.*

CHAPTER 4

"But what, *is* thy servant a dog,
that he should do this great thing?"
—2 Kings

The Wisdom of the Dogs: Jack London

A frozen earth lies void beyond the path of the sun. A dead tree falls and crushes a man. Gold dust is exchanged for an egg. The legend goes that in making the world God grew weary with his last barrowload and just dumped it. This is the Far North, the deathlike nature of Jack London's Klondike stories, where dying may be slow and unheroic in the snow. The most "stupefying" trick by which nature "convinces man of his finity" is the "the passive phase of the White Silence. All movement ceases. . . ."[1] A sign of life in this land is the footprint of a rabbit. Against a world of lifeless white move the dark specks of the living, men and dogs.

All animals face the common enemy in the "battle with frost and famine."[2] In "The Law of Life," which might as well be called the law of death, nature is the image of death for old Koskoosh, who envisions his limbs going numb as in the snow, his head nodding until he is stiff. Nature is "not kindly to the flesh,"[3] he reflects. The weaker animals go quickly—mosquitoes vanishing with the first frost. The man with intelligence and imagination need not be defeated, but he who is ignorant of the elements brings on a grim fate. And the animals who survive him are evidence that the race is no more to the powerful than it is to the wise.

London has been placed both in and out of the naturalistic

tradition in American literature. Charles Walcutt includes him on
the basis of his advocacy of Spencer's *First Principles,* that blind,
inexorable law is the operating force of the universe. Walcutt discovers, however, the discrepancy between London's ideas and the
naturalistic use he makes of them.[4] In a version of unfeeling nature
in which man's death is insignificant, London's snow works as
mechanistically as Crane's ocean in "The Open Boat." But against
that snow a subtle distinction exists in the death of London's characters: they commit a misstep of pride, an error in judgment. If
naturalism precludes free will, London is not one of its followers.
While his characters are limited by the conditions of the Klondike,
they are there by choice. And it is possible to adapt. If they were
doomed on arrival, the critical test of survival would not exist, a
struggle that follows not as the unfolding of sheerly deterministic
forces but as a result of individual instinct, imagination, and will.

Vernon Parrington excludes London from the naturalistic tradition on the basis of his revolutionary Nietzschean spirit that contradicts determinism, which Parrington sees as the key tenet of
naturalism.[5] And he is correct in doing so. The grim cosmos of
Crane, Norris, and Dreiser, where Darwinism is applied almost
exclusively as a social principle, shows man as an inevitably debased
and defeated animal in an urban jungle. London's animalistic humans, even in the wilds where they are more visceral than city
man, do resemble Norris's McTeague and similar hairy beasts. But
London's men and other animals flare with will. While a prime
determinant of the naturalistic protagonist's doom is his sexual ap-
petite, that instinct is strikingly absent in most of London's people.
Their physical drive is for food, a quest that does not always lead
to disaster.

What most dramatically sets London apart from the mainstream of naturalism in his Klondike stories—something so obvious
it is surprising to find it so rare—is that he makes Darwinism literal
and presents the *animal characters themselves.* Jay Gurian makes the
case that since "a *wholly* naturalistic human hero is an impossibility," London solves a dilemma by creating the nonhuman hero,
thus fulfilling a "romantic necessity" in naturalistic literature.[6] But
the very creation of a genuine hero dispenses with naturalism itself.

The rare survivor in deterministic fiction, if considered heroic at all, is a cynical remnant of the struggle: Sister Carrie, for example.

London creates, instead, romantically realistic heroes in his dogs—and naturalism is dispelled. It is his socialistic works that reek of pessimistic determinism. His dogs not only survive but they triumph. Within the realm of actual behavior, the exceptional dog is capable of deeds that humankind finds noble. Because adaptability is more important than sheer savagery, the triumphant animal is much more than the most powerful predatory beast. On the other hand, where he does follow the laws of survival that offend the morality expected of the human hero, he may be excused.

Had London decided upon dogs sheerly for illustration of his Darwinist views, he could not have presented them more successfully. Yet he maintains he was simply writing stories about dogs, and his least ideological writing is his best. In response to the reader who finds a human allegory in his animal characters, London maintains that when he created them he was " 'unconscious of it at the time. I did not mean to do it.' "[7] London's affection, respect, his *passion* for dogs makes them better characters than his supermen, whose superiority is always in doubt and who must mouth ideas. In releasing his lushest poetry with his animals London is further removed from naturalism, in which emotions are as pared off as opportunities are. He not only makes Darwinism literal (interpreting survival as partially a matter of will), but in his writing of dogs London shares the exultant spirit of Darwin himself, a spirit that was darkly altered by naturalism as his theories were applied to social man.

The story of a dog that comes closest to the pessimistic conclusions of naturalism is "Diable—A Dog" (1903), in which the animal is conditioned to viciousness by a vicious master. A better Pavlovian example in fiction would be difficult to find. No one shows us more effectively than London not only *that* an animal develops in response to stimuli but just *how* that development takes place, as a natural process occurring in the dog's association with man rather than as a controlled experiment.

Motivated by hate for the meanest of the litter, Black Leclère purchases the pup Diable, bred to savagery by a male wolf and to

tenacity by a female husky. While London proposes pure breeding
for his supermen, his dogs are mongrels—not just this devilish dog
but the nobler ones as well. All forces working on Diable foster
brutality, so when the first kindly hand reaches his way Diable bites
it as he would any other. Evidence for his behavior may be presented directly, without entering the dog's consciousness: "Once a
man did kick Diable, and Diable, with quick wolf snap, closed his
jaws like a steel trap on the man's leg and crunched down to the
bone." Unlike Diable's reactionary brutality, Leclère's hatred is a
product of "understanding and intelligence."[8] In mutual animosity
man and dog roll on the ground tight as lovers. But while the dog's
part in the struggle is a credible defense, Leclère's imitation of a
beast is ludicrous. One is inclined to smile when a man bites back
at a dog.

Leclère's will to dominate is all too darkly believable. His cruelty to the dog successfully fosters ferocity, whereas "with a proper
master the puppy might have made a fairly ordinary, efficient sled
dog" (90). Still, Leclère's drive to make Diable "wilt in spirit and
cringe and whimper at his feet" (91) fails. Heredity and conditioning count for much in his behavior, but an individual will drives
him on where another dog would be broken.

In an attack on the "nature" writing of his time, London
denounces the view that all animals below man are "automatons
and perform actions only of two sorts—mechanical and reflex—
and that in such actions no reasoning enters at all." The belief that
man is the only animal capable of reasoning, he says, "makes the
twentieth-century scientist smile. It is not modern at all. It is distinctly mediaeval . . . homocentric." As an example of animal
reasoning London cites the case of a dog who liked to ride in a car
so much he left his food when he heard the horn. "In thus forsaking
his breakfast for the automobile he was displaying what is called
the power of choice." When the horn was sounded twice more as a
joke, the dog grew wise and stayed with his meal. "Thus once
more did he display power of choice, incidentally of control, for
when the horn tooted it was all he could do to refrain from running
for the barn"[9] where the car was kept.

Even conditioned as he is, Diable is capable of choice, which
he exercises in one case by attacking his master in his sleep. The

dog's final, willed gesture against his enslaver is to push the box out from under Leclère, who stands condemned for murder with a noose about his neck. Even after the dog is shot, his jaws will not let go of the man's leg.

As a companion piece to "Diable—A Dog," London set out to write a short story of a dog who triumphs within his environment. But here the author found the subject of his heart—Buck—and the tale grew into a novel that has become one of the most popular American stories in the world, *The Call of the Wild* (1903). In his thrilling atavistic ascent to become the "triumphant primordial beast," Buck is as exuberant a hero as may be found in our fiction. The call that drives him might be the motto for other animals in American literature as well.

If *The Call of the Wild* is not London's most perfect work, it is as powerful as anything he wrote, with a mystique that, if anything, deepens the more civilized we become. Although written from Buck's point of view, the story is faithful to the accurate behavior of a dog. The tendency to enter the animal's consciousness in a well-developed portrayal is almost unavoidable, and London achieves that point of view with varying degrees of success. The awkward beginning, "Buck did not read the newspapers, or he would have known that trouble was brewing,"[10] gives the impression that the reader might have expected that the dog could read. To say that Buck is sent north to help men find "yellow metal" rather than gold does not solve the narrative problem of the non-verbal animal, for he no more knows the words *yellow* or *metal* than he knows the word *gold*. While one does not doubt that Buck "could not understand what it all meant" (16) when he is choked and thrown into a cage-like crate—either because such cruelty is incomprehensible *or* that a mere dog cannot grasp its meaning—this explanation lends a juvenile cast to a story which rises to much more than that. The terminology selected to represent the dog's mental processes, however, is carefully chosen according to the following theory: "I wrote, speaking of my dog-heroes: 'He did not think these things; he merely did them,' etc. And I did this repeatedly, to the clogging of my narrative and in violation of my artistic canons; and I did it in order to hammer into the average human understanding that these dog-heroes of mine were not directed by abstract reasoning, but by instinct, sensation, and emotion, and by simple reasoning."[11]

After one's initial skepticism in response to an author's entry into a dog's consciousness, Buck's point of view soon becomes acceptable, unobtrusive. He is forever a real dog, while most of his emotions, particularly his passion for freedom, are convincingly drawn. If London is guilty of the occasional cliché in *The Call of the Wild*—Buck "was beaten (he knew that); but he was not broken" (19)—it is so fused with a passionate and original story that it may be forgiven. When London's fires of injustice rage, as they do for the beaten and caged Buck, that reader would be hard who did not feel something for him. The buoyant emotions that triumph in the dog despite his acquaintance with the brutality of man and nature— which make most modern protagonists cynical—may be accepted as genuine, for the animal does not simulate emotions.

Buck is that classic American frontier hero—rugged, male, celibate, and free. As Raymond Benoit points out, in his escape to freedom Buck is as American as Rip Van Winkle.[12] But while Rip's call of the wild is an escapist's fantasy, Buck makes the dream of going into the wilderness actual. What is more, London ingeniously makes him a *proletarian* hero. Uncommonly versatile, Buck may be domestic or wild, restrained or impassioned, accepting or rebellious. While adaptability is his overall strength, a quality potentially damaging to his individuality, Buck maintains his integrity by holding to obedience under necessity without becoming subservient: "a man with a club was a lawgiver, a master to be obeyed, though not necessarily conciliated. Of this last Buck was never guilty, though he did see beaten dogs that fawned upon the man, and wagged their tails, and licked his hand" (20).

Exemplar of Darwinism, Buck also becomes a revolutionary for the working class before London had officially put Marxism to work. Through it all Buck emerges as that rarity—a fulfilled character. The "me" generations of the latter twentieth century in the quest for physical and psychological wholeness, even in the search for vocational fulfillment, might find in Buck a kind of perfection, a sense of self-completion that reaches to joy according to that Greek definition of happiness—the exercise of vital powers along lines of excellence in a life affording them scope. Buck also touches the case of the modern in another powerful way: his experience is a triumph over a subtle but significant dread—the fear of fat living.

All of this is achieved through Buck within the bounds of a realism that revolutionized popular fiction in the 1900s.[13] London defends his faithfulness to factual reality against a charge of " 'gross falsifying of nature's records,' " of *nature fakery,* by a reader none other than the president of the United States, Theodore Roosevelt (whose charge that *White Fang* [1906] errs in having the lynx kill the wolf is based on a misreading—it is the other way around). London maintains that his books about dogs are "a protest against the 'humanizing' of animals, of which it seemed to me several 'animal writers' had been profoundly guilty." His chief target is John Burroughs, the popularizer of animal lore, who despite "well-exploited and patronizing devotion" to the "lower animals" considers them "disgustingly low." His homocentric view follows from the "self-exalted ego" that requires a vast distance between man and the other animals.[14] London's strong fellow feeling for dogs is evident, but even more striking is his respect for them as remarkable individuals—capable of pain and fear, surely, but creatures unlike and often superior to man.

Only in the Alaskan frontier do London's dogs reach their fullness, a frontier whose time came perfectly for the wildly adventurous young man who went for gold and admittedly found himself in the Klondike. In 1890 the United States census had declared the last frontier officially dead, but the discovery of gold in 1896 overturned that obituary, and incidentally made possible London's literary world of the North. The rigors of the new frontier had been the myth of the poetry read to Congress prior to the purchase of the territory in 1867. In London's version, that far country becomes even more severe.[15]

Only the strongest dogs were sent to the territory from the United States and Canada. London's Buck, son of a St. Bernard father and a Scotch shepherd mother, is a large dog, whose size is matched by an equally important fitness. Although life was easy in the Santa Clara Valley, Buck's hunting sprees kept his muscles firm. Still, fitness as a pastime found no true test. In the grueling

North his muscles become hard as iron, and he grows "callous to all ordinary pain" (29). He also learns to conserve and to care for himself—how to bite ice out with his teeth when it collects between his toes and how to strike through the crust over the water hole. The old life is remembered as one of boredom; there he was easily king of the whole realm of house and kennel. Now he must earn his place at the top. He waits, and when the time is right he defeats the team's head dog, Spitz, in a death struggle that calls not only for every ounce of his new-found strength but for great ingenuity as well.

As Buck's powers increase and the inhibitions of civilization are sluffed off, this mighty young male character lacks one thing that might certainly be expected in a return to nature, particularly an animal's return to nature—an uninhibited sexual life. Yet not only does Buck escape the entanglements of mating, but he is free from the bothersome urge altogether. His unquestionable sense of virility is evidenced instead through size, strength, prowess as a fighter, and the sheer energy of his joyful gallop across the snow which takes the place of breeding as the perpetuation of life. Buck's purifying passage to the primitive calls for the abandonment of all encumbrances (such as the woman who adds the last impossible weight to the sled). No troublesome female will travel with his pack.

The threat of the female is made emphatic in the example of the dog Dolly who goes "suddenly mad," announcing her condition by a "heartbreaking wolf howl that sent every dog bristling with fear." She goes straight for Buck, who knows only that "here was horror, and fled away from it in panic" with the frantic female "panting and frothing, one leap behind." Nor does she "gain on him, so great was his terror." Buck is never so frightened as he is here—and nowhere else does he run away. Even when he was kidnapped he did not panic. The spirit of the neurotic, destroying female is at large even in the Klondike, and Buck must go deeper into the wilderness to escape her—plunging through woods and across channels "in desperation" (34–35). He is safe only when the dog-driver crushes Dolly's head with an ax.

If in the American grain Buck is predictably powerful, wilderness-loving, and celibate, he is uniquely a proletarian hero at the same time. The fact that the necessity for dogs in the Klondike took them both to the frontier and to unbearable working conditions allows for a call of the wild along with an appeal to workers of the world—in this case those who are literally enchained. When the dogs are first harnessed to the sleds they go at their task eagerly, suited as they are for long journeys in the cold. A team of huskies raising a spray of snow as they rip a sled out of place is a thrilling sight—and a triumph for them. When the dogs are fresh, all "passiveness and unconcern" disappear; they become "alert and active, anxious that the work should go well, and fiercely irritable with whatever, by delay or confusion, retarded that work" (26).

But extenuating labor is a greater killer than the cold. Buck turns rebel to incite the other dogs to protest their conditions and to overthrow the tyrannical leader, Spitz, a sort of class revolution that backfires into friction within the group. "The insidious revolt led by Buck had destroyed the solidarity of the team. It no longer was as one dog leaping in the traces. The encouragement Buck gave the rebels led them into all kinds of petty misdemeanors. No more was Spitz a leader greatly to be feared. The old awe departed, and they grew equal to challenging his authority" (38). Yet when Buck becomes head dog himself (a more just leader than Spitz, but an authority figure, nevertheless), being at the front of the sled only means more debilitating toil than before.

Most of London's dog-drivers do not learn the rule of the trail: that a man must first care for his dogs and then for himself. The old-timer knows for practical fact, not sentiment, that "as with our dogs, so with us." It would be difficult to imagine a place where people were more dependent on animals than in the Klondike of the late 1890s, where sled dogs were *the* form of transportation, food consisted mainly of meat (at least it would seem so in London's work), a fur coat was a necessity, not to mention leather moccasins, and the dogs also provided entertainment by fighting and racing. And yet "callous to the suffering of their animals" (58), their drivers wield the whip, regardless of the whines that indicate danger as well as hunger and fatigue. Under these conditions Buck's "heart was not in the work nor was the heart of any dog" (55). He has gone from 140 pounds to 115, staggering at the head of the team, "as in a nightmare. He pulled when he could; when he could no longer pull, he fell down and remained down till blows from whip or club drove him to his feet again. All the stiffness and gloss had gone out of his beautiful furry coat. The hair hung down, limp and draggled, or matted with dried blood where Hal's club had bruised him. His muscles had wasted away to knotty strings, and the flesh pads had disappeared, so that each rib and every bone in his frame were outlined cleanly through the loose hide that was wrinkled in folds of emptiness" (58). Buck would likely have died under the whip if John Thornton had not intervened to keep him in his camp. Together they watch as the foolhardy and cruel driver forces the remaining dogs across the spring ice—where the sled cracks through, taking dogs, men, and that extra weight, the woman, down to a justified death.

The stages leading to Buck's freedom, ironically set in motion when he is kidnapped from the sweet bondage of home, take a new turn in his allegiance to Thornton, a loyalty that is the exception for the animal in American literature. To the credit of the many-faceted Buck, he is capable of affection and devotion, and in this he resembles the dog of traditional lore, man's best friend. This passage in Buck's life is saved from sentimentality by the harsh struggles that precede it and the salutary rush to the wilds which follows. Buck's loyalty to Thornton, too, has in it the honoring of a debt. As conditions are turned to opportunities with Buck, his association with Thornton presents the occasions for the dog's most spectacular feats. The dramatic rescue of his master from the river comes closer than any other episode to the expected role of the dog hero of juvenile literature. But it is nicely held in bounds as Buck pulls Thornton only part way across the torrent and the full rescue requires help from the men on shore.

Buck's most wonderful performance is breaking out the sled weighted with a thousand pounds of flour at sixty degrees below zero. Not only is this more essentially a London event than the river episode because of the author's special touch with the cold, but being centered in self-fulfillment rather than altruism, it flares with his Nietzschean spirit. Buck may not know that Thornton's one thousand borrowed dollars are on the line, not to mention his pride, and the dog may get into the harness as an act of loyalty. But once he is there, the challenge is everything.

> Buck threw himself forward, tightening the traces with a jarring lunge. His whole body was gathered compactly together in the tremendous effort, the muscles writhing and knotting like live things under the silky fur. His great chest was low to the ground, his head forward and down, while his feet slipped, and one man groaned aloud. Then the sled lurched ahead in what appeared a rapid succession of jerks, though it never really came to a dead stop again . . . half an inch . . . an inch . . . two inches. . . . The jerks perceptibly diminished; as the sled gained momentum, he caught them up, till it was moving steadily along. (73)

That Buck's supremacy should become a matter of public record is appropriate and satisfying. But at the same time the episode reminds us that only humans need applause. The event also reveals the weakness of vanity in Thornton, who boasts of his dog with no idea of how much weight he can pull. Thus Buck is given a kind of moral edge over his master. Plus—in saving face and money for him, the dog more than pays his debt in full. Although the prize goes to Thornton, the fact that Buck earns $1,600 for five minutes' work clearly raises him from the ranks of proletarian laborer.

If Buck had stayed with Thornton, the call of the wild would have remained a myth. No matter how far into the wilderness the two might go, the dog would still be bound to the man. Growing restless, Buck strays from Thornton to hunt with a wolf, sensing a new blood longing and pride: "He was a killer, a thing that preyed, living on the things that lived, unaided, alone, by virtue of his own strength and prowess, surviving triumphantly in a hostile environment where only the strong survived. . . . Every part, brain and body, nerve tissue and fiber, was keyed to the most exquisite pitch" (80–81). When he returns to find Thornton slain by Indians, in a frenzied attack Buck kills them too.

And so the mighty dog is free at last for the passionate, essential life of the wild, which for him becomes literal and absolute: "There is an ecstasy that marks the summit of life, and beyond which life cannot rise. . . . He was mastered by the sheer surging of life, the tidal wave of being, the perfect joy of each separate muscle, joint, and sinew in that it was everything that was not death, that it was aglow and rampant, expressing itself in movement, flying exultantly under the stars and over the face of dead matter that did not move" (39).

No form of tooth and claw savagery is more ecstatic than London's version of the life of animals. While the violence of men may be secretly approved by some who write of it, human brutality is rarely, if ever, so completely sanctioned. So volatile is the life of London's animals that other versions of violence, Kipling's cult of savagery, for example, which was a major influence on London, is tame by comparison. The Anglo-Indian's jungle animals do lead an enviable life beyond the rule of men, but that life is civilized, almost gentle in tone. It is a jungle society that turns back on man. Animals are referred to as "Free People," and the bad animals are those who refuse to submit to authority,[16] the antithesis of the ultimately anarchic Buck.

The bloody violence that London injected into the pale literature of his time is generally considered a law of "club and fang" for all animals alike. But the approach to the brutality of men and of the other animals varies sharply. Rather than being tragic or even well motivated, the killing of man by man, especially in the Klondike where life is so scarce, is incredibly foolish. "In a Far Country" (1899) shows a man axing his cabin mate for accidentally taking sugar from the wrong bag. This rash act is not to be equated with the survival of the fittest, for the murderer is more irked than hungry. Given the power of reason to investigate, he is the stupid animal for not using it. In another instance a bride-to-be refuses to marry the man who will not kill. The bloodthirsty woman prevails, and he presents her with the heads of four of his tribesmen. Suicide is even more absurd. A hustler from California carries a thousand dozen eggs north that sell at a dollar and a half apiece, and when they turn out to be spoiled he hangs himself, a denouement more amusing than it is awful.

The physical abuse men inflict upon animals carries a power of another order. London's most flawed characters not only attempt to manipulate animals for economic purposes, but they are often sheerly sadistic. No sign of a deeply flawed human character announces itself more certainly than the gratuitous abuse of a dog.

Black Leclère's viciousness is flaunted in his treatment of Diable. Mason of "The White Silence" (1899) exhibits his twisted nature in his malicious whipping of the dog Carmen—whose name is too fancy. If one didactic thread runs through London's Klondike stories, it is that a man who ill uses dogs will suffer for it. A dead pine crushes Mason, who convinces Malamute Kid, the sourdough hero, to kill him rather than leave him to die. If it seems too pat that justice is wrought upon Mason by the fall of a tree, it would not be by chance that a man who mistreats his dogs might be stranded in the snow. Malamute Kid is in no way more clearly contrasted to Mason and men like him than by the Kid's respect and affection for the sled dogs: "Strong man, brute that he was, capable of felling an ox at a blow, he could not bear to beat the poor animals, . . . nay, almost wept with them in their misery."[17] Mason is relieved of his life, but a wounded dog must follow along behind the sled for as long as he can crawl.

Although the necessity of killing for meat is unquestioned, London rarely writes of the hunt. He personally hated to kill animals and was haunted by the sight of a beautiful bird reddening the snow.[18] The delicacy of his version of a master hunter may be surprising to the reader who knows London only for his tooth and claw battles. The elder Keesh is renowned by his tribesmen for his skill in the hunt, although no one has ever watched him kill. He always returns with a good supply of meat, properly quartered (a frozen food that is far removed from the living animal), which he distributes fairly to members of the tribe. Still, they send spies who watch him drop small balls of food to a bear who eventually falls, and Keesh spears him. Against a charge of witchcraft, Keesh reveals that he practices only headcraft: a coiled strip of whalebone was frozen into the whale blubber fed to the bear. By this intelligent, minimally violent method of hunting, a superior man survives in the North as he must. But killing an animal is not an exhilarating act.

The most dramatic slaying of an animal comes in "Love of Life" (1906), where a starving man survives on the vile-tasting blood of a wolf. This grisly account is anything but a buoyant hunting story. A skeleton of a man claws his way across the ground to suck the bones left by other animals, and the only reason he is able to kill a wolf is because the beast is diseased. They wait each other out in "as grim a tragedy of existence as was ever played—a sick man that crawled, a sick wolf that limped, two creatures dragging their dying carcasses across the desolation and hunting each other's lives."[19]

The form of violence that is exhilarating in London's work is the kill of one wild animal by another, especially in the world apart from man. London's dogs justifiably wound men—their teeth against his clubs, cages, the whip—although they almost never kill humans. But it is the hunt for food that exhilarates. Motivated by a hunger not so severe as to debilitate—and hunger is a subject London knows well from his poverty-ridden days of "meat hunger" as a child—the wild animal's energized attack is a sight of raw beauty. As being a killer in the wilds is the epitome for Buck, so is it for White Fang, who takes up where Buck leaves off.

Reversing Buck's story, London takes the three-quarter wolf, one-quarter dog from the primitive Far North to California. And as *The Call of the Wild* rises to a climax, *White Fang* dies down from one. What the author intends as the virtue of adaptation comes across instead as the case of a character who sells out, at least so it seems to the American reader. The case for civilization is apparently viewed differently in Europe, however, where *White Fang* outsells *The Call of the Wild*.

The awesome deathlike North takes up the whole first paragraph of *White Fang*: "the land itself was a desolation, lifeless, without movement. . . ." The second paragraph answers with the antithesis: "But there *was* life, abroad in the land and defiant. Down the frozen waterway toiled a string of wolfish dogs."[20] Their toil is that of the individual struggle for life, which is finally the only valid labor. Here is the world without men—where the force of death and the force of life are held in critical balance. But the men come with the enticements of a softer existence that will curtail the hunter accustomed to going after his own warm meat.

The joy of the hunt is never shown with a finer pristine beauty than in the wolf cub's first kill, his rite of passage from the cave where he has lived on meat disgorged by his mother. No experience quite matches the feel of the live ptarmigan chick he gets for himself—"alive between his teeth and therefore better" (65). How good life is! Overcoming his fright, the cub earns the delicious satisfaction that comes only in a fearful challenge well met: "The pitch to which he was aroused was tremendous. All the fighting blood of his breed was up in him and surging through him. This was living, though he did not know it. He was realizing his own meaning in the world; he was doing that for which he was made—killing meat and battling to kill it. He was justifying his existence, that which life can do no greater; for life achieves its summit when it does to the uttermost that which it was equipped to do" (66).

White Fang's coming of age lacks all caution, but the thrill of knowing what to do the first time out is the animal's special gift. And how swiftly the core experiences follow—hunger, attack, fulfillment. The appetites of body and spirit are satisfied at once in this form of the hunt, and this form alone, as it combines the elements of independent struggle (no accessory weapons), the thrill of the chase, violence, triumph, and—innocence. Here is London's beauty in violence, life at the pitch, which falls off sharply in the move toward civilization.

A key element in *White Fang*'s leanings to society is the importance of the female animal. In an opening episode a she-wolf acts as a decoy to draw dogs away from camp so the wolves of her pack can attack. Not only does she lead the enemy to danger, but she wounds each of her suitors (who treat her with nothing but gentleness). Old One Eye tries to keep free of this she-devil who is the affliction of his life, but she stays on his tail, nipping him when he makes a mistake. "The business of love was at hand—ever a sterner and crueler business than that of food-getting." The she-wolf turns wolf against wolf until the weaker ones fall, reddening the snow in the "sex-tragedy of the natural world" (39–40), which inevitably leads to socialization and the family. One Eye's victory over his companions earns him a nagging mate whose fangs are quick to sink into him when he misses a rabbit. The male wolf is ferocious; the female lynx and the she-wolf are mean-tempered. One Eye is "more in fear of his mate" (44) than of any other threat of the wild.

The she-wolf is at her fiercest and most effective as the mother of White Fang. But like any wholesome young male, he builds for the day of his independence. Unfortunately, that day is short-lived, as he tends toward human society for warmth, regular meals, and protection—the things Buck boldly forgoes. White Fang's motivation is understandable, but it is not heroic. The use of the term *god* for man as seen by White Fang has an almost sarcastic ring, and the acknowledgment that "it is always easier to lean upon another than to stand alone" (91), which apparently is meant as a wise realization, is rather a major confession of White Fang's weakness. The death blow to his character comes in the recognition of the price of his "covenant": "For the possession of a flesh-and-blood god, he exchanged his own liberty. Food and fire, protection and companionship, were some of the things he received from the god. In return, he guarded the god's property, defended his body, worked for him, and obeyed him" (118).

The conversion to domesticity represses rather than alters White Fang's basic nature; the wild creature is never truly at home again. In the North his abdication to the society of man inspires hatred from his own kind, and the civilized dogs arriving in the Yukon want to destroy him from envy. Although he is exhibited as "The Fighting Wolf" by his Indian owner, organized battle is an atrocity set up for human entertainment. As a result of a decisive defeat by a bulldog, White Fang is purchased out of mercy and taken to California, where opportunities for sanctioned violence are almost nil. There his wildness is thoroughly frustrated, as he is punished for stealing chickens and taught not to respond to his urge, and ostracized when he takes food from the other dogs.

The ultimate squelch of his wild spirit comes from the female, Collie, who "took advantage of her sex to pick upon White Fang and maltreat him" (205). Like "a policeman following him," this "pest" (216) nudges like a prickly conscience, never forgiving him for the chicken-killing episode. Although White Fang's father One Eye had been pursued and restricted by the female in a similar manner, his role as father required that he be a better hunter than ever, so his essential nature was fulfilled. Many are the restraints of White Fang's new environment, but Collie is "the one trial" (216) in his life. He is doomed. The pursuant female triumphs: one afternoon White Fang "ran with Collie" (221). How discreet—how bland—how asexual. What puritans are London's mighty male dogs.

Thus the final door is closed on the splendor of White Fang.

The next time we see Collie she is snarling her timid mate away from the inevitable litter. A fellow cannot fool around once without becoming responsible for a family. And society is ever present here to make sure a male does his duty, whatever tame activities that entails. A last contrived episode allows for White Fang's ferocity—he attacks an escaped convict. But he is pretty much out to pasture when he weakly drags toward his family at the novel's end, closing a story that is finally as much a testament to wildness as *The Call of the Wild.*

If London is best known and loved for the passionate animal, he is no less talented in capturing the classically restrained dog in his finest short story, "To Build a Fire" (1908). A boy's version of this tale, minus the dog, was written in 1901 as an exemplum to the uninitiated who would travel in the far country of the North. It resolves with the happy ending editors sought, as the struggling man in nature survives. The transformation of that story into the masterpiece published in 1908 has much to do with the brilliant touch of adding the dog. This ironic "reflector" is generally considered the story's master stroke.[21] The technique of having a dog simply watch a man die his lonely death is more powerful commentary than anything that could be said.

More profoundly and specifically than in any other Klondike tale, the frozen world here is a place of death, and the life that shows against that stark plane is, or should be, precious. But a man wastes his life because, heedless of the warnings, he insists on traveling alone (although he does have a dog with him), at temperatures colder than the prohibitive fifty below. "Any man who was a man could travel alone."[22] Indeed, the story opens as if there were no other life about, since to this traveler a dog does not count. There is "nobody to talk to" (145), he reflects. No words pass to the dog. The man does not refuse to share his lunch—it just never occurs to him to toss the dog a piece of his biscuit. Only when he compels his "toil slave" (148) to test the snow does the animal become significant, and even then only as an instrument, referred to by the impersonal pronoun. "The dog did not want to go. It hung back until the man shoved it forward . . ." (146). The verb *shove*, inclining one to think of baggage, insults more profoundly than a curse.

Even when the man realizes he is freezing to death and with "a great surge of envy" regards the creature that is "warm and secure in its natural covering" (152), he sees the dog as no more than useful matter, an attitude that as much as the man's lack of respect for the elements indicates a deficiency in imagination. His decision to kill the dog and use the body for warmth, as someone was once saved when he crawled into the carcass of a steer, is an indication not only of unthinking cruelty but of naiveté. Who is he to kill this powerful dog? His numb hands are not even capable of holding onto the animal, who plunges wildly away from the new danger.

This dog need not demonstrate spectacular qualities to be the superior form of life here. The animal simply has the sense to resist going on in the extreme cold. As with London's other dogs, instinct and physical fact are not in opposition—the one is based on the other. It is in a passage where the point of view shifts to the dog's sensations of the cold that the actual temperature is given, seventy-five below zero. "Its instinct told it a truer tale than was told to the man by the man's judgment" (144). And if he had known the temperature, he would not have been wiser.

In this one deft touch London reveals the wisdom of the dog that is elaborated in the novels. Buck and White Fang are spectacularly powerful and adaptable. But his unnamed, understated dog is also amazing. He is a more modern character than they—in a world that no longer holds such heroes. In his sheerist realism London presents a nonviolent dog, one who is not the central character. Neither rebellious nor domesticated, he is poised with a classically realistic balance between the two. Obeying the man with the whip, he also takes satisfaction in his fire, at the same time keeping his distance from that man. And this dog is vulnerable. We cannot be so certain he will get the ice out from between his toes before it is too late. But it is the man's feet that freeze. A mock similarity of the characters is suggested even in the way they look—the dog's breath forms a powder of frost on his fur just as the man's beard and moustache are crusted with ice. But their differing perceptions, contrary fates, only make any similarities ironic.

More profound than a physical attack or even abandonment is the way the objective dog witnesses the man's death. In that last terrified stumbling down the trail as the man realizes he is freezing, the dog follows as one who shares his master's suffering to the last.

But "when he fell down a second time, it curled its tail over its forefeet and sat in front of him, facing him, curiously eager and intent" (156). It is too late for the man who cared nothing for a dog. As the strange figure drowses off for the last time, "the dog sat facing him and waiting." At last, scenting death, it "turned and trotted up the trail in the direction of the camp . . ." (157). Thus ends one of London's darkest Klondike tales. Nature is a killer, and a man is dead. Yet, the dog lives.

London's dogs are indeed rich with life. Violent, rebellious, splendidly free, or restrained, they are ultimately adaptable, and they survive better than man, with or without heroics. The dog in "To Build a Fire" is nothing more than a natural dog—and yet nothing less awesome than the only living being left in a crypt of snow.

Notes

1. Jack London, "The White Silence," *The Bodley Head Jack London,* ed. Arthur Calder-Marshall, I (London: Bodley Head, 1963), 41.

2. Jack London, "Gold Hunters of the North," *The Bodley Head Jack London,* ed. Arthur Calder-Marshall, IV (London: Bodley Head, 1966), 27.

3. Jack London, "The Law of Life," *Bodley Head Jack London,* IV, 34.

4. Charles Child Walcutt, *American Literary Naturalism, a Divided Stream* (Minneapolis: University of Minnesota Press, 1956), pp. 89–90, 107.

5. Vernon Louis Parrington, *Main Currents in American Thought: An Interpretation of American Literature from the Beginnings to 1920* (New York: Harcourt, Brace & World, 1930), III, 324, 352.

6. Jay Gurian, "The Romantic Necessity in Literary Naturalism: Jack London," *American Literature,* 38, no. 1 (Mar., 1966), 114.

7. Joan London, *Jack London and His Times: An Unconventional Biography* (Seattle and London: University of Washington Press, 1939), p. 252.

8. Jack London, "Diable—a Dog," *The Call of the Wild and*

Selected Stories (New York: New American Library, 1960), pp. 90–91. Subsequent references to this edition of "Diable—a Dog" will appear in the text.

9. Jack London, "The Other Animals," *No Mentor But Myself: A Collection of Articles, Essays, Reviews and Letters on Writing and Writers,* ed. Dale L. Walker (Port Washington, N.Y., and London: Kennikat Press, 1979), pp. 110, 115–16.

10. Jack London, *The Call of the Wild and Selected Stories,* p. 13. Subsequent references to this edition of *The Call of the Wild* will appear in the text.

11. London, "The Other Animals," p. 109.

12. Raymond Benoit, "Jack London's *The Call of the Wild,*" *American Quarterly,* 20, no. 2 (Summer, 1968), 246.

13. See, for example, Maxwell Geismar, *Rebels and Ancestors: The American Novel, 1890–1915* (Boston: Houghton Mifflin, 1953), p. 199.

14. London, "The Other Animals," pp. 108–9, 118.

15. Frank E. Buske, "The Wilderness, the Frontier and the Literature of Alaska to 1914: John Muir, Jack London and Rex Beach" (Dissertation, University of California, Davis, 1976).

16. James Richard Giles, "A Study of the Concept of Atavism in the Writings of Rudyard Kipling, Frank Norris, and Jack London" (Dissertation, University of Texas, 1967), pp. 48–49.

17. London, "The White Silence," p. 40.

18. Franklin Dickerson Walker, *Jack London and the Klondike: The Genesis of an American Writer* (San Marino, Calif.: Huntington Library, 1966), p. 147.

19. Jack London, "Love of Life," *The Call of the Wild and Selected Stories,* p. 174.

20. Jack London, *White Fang and Other Stories* (New York: Dodd, Mead, 1963), p. 3. Subsequent references to this edition will appear in the text.

21. See, for example, Earle Labor and King Hendricks, "Jack London's Twice-Told Tale," *Studies in Short Fiction,* 4, no. 4 (Summer, 1967), 340.

22. Jack London, "To Build a Fire," *The Call of the Wild and Selected Stories,* p. 150. Subsequent references to this edition of "To Build a Fire" will appear in the text.

CHAPTER 5

"Among animals, one has a
sense of humor."
—Moore

Controlled Creatures:
Marianne Moore

The apartment in Brooklyn where Marianne Moore lived for thirty-six years was furnished with minuscule mice of carved ivory, pictures of kangaroos, and an ebony sea horse. A box of wild bird feathers graced the home, and the poet was known to offer eagle down and a bluejay claw to one of her guests.[1] Here was a brick with the imprint of a cat's paw brought from Pennsylvania. And in this apartment she kept Tibby, her pet alligator.

Moore's reputation for the exotic elicited a request from the Ford Motor Company for assistance in the "ethereal" matter of naming a 1955 series of cars, for which the company's tally of labels was "characterized by an embarrassing pedestrianism." The poet's supply of titles was predictably rich with odd animal names, her first line of thought being that of a bird series: Hurricane Hirundo (swallow), aquila (eagle), or accipiter (hawk). MONGOOSE CIVIQUE, cresta lark, and TURCOTINGO (finch or sparrow) followed. For UTOPIAN TURTLETOP, Ford sent back a bouquet of roses addressed "To Our Favorite Turtletopper." But the company did not select one of the poet's rare species, although perhaps if they had, their car would have been a success. Instead, they called it the Edsel.[2]

Queer creatures populate Moore's poetry—dikdik, echnidna, tuatera—drawn from scientific sources by the poet who was first a biology student and then a librarian. No stereotypes come to mind with these subjects. By handpicking them from afar, she takes a control not assumed with the surprise appearance of animals nearby. Moore's characters are kept at an emotional distance, just as most of them are geographically remote. They are strange but not frightening. As if viewed through a microscope, clear-edged shells or heavy hides, stripes or neatly arranged scales, and geometrical designs give a comforting sense of order. Moore's animals rarely attack; in fact, many of them barely move. Those who do are usually in flight, and motion is brought under control. The animal comes safely to rest.

Moore's stable, often hard-crusted animals more closely resemble *things* than any in American literature. Although she disclaimed herself as an imagist, Moore's emphases on the exact word, new and freer rhythms, clarity, and concentration are inevitably linked with imagism. And Ezra Pound's call for the direct treatment of a thing has a particularly literal bearing in terms of her animal subjects. Not only does Moore bring fresh vision to the object before her but she puts new objects into the light. The clear-edged brilliance of her images has been made the subject of a study by Kingsley Weatherhead, who finds in her clarity a kinship with Homer.[3] She cites the Greeks for "distrusting what was back / of what could not be clearly seen."[4] For Roy Harvey Pearce, she "more than any other American poet of her time respects (in a phrase dear to Stevens) 'things as they are.' "[5] And no group of "things" is more prominent in Moore's poetry than her animals. A fourth of the *Collected Poems* (1951) are specifically devoted to animals, and they appear in almost all the others. The animal may serve as metaphor, but in most cases he walks away as himself, especially when the poem extends beyond two or three stanzas.

By Kenneth Burke's definition, Moore is an objectivist rather than an imagist, for by his analysis the symbolist makes the subject more important than the object; the imagist establishes equality between subject and object; but it is the objectivist who studies the object in its own right.[6] Not only do Moore's animals have their own lives, but a persona is rarely present in the poetry to record a subjective response. To say that the objectivist *studies* a subject is also descriptive of Moore's technique, as facts are turned to poetry under her hand. Burke's linking of Moore with Henry James on the basis of a gratitude that invests their subjects with a "secular equivalent to the religious motive of a glorification"[7] is also applicable to Moore's animals. In fact, Burke's analysis of Moore pertains to animals in American literature generally: they are secular subjects valued in their own right, yet sensed with a spiritual wonder. The intent of imagist and objectivist to eschew traditional symbolism is also pertinent, for even with the most prominent symbolic animals, at some point metaphor is stripped away to reveal the magnificently actual. As Moore puts it, "No anonymous / nightingale sings" from "palm-trees blurring at the / edge."[8]

The relationship of live animals to things calls for a careful distinction. "No Swan So Fine" would give the edge to the Dresden china swan of Louis Fifteenth. But as the opening image of the poem is that of the " 'dead fountains of Versailles,' " the word *dead* also closes the poem, contradicting the claim raised by the title. The "toothed gold / collar" indicating "whose bird it was" hints at the tyranny of ownership. A comical twist comes with the swan's being put "at ease," a gentle mockery of the poet's own inclination to the serene—even deathlike—state of her living animals. The repose of a china swan is not so fine.

In "Critics and Connoisseurs" the "unconscious / fastidiousness" of "certain Ming / products" is bettered in a "mere childish attempt to make an imperfectly bal / lasted animal stand up." As a literalist of the imagination, Moore puts that real toad in the imaginary garden, where balance in the living subject carries an aesthetic rightness of its own. While the artist models after nature, living animals merely appear to imitate art as they surpass it: "copying the / Chinese flower piece" is an incredible "brass-green bird with a grass- / green throat";[9] splendidly topping the man-made is the reindeer's "candelabrum-headed ornament."[10]

Actual and mythical animals are practically interchangeable in "The Plumet Basilisk," where the fabled basilisk, a reptile whose breath and look were said to be fatal, is no more spectacular than the tropical American lizard with an erectile crest and a dilatable pouch on the head. Moore's sources of information are also a weave of the fictional and the factual; her data for the mythical Chinese dragon come from the *Illustrated London News*. From a natural history text, *Animals of New Zealand,* a bizarre creature is unearthed, the only living representative of an order having the appearance of a lizard, characteristics of a tortoise, the uncinate processes of a bird, and crocodilian features.[11] The fabled creature is forever bettered by the more peculiar actual one. The failing of explorers to the New World was in overlooking the living indigenous prize, the tropical American basilisk, "our Tower-of-London / jewel that the Spaniards failed to see."[12]

The various roles of animals—art object, slave, hunter, plaything, by-product, guard, and free being—are all included in "The Jerboa," all but the last under the heading "Too Much." Roman society is so lush with the accumulation of animals that one might be satisfied with its levels of artistry, were it not for the stunning appearance of a single desert rat, the subject of "Abundance." Art commissioned makes for the doubly contrived animal's form, "the peacock / statue in the garden of the Vatican." More appealing is the sight of baboons, not enslaved exactly but "put" on the necks of giraffes to pick fruit, and "dapple dog- / cats" engaged "to course antelopes." Without indignation, the poet quietly states the case: the Romans "looked on as theirs, / impallas and onigers, / the wild ostrich herd." While animals are considered possessions, without rights or sensations, a wealth of wild life is appreciated in a variety of ways. "Tame fish, and small frogs" ornament the garden, and the toy ichneumon (a weasel-like creature) and snake are given to the young boys. Animal by-products epitomize the life of luxury—goose-grease paint in bone boxes, honey, milk. And the king over all this, in his fear of snakes, must turn for protection to yet another creature, the mongoose.

The unique qualifications of animals are featured, not ignored, by the Romans—the height of the giraffe and the tensile ability of the baboons. They are not mistreated or even severely limited. But it is Moore's brilliance to draw a seductive picture of conditions that are nonetheless a graver danger than force—the affluence which calls increasingly for the domination of animals by man.

To remain free, the animal must protect himself. The most striking feature of Moore's animals is their armor—both an immediate physical defense and a long-range prevention against the more insidious penetration of the spirit. A philosophy of the shield is built on the principle of an inner discipline, manifest in the tough exterior that provides privacy and its accompanying freedom. In the exceptional case of armor as a weapon—the "battle-dressed" porcupine, for example, who wears a "pin-cushion thorn-fur" coat[13]—the image is not aggressive. The quill is softened in its equation with fur and with coat; the analogy with a pin cushion puts the sharp end of the quill to the inside, a blunt end pointing out. But make no mistake: the animal intends not to be disturbed.

If not a material covering, protective coloring, odor, or swiftness, then inner restraint alone serves as a shield. Donald Hall's theory that Moore's armor is used as a cage to check the wild spirit inside[14] simply does not describe Moore's genuinely peace-loving animals. Their solid surfaces *reveal* an inner security rather than contradict it. The "patina of circumstance can but enrich what was / there to begin / with."[15] The concept of power in stasis is indeed the uncommon view in American literature—this vision of a poet who maintains that "a Chinese 'understands / the spirit of the wilderness.' "[16]

Moore's fascination with animal coverings goes for the furnishings themselves, irrespective of the life of the animal. In a prose selection, "My Crow, Pluto—a Fantasy" (a crow who reverses gloom by answering only "Evermore"), Moore tells of her desire to own a crow that would accompany her on errands and then provide plumage for her hat (with no mention of the fate of a bird whose feathers are taken).[17] New York is saluted as the center of the wholesale fur trade, not as a place of plunder but as the incarnation of " 'accessibility to experience' " (Henry James's phrase), which for Moore is called up in the splendor of fur: "tepees of ermine" and "picardels of beaver-skin; white ones alert with snow." As the "savage's romance," New York is "peopled with foxes," worn not in the spirit that " 'if the fur is not finer than such as one sees / others wear, / one would rather be without it' "[18] but with unalloyed pleasure in the incomparable. The unusual case where Moore does meet the issue of the kill is coolly phrased in a poem based on an essay by a farmer of musk oxen: "To wear the arctic fox / you have to kill it. Wear / *qiviut*—the underwool of the arctic ox— / pulled off it like a sweater; / your coat is warm; your conscience, better."[19] The easy transition from attainment of fur by the fatal method to one shown to be as harmless as undressing puts the graver issue at a distance, just as other threats are made remote.

Armor is frequently described in architectural terms. A vulnerable maternal care is displayed in the paper nautilus's rooms of thin glass shell where the eggs are kept. The lizard's shield is fireproof asbestos. Best known is the snail's quaint house, that charming model of compression, " 'the first grace of style,' " achieved through a contractility which is "a virtue / as modesty is a virtue." This house moves as a well-oiled machine run on the snail's own lubrication, a structure that like other armor *is* the animal himself, not an adornment. The only protrusion reaches out for perception, not locomotion—"the curious phenomenon" of the "occipital horn." The "absence of feet"[20] is a benefit; feet are vulnerable, frequently superfluous. Besides, what's the hurry?

The hide that most graphically registers experience weathered is the wonderfully homely skin of the elephant. "Melancthon" shows age as a form of armor in itself, translated to the visible in the deeply rutted but carefully patterned hide "cut / into checkers." An analogy with a coconut shell accurately captures color and texture, while exaggerating solidity. More specifically than elsewhere, a definite threat is identified here: the soul shall not be "cut into / by a wooden spear"; the elephant (synonymous with his hide) is "that on which darts cannot strike," both images suggesting an abstract as well as a tangible encroachment. The more inclusive need for armor is, if not to resist, to absorb "unpreventable experience." The elephant is not merely earthbound; he is "black earth preceded by a tendril." But even the metaphor turns back on the literal, for the elephant's hide is incorporated with dirt. As atypically stated in the first person, "The sediment of the river which / encrusts my joints, makes me very grey but . . . do away / with it and I am myself done away with." Here is illustration not only of the exemplary hide but of the necessity for protection, as crucial for the massive as for the minute animal.

The most perfectly completed form of armor is that of a toothless, scaly mammal of Asia and Africa, the spherical pangolin.

Another armoured animal—scale
    lapping scale with spruce-cone regularity until they
form the uninterrupted central
    tail-row

. . .

[He] rolls himself into a ball that has
    power to defy all effort to unroll it; strongly intailed, neat
    head for core, on neck not breaking off, with curled-in feet.
        Nevertheless he has sting-proof scales; and nest
           of rocks closed with earth from inside, which he can
                            thus darken.
    Sun and moon and day and night and man and beast
        each with a splendor
           which man in all his vileness cannot
           set aside; each with an excellence!

. . .

In a note to "The Icosasphere" Moore shows a fascination with a problem which had baffled engineers, in a layman's image that of the impossibility of wrapping a rubber ball without wrinkling or wasting material. Steel and plexiglass, delivered only in rectangles, would writhe back to their original shape when heated. The solution was found in a design of twenty equilateral triangles that could be grouped into a sphere with negligible scrap loss. The more perfect model in nature, the pangolin is a "night miniature artist engineer" who makes of himself that perfected sphere, complemented with regularly arranged scales. Rolled into a ball, the pangolin secures even the "small eminence," the ear; "similarly safe" are "contracting nose and eye apertures, / impenetrably closable." Protected not only from physical attack, the pangolin is shored up against violation through the senses.

"Pangolins are not aggressive animals"—nor are any of Moore's characters. When left to himself, the pangolin "cautiously works down the tree" with the help of that most valuable appendage, the tail, "graceful tool, as prop or hand or broom or ax." Stepping in the moonlight on the outside edges of his hands (no feet), he saves his claws for digging. Fully "mechanicked," safe, sound, the pangolin is the character most explicitly associated with humor:—"humor saves a few steps, it saves years,"[21] a concept that might be taken literally in the poetry of one who cares little for feet. The pangolin does not need to run—not this marvelously whole artist-engineer-machine who looks like an artichoke.

Whatever fabric Moore's animals are made of, they show no flesh. And none could be more virginal (although eggs do hatch). As R. P. Blackmur observes, "there is no sex anywhere in her poetry. No poet has been so chaste; but it is not the chastity that arises from an awareness—healthy or morbid—of the flesh, it is a special chastity aside from the flesh—a purity by birth from the void."[22] In Moore's words chastity "confers a particular strength."[23] As such, it is not dramatized as a matter of restraint; it is simply one of the intrinsic disciplines that protect. Neither is a life force that might go for breeding channeled elsewhere, for her animals have little excess energy. In a rare reference to mating in "The Arctic Ox (Or Goat)" the subject is at the same time equated to torture and lightly dismissed.

> While not incapable
> of courtship, they [Arctic oxen] may find its
>   servitude and flutter, too much
> like Procrustes' bed;
> so some decide to stay unwed.
>
> . . .

In addition to formally arranged armor and internal controls, numbers systematize Moore's menagerie. The paper nautilus guards eggs "buried eight-fold in her eight / arms";[24] seagulls sail in twos and threes; eight green bands mark the basilisk's tail; and three mocking-birds stand in a row. While numbers applied to poetry generally proclaim nothing but the death of the spirit, as they do so memorably for Auden's unknown citizen, for example, in Moore's poetry they are used to quantify animals' achievement, the way statistics are used for athletes. Reindeer ("Rigorists") "can run eleven / miles in fifty minutes." The recorded fact, certifying action and giving it permanence, takes precedence over a dramatic display of the deer's ability.

The comfort Moore reflects through order does not stop at

armor, formal arrangement, and factual data. Dead animals, properly arranged, make a thoroughly satisfying aesthetic image, as in
the opening lines of "The Steeple-Jack": "Dürer would have seen a
reason for living / in a town like this, with eight stranded whales /
to look at." There is no melancholy in this image of whales, who
do not even produce an odor: sweet air flows through the house
nearby. Death is not Moore's subject; she is simply at peace with
death. Evenly numbered, lined up, the impacted figures whose
organs tend to the inside, bodies an extension of tail, provide a
pleasure altogether apart from the life of whales. The apparent
finality of their forms contrasts favorably with the dangerously
tentative situation of the steeple-jack attempting to balance his star.

Animals work as a stabilizing pattern generally in this poem,
from the aesthetic ideal embodied in the whales to the spider metaphor for the steeple-jack, with its reassurance of the spider's competence as the man works his way along a thread. At the pedestrian
level "a twenty-five / pound lobster" provides fisherman and shopper
with the pleasure of a prize whose value may be quantified. Animals are also central in the arrangement of the town's structures—
"a schoolhouse, a post-office in a / store, fish-houses, hen-houses,
a three-masted / schooner on / the stocks"—with food stores at the
core. The church, being "a fit haven for / waifs, children, animals,
prisoners, / and presidents,"[25] puts live animals at the center. An
artistic distance from Moore's subject is never more evident than
here where she who reveres the lives of her pangolin, her jerboa, is
also capable of showing the various ways animals are integrated
into human society, where the incongruity of affection for the living on the one hand and casual utility on the other is of no
consequence.

Dead animals are, however, the exception. While the distinction between animals as matter and as living beings is often subtle,
the revelation of life as motion is at last exquisite. The astonishing
manifestation of the living is dramatized in the delicate unfolding
of "The Fish," where the mysterious combination of plant, mineral, and animal under water makes identification a compelling
adventure. As animals are likened to objects or even to machines
throughout Moore's poetry, here are "crabs like green / lilies."
From one who inclines rather to adjective complexes than to met-

aphor, this simile does not represent the poet's ingenious linking of two unlike things: the analogy occurs in nature, where animal and plant (or mineral) are well disguised. Jellyfish, crab, and toadstools "slide each on the other." But "of the crow-blue mussel-shells," one opens and shuts itself—minimal movement, yet an indication of the self-willed life. That the inanimate shell moves is an enchanting puzzle (not unlike the miracle of machines). And the form of movement is characteristically gradual and directed by the urge for resolution: the mussel shell "keeps / adjusting the ash-heaps." Whatever the motive for action, the sign of life is exhilarating—the thrill of seeing a stone move. My God, the thing is alive!

Still, for Moore most movement is disturbing and must be controlled. After all, "a good brake is as important as a good motor."[26] Speed indicates danger. Similarly, solid matter comforts, while the sea is "A Grave": "you cannot stand in the middle of this." The quick gesture is brilliantly awkward, a mode of escape toward a home where the animal may stand or sit.

The most dangerously active creature is the basilisk, "one of the quickest lizards in the world," who goes like "a living fire- / work" when he must or lies "basking on a / horizontal branch" when he may. Action serves somewhat the same function as armor, yet it produces the opposite effect—panic instead of peace. Meeting his "likeness in the stream," not only in the reflection but because of the ability to effect the blue-green colors of deep water, the basilisk dives to hide. In this brilliant reptile, a "nervous naked sword on little feet," is the culmination of movement as tense, exposed, even unnatural activity. Running is "a thing / difficult for fingered feet." When he is stopped, captured, the texture of the lizard turns substantial, putty-like. The force of gravity that keeps Moore's weightier animals in place is generally a reassuring factor, but the trip to earth suggests a crash. The falling dragon *smites* the water (or *faints* on the air). In a chillingly suicidal image the Malay Dragon "knows how to dive head-first from a tree-top / to something dry." The flying of lizards charges the poem with excitement, but flight without wings is unnatural, terrifying. An unnerving movement is matched to the uneven structure of "The Plumet Basilisk":

a scared frog screaming like a bird, leaps out from weeds
    in which
it could have hid, with curves of the meteorite,
    wide water-bug strokes,
in jerks which express
a regal and excellent awkwardness,

    the plumet portrays
mythology's wish
to be interchangeably man and fish—

travelling rapidly upward, as
spider-clawed fingers can twang the
bass strings of the harp, and with steps
as articulate, make their way
back to retirement on strings that
vibrate till the claws are spread flat.

. . .

The wildly irregular stanza for fright smooths to a more even
whole as motion slows and the lizard retires, a resolution of movement as well-defined for him as it is for the sedate animals. Peace
exists where sea lizards congregate "with tails laid criss-cross,
alligator-style, among / birds toddling in and out—," the participle
slowing and lightening the otherwise tense line of action. And the
quick, irregular dash of the basilisk is resolved. In the opening
section "he runs, he flies, he swims, to get to / his basilica—." As
the poem closes, he is "nested," "thinking himself hid," yet "alive
there / in his basilisk cocoon."

Even the bird in flight moves with frantic necessity. Above the
sinister wrinkling "progress" of the sea, "birds swim through the
air at top speed,"[27] the verb accurately illustrating flight but transforming it from the classically free-spirited form to a desperate
journey. The weightier frigate pelican *lies* on the air, his wings
"uniting levity with strength," a brilliant occupation deactivated in
the noun compound: this "hell-diver" prefers taking his fish from
other birds to attacking for himself. The pelicans "move out to the
top / of the circle and stop." Then this "most romantic bird flies /
to a more mundane place, the mangrove / swamp to sleep."[28] A

bird may hide in the sky or escape back to earth, but he does not fly for fun.

The flightless bird is a more characteristic Moore subject, the kiwi, whose wings are used for an umbrella, and the ostrich, the world's largest bird, who "Digesteth Harde Yron."[29] Moore finds in this bird as he swallows gravel for digestion the substantiality she seeks in all her animals—the size that works as a stabilizing, not a power, factor. With "leaden-skinned back," the big bird is solid enough to carry a man. That he is the symbol of justice interests the poet only as it ironically works to the detriment of the ostrich: his feathers are taken so man might appear just. Being valued by man is only a liability for an animal.

While the ostrich is a mighty runner, "swifter than a horse," Moore does not show him running. His speed as the potential for escape is enough. First noted as the "large sparrow . . . walking by a stream," he then stands guard over his chicks. That he "will wade / in lake or sea till only the head shows" makes even slow motion dangerous. Motion as an indication of vulnerability rather than might is expressed in the "compass-needle nervousness" of the neck, a delicately precise image built on the quivering of an instrument that points the way home. A strange mix of solidity and pregnability furthers the comic impression of this camel-sparrow with the "comic duckling head."[30]

The most stable and serene of Moore's animals is the elephant. With the security born of massiveness and a super thick hide, he is "the Socrates of / animals." His trunk is that protuberance of perfect circumference, which, while it may extend in aggression, is sensibly contractile, raining a siphoned pool back upon himself. Two elephants poise in the guise of battle, proboscises entwined. But their "mouse-gray" weapons are "immobilized / wistaria-like" as Moore turns what might be a "knock-down drag-out fight" to "just / a pastime." Instead of fighting, one elephant sleeps, "with the calm of youth, / at full length in the half dry sun-flecked stream-bed," resting his "hunting-horn-curled trunk on shallowed stone." And in the hollow of the massive figure lies his sleeping mahout, far from master of the huge animal oblivious of his feather-weight passenger. Rather, the creature's security is transferred to his rider: "asleep on an elephant, that is repose."

Less fortunate, although as serene as the sleeping elephant, is the prize white one carrying the Buddha's Tooth, "a life prisoner but reconciled." Although "white is / the colour of worship and of mourning, he / is not here to worship and he is too wise to mourn,"[31] a statement that might stand for the poet herself. Being destined by nature with the handsomer hide, the more conspicuous white elephant is not as fortunate as the commoner grey one left alone to sleep in the sun.

Moore's other expert slumberer is the cat, "Peter," her only domesticated animal, for whom sleep, "epitome of what . . . to / him as to the average person," is the "end of life." In classic cat posture Peter naps with claw "retracted to its tip." Like the elephant asleep on the ground, he is at ease on this earth, comfortably "flat- / tened out by gravity." Supine, he may be viewed in detail, down to the whiskers ordered as "shadbones regularly set about the mouth, to / droop or rise / in unison like the procupine's quills— motionless." So armored, he is yet largely pliable, not eager to assert himself in movement, but in relaxed security allowing himself to be "dangled like an / eel."

Jarred awake by an aberration, a dream of a fight, Peter springs about with "froglike ac- / curacy," a skilled but uneven reaction that yields to the smoother "extension of trunk into tail" as balance is established. Conceding that such an animal "with claws wants to have to / use / them; . . . To / leap, to lengthen out, divide the air— / to purloin, to pur- / sue," the poet, nevertheless, makes action hypothetical in the string of infinitives. And in one of her most memorable images, that of the self-reliant cat in "Silence" who "takes its prey to privacy, / the mouse's limp tail hanging like a shoelace from its / mouth—," the attack is kept off stage, and what might be a grim aftermath is familiarized into a comic picture. It is not the death of animals that is distressing: it is their flight that shocks. Peter offers composure rather than a chase, his claws sufficient as a deterrent "to tell the hen: fly over the fence." Like the elephant, he prefers sleep to battle, the cat fight, which in Moore's version is turned to a "midnight grass-party."

Like others whose potential for violence works more as a deterrent than as a dramatized act, the Indian buffalo will, if a tiger so much as coughs, "convert the fur / to harmless rubbish." But rather than show him charging toward a target, Moore pacifies the beast with "compactly incurved horns" who is led to a stable by "bare-leggèd herd-boys." In him, "black in blazonry means / prudence; and niger, unpropitious." In his strength he is safe. At the same time he is a sparse-haired, modest beast who meets "human notions" better than the ox of the famous portrait (decreased to cat size) or the more elegant "white-nosed Vermont ox" yoked in labor with a twin. "Standing in a mud-lake with a / day's work to do"[32] (even labor being defined as a stationary activity), the unyoked buffalo takes his ease.

Even the most hair-raising creature in the kingdom is controlled—the snake—in "Snakes, Mongooses, Snake-Charmers and the Like." While Moore is the first to see the wisdom in avoiding what we dislike, which usually includes the animal with "hypodermic teeth,"[33] under the spell of snake charmer the reptile is no longer frightening. Nor is the mongoose shown in its predatory function but for the soothing order in the "fingers all of one length—." While generally given to reasonable means of achieving order, the poet accedes to mystic authority in the case of the snake charmer, who "gazes as if incapable of looking at anything with a view / to analysis." Transformed to "distinguished worm" by the snake charmer's art, the snake "stands up from its traveling basket." As it is steadied, resembling a plastic animal "all of a piece from / nose to tail," a long close look at the serpent makes the altering of a prejudice possible. Danger is not omitted—one is "compelled" to look at the snake as "at the shadows of the alps / imprisoning in their folds like flies in amber, the rhythms / of the skating rink"—but the image of destruction yields to one of graceful recreation that does away with the *motive* for violence. The snake is taught peace.

As Pearce sees it, poets such as Williams, Aiken, and Cummings in their "chest pounding" conceal a "fear of the unknown" that is not to be found in Moore's poetry.[34] Instead, in her assumption of the need for armor, the acknowledgment of threat as a first fact of life works to minimize fear or even to avoid it. As successful controls are imposed, a new sense of security becomes possible.

With scant physical armor, the jerboa, a tiny nocturnal rodent of Asia and North Africa, is the supreme case of inner discipline.

Exemplar of abstinence, the jerboa is master of the enemy Moore has referred to as "fat living and self-pity."[35] With no ivory bed, no palm trees, not even any water, the spare desert rat knows abundance—it knows *happiness.* Anything more than the stark self is "Too Much." Certainly being without companions is no detriment. As the wisely witty line from "If I Were Sixteen Today" maintains: "The cure for loneliness is solitude."[36] The frontier of "boundless sand" armors the jerboa against civilization, serving as the bare stage upon which the individual stands. "Not famous" or of value to man, without material abundance, the jerboa is bared to a state requiring sheer self-reliance, a "sand-brown jumping-rat—free-born."

One of Moore's most notably adaptable animals, the jerboa is uniquely composed of what appear to be features of other animals: the "buff-brown" coat of the "bower-bird," "chipmunk contours," a "bird head," and a "fish-shaped" body. But "the fine hairs on the tail, / repeating the other pale / markings" bring disparate elements into a unique unity in the fragile exterior. At the same time, the jerboa, harmonizing with earth,

> honours the sand by assuming its colour;
> > closed upper paws seeming one with the fur
> > in its flight from a danger.
>
> By fifths and sevenths,
> in leaps of two lengths,
> > like the uneven notes
> > of the Bedouin flute, it stops its gleaning
> > on little wheel castors, and makes fern-seed
> > foot-prints with kangaroo speed.
>
> Its leaps should be set
> to the flageolet;
> pillar body erect
> on a three-cornered smooth-working Chippendale
> > claw—propped on hind legs, and tail as third toe,
> > between leaps to its burrow.[37]

This disproportionate creature leaps straight, as if inner spirit alone resolves exterior imbalance. And by setting irregular jumps to a musical measure, however unseemly the half-note effects, an underlying pattern leading to resolution is established. Likening the fragile bounce to the tune of flageolet catches an errant rhythm but also the pure tones of the flute-like instrument. Thus disturbing movement in the jerboa is brought under control, resolved in the final note, which Moore draws as a whole note. Delicate though they are, footprints show the beginnings of rootedness. Freed by obscurity, inner restraint, and stops between leaps, the sound little rodent makes it home.

Poetry has "a place for / the genuine,"[38] and Moore's favoring of animals as poetic subjects is a tribute to their genuineness. "Why an inordinate interest in animals and athletes? They are subjects for art and exemplars of it, are they not? minding their own business. Pangolins, horn-bills, pitchers, catchers, do not pry or prey—or prolong the conversation; do not make us self-conscious; look their best when caring least."[39]

The obscurity of Moore's animals bestows the virtue of modesty, the gift of freedom. No less inclined to individual liberty than those who dramatize it more actively, she shows independence as the result of self-protection and discipline. In this, her animals incline to the stationary rather than to the expansive. Indeed, they would rather sleep than attack. And with the proper controls, they are free to do just that.

Notes

1. Daniel Louis Guillory, "A Place for the Genuine: The Poetics of Marianne Moore" (Dissertation, Tulane University, 1972), p. 2. The guest was Marguerite Young.

2. Marianne Moore, "The Ford Correspondence," *A Marianne Moore Reader* (New York: Viking Press, 1961), pp. 215–24.

3. A. Kingsley Weatherhead, *The Edge of the Image: Marianne Moore, William Carlos Williams and Some Other Poets* (Seattle and London: University of Washington Press, 1967), p. 21.

4. Marianne Moore, "An Octopus," *Collected Poems* (New York: Macmillan Company, 1959). Unless otherwise noted, subsequent references to the poetry will be to this edition.

5. Ray Harvey Pearce, "Marianne Moore," *The Continuity of American Poetry* (Princeton, N.J.: Princeton University Press, 1961), p. 374.

6. Kenneth Burke, "Motives and Motifs in the Poetry of Marianne Moore," *A Grammar of Motives* (Berkeley and Los Angeles: University of California Press, 1969), p. 486.

7. Ibid., p. 489.

8. "The Plumet Basilisk."

9. "Smooth Gnarled Crape Myrtle."

10. "Rigorists."

11. Notes to "The Plumet Basilisk."

12. "The Plumet Basilisk."

13. "His Shield."

14. Donald Hall, *Marianne Moore: The Cage and the Animal* (New York: Pegasus, 1970), p. 16.

15. "Melancthon."

16. "Nine Nectarines."

17. *Marianne Moore Reader,* p. 193.

18. "New York."

19. "The Arctic Ox (Or Goat)," *Marianne Moore Reader.*

20. "To a Snail."

21. "The Pangolin," *Marianne Moore Reader.*

22. R. P. Blackmur, "The Method of Marianne Moore," *Form and Value in Modern Poetry* (Garden City, N.Y.: Doubleday, 1957), p. 250.

23. "If I Were Sixteen Today," *Marianne Moore Reader,* p. 196.

24. "The Paper Nautilus."

25. "The Steeple-Jack" (revised, 1961), *Marianne Moore Reader.*

26. "People's Surroundings."

27. "A Grave."

28. "The Frigate Pelican."

29. From Lyly's *Euphues.*

30. "He 'Digesteth Harde Yron.' "

31. "Elephants."

32. "The Buffalo."

33. "The Hero."

34. Pearce, p. 372.

35. " 'Keeping Their World Large.' "
36. *Marianne Moore Reader,* p. 195.
37. "The Jerboa."
38. "Poetry."
39. "Foreword," *Marianne Moore Reader,* p. xvi.

CHAPTER 6

"As flies to wanton boys are we to the gods, They kill us for their sport."
—Shakespeare

The Cycle of Death: John Steinbeck

By one means or another, John Steinbeck's animals are put to death. Marine invertebrates are gathered as specimens; pigs and chickens are slaughtered for provision; a colt succumbs to pneumonia; a mare is sliced open to save her foal; mice are squeezed to death by a half-wit; insects are squashed; dogs and rabbits are struck by swerving cars. The violence of Steinbeck's world generally takes a peculiar turn in the case of animals, who meet death in an ingenious variety of ways, drawn out with the graphic detail and detachment of a biologist. A spirit of harmony belies the customary posture of man poised with a knife over an animal. Although Steinbeck's simple folk turn to animals directly for survival, the approach is not simply primitive: it is, as Alfred Kazin says, "primitive, with a little cunning."[1] While metaphors align the lower species with underdog man, the actual animals have little in common with him. And the tenderness expressed for human suffering does not extend to animals—nor does Steinbeck's sentimentality—as he maintains an almost perfect detachment from their sensations.

The nonteleological doctrine set forth in *The Sea of Cortez* (1941), the record of an expedition with biologist Ed Ricketts to collect marine species, leads to an easy utility of animals—which contradicts the work's concept of cosmic unity. The central image of a biological universe, the tidepool, is devoid of the humanity that Steinbeck makes the basis for union in human society, a humanity his people do not extend to animals. The *Log from the Sea of Cortez* (1951), with its personal account of Ricketts, reveals a biologist's outlook that suggests not the harmonious inclusion of animal life into a universal scheme but quite another posture. And it is this which remains constant as Steinbeck's style varies and a deterministic view of man yields to a more humanistic one. Throughout, animals exist to be used by man.

In the *Log* Steinbeck reflects nostalgically on the luxury of leisure available to Darwin on his *Beagle* voyage, as he had the time to care for living specimens. The contemporary expedition, however, calls for the expedient relegation of species to a formalin solution. "Why do men, sitting at the microscope, examine the calcareous plates of a sea-cucumber, and, finding a new arrangement and number, feel an exaltation and give the new species a name, and write about it possessively?" With Ricketts, Steinbeck determines that satisfaction has nothing to do with the " 'services to science' platitudes," not even necessarily with the observation of how species live. The greater urge of the biologist is to establish patterns. If the fish strikes hard on the line and nearly escapes, "a whole new relational externality has come into being—an entity which is more than the sum of the fish plus the fisherman. The only way to count the spines of the sierra unaffected by this second relational reality is to sit in a laboratory, open an evil-smelling jar, remove a stiff colorless fish from formalin solution, count the spines, and write the truth 'D. XVII-15-IX.' " Although this may be the "least important reality"[2] concerning the fish, it is essential to Steinbeck's fictional treatment of animals.

Ricketts demonstrated to his friends exactly how animals should be killed. While the biologist hated to see unnecessary brutality, "when the infliction of pain was necessary, he had little feeling about it." He could cut a sheep's throat with "no emotion whatever, and even explained to the rest of us who were upset that bleeding to death is quite painless if there is no fear involved. The pain of opening a vein is slight if the instrument is sharp, and he had opened the jugular with a scalpel and had not frightened the animal" (xviii). Acquaintance with Ricketts and his commercial laboratory not only reinforced a sense of a biological universe but of man's relationship to the lower animals, one which is followed in its detachment not only by Steinbeck's most pragmatic characters but by his casual ones as well.

On their Sea of Cortez expedition the biologists are clearly in control. Brilliant red rock lobsters show up for them against ultramarine water, with "no protective coloration here." The climax of the catch comes as "finally, we immersed them in fresh water and when they were dead, preserved them in alcohol, which promptly removed their brilliant color" (48–49). Moving pictures are taken of the changing hues of the bonito in its death struggle. Most dramatic is the procurement of a tortoise shell turtle, an operation in which "we were able to observe the tender hearts of our crew," says the professionally detached Steinbeck persona. At the same time, through an observation of the emotionalized attack of the harpooner Tiny, the biologist-viewer finds occasion to embellish a bloody struggle. Wounded by the harpoon, the turtle "waved its flippers helplessly and stretched its old wrinkled neck and gnashed its parrot beak" (45), but it does not die. Two tries with the ax are necessary before the head is severed, bringing "a large quantity of very red blood" from the still lively trunk. Eager to examine the turtle, the biologists "put Tiny's emotions aside for the moment" (46) as they open the body cavity and examine the digestive track from gullet to anus, while the turtle's heart continues to beat regularly. The scene is presented with an unmistakable relish in the entire process, which may be drawn out because a turtle is so hard to kill. Its execution is, however, part of a man's job, a subject Steinbeck treats not merely for proletarian argument but as it is truly the center of people's lives—and not simply as a necessity but as a means of earning respect. Thus the effect of the turtle's death is outweighed both by Tiny's arduous accomplishment and by the more restrained enterprise of the biologists.

Steinbeck has been faulted for taking the sting out of reality while offering all the trappings—a valid contention as it applies to his protagonists. But the absence of profundity in the case of animals is a function of his detached realism: one may observe but not experience what they feel. The philosophy of acceptance—an "is" rather than a "why" approach—is thus literally and effectively applied to animals: they exist, they may be taken, and, indeed, he does not raise questions as to the nature of their sensations. While the reader might wish for or even expect compassion for the victimized creature, the author does not take the literary license to provide it. What one cannot help but consider is the impetus for such frequent violations of animals—so frequent and so eloquently described as to suggest more than the acceptance of death as part of the cycle of nature. Animals most often die at the hand of man. Necessity may be the primary drive for Steinbeck's characters, but in the killing they experience power—and, frequently, pleasure.

Animals as specimens distributed through the commercial laboratory are put to literary use in the successful comic novel, *Cannery Row* (1945). Doc, a fictionalized version of Ed Ricketts, supports himself and a band of followers in the business of selling living and preserved specimens. The vagabonds of the neighborhood are paid for the dead cats and dogs they drag in by the bag, most of them stolen from neighbors. In his more sophisticated fashion, Doc collects samples with the rarefied appreciation of one who wields a quiet knife. "When you collect marine animals there are certain flat worms so delicate that they are almost impossible to capture whole, for they break and tatter under the touch. You must let them ooze and crawl of their own will onto a knife blade and then lift them gently into your bottle of sea water."[3]

This lyrically seductive approach diffuses the concept of death, which is doubly removed in invertebrates as they lack the sensory apparatus of man. In a seemingly intimate spirit anemones "invite" other creatures to "lie for a moment in their arms" where "the stinging cells shoot tiny narcotic needles into the prey and it grows weak and perhaps sleepy while the searing caustic digestive acids melt its body down." Through the range of imagery, from lover to chemical, a softening tone is sustained. Even the octopus as "creeping murderer" enchants as the analogy flows from one form of matter to another: the octopus "steals out, slowly, softly, moving like a gray mist, pretending now to be a bit of weed, now a rock, now a lump of decaying meat while its evil goat eyes watch coldly. Then suddenly it runs lightly on the tips of its arms, as ferociously as a charging cat. It leaps savagely on the crab, there is a puff of black fluid, and the struggling mass is obscured in the sepia cloud while the octopus murders the crab" (18). The elegance of this intriguing drama ameliorates the harsh facts, and danger-loaded words that might personify—*murder, steals, evil*—exaggerate beyond personification in the biologist's wry application of them to an amoral situation. In addition, the terms of destructiveness are countered by gentling concepts—*softly, mist, bit of weed, lightly on the tips of its arms*—as the predatory event is made a graceful happening.

For the regular folk of *Cannery Row,* the sea creatures that provide their living are viewed as pleasing matter. Sardines for the canneries pour from the boats as "silver rivers of fish" (1). The specimens that bring a price from Doc are treated similarly, comparable to supplies in Lee Chong's grocery across the street. The most lucrative project is the collection of frogs for cancer study—they go for five cents a head. With this incentive, the hunt, of unquestioned ancient origin, is carried out with the high spirit of adventure and profit. The frantic frogs head down the pool until they are "bunched and crowded against the end. . . . A few frogs lost their heads and floundered among the feet and got through and these were saved." The rest clamber onto the bank; "little ones rode on big ones. And then—horror on horror—the flashlights found them. Two men gathered them like berries. . . . Tens and fifties of them were flung into the gunny sacks, and the sacks filled with tired, frightened, and disillusioned frogs. . . . never in frog history had such an execution taken place" (58). The attributes *tired* and even *frightened,* which may be applied fairly objectively to animals, yield to *disillusioned,* a term that goes beyond a sympathetic view in its mockery. The frogs' "horror" is obscured by the triumph of the good-natured gang who seek only a bare living and a little fun. With six or seven hundred frogs, "happily Mack tied up the necks of the sacks." And it is doubtful whether the captain who permitted them to trespass on his property "had ever had so much fun" (58). In Doc's absence the frogs are put to a utilitarian purpose even before they arrive at the scientist's lab: Lee Chong accepts them as a medium of exchange, in the process upping his prices. Coca-Cola goes for two frogs, canned peaches for eight, and the price of good steak jumps from ten to twelve and a half frogs.

While gaining a livelihood is made an escapade for Mack's

gang, it reflects a proficiency and a healthy orientation to workaday reality, which happens to be based on the utilization of animals. Even the fat gopher that apparently mirrors the prosperity of the protagonists lives where "they put out traps every night" (121). The gang's parties may fall flat, but a hopeful spirit of survival prevails for these lowbrows, whose fortunes depend on animals. The more esoteric loner, Doc is sustained by music and poetry— but finally by the work with animals that feeds both body and soul. As the novel closes, to his back "the white rats scampered and scrambled in their cages. And behind the glass the rattlesnakes lay still and stared into space with their dusty frowning eyes" (123).

In "The Snake" (1938) a line is drawn as to the proper use of animals in a commercial laboratory as a woman purchases a male rattler to satisfy a prurient urge. But even her satisfaction depends on the death of an animal—the snake's devouring of a rat—not a display of snakes in coition. The lab director, too, is spellbound by the performance. Surprised that at first "for some reason he was sorry for the rat," Dr. Phillips is caught up in admiration for "an operation as deft as a surgeon's job." The snake's fangs enter exactly between the rat's shoulder blades, nearly reaching to the heart. The rat stands still, "breathing like a little white bellows. Suddenly it leaped in the air and landed on its side. Its legs kicked spasmodically for a second and it was dead."[4] Approaching to eat the rat, the rattler appears "to measure the body and to kiss it"—a kiss-of-death suggestion which is rather a mocking reminder that this is no subtly motivated beast—no symbolic snake—nor is it even a wild creature caught in a predatory act. It is a controlled specimen performing for man's benefit. The image of deceiving lover accordingly shifts to a more scientific account as the snake unhinges the jaws that fit over the rat's head and, with a "slow peristaltic pulsing" (56), engulf the rat. The woman's rhythmic weaving in response so disturbs Phillips that he must look away. But he has no trouble watching the rat—which he did not, by the way, refuse to deliver. The chillingly clinical nature of the biologist's work is established with the introduction to the doctor, who gently strokes a tabby cat before dropping it into the black box and flipping on the gas that brings the "short soft struggle" (48).

If the death of an animal is necessary to satisfy one woman's erotic urge, it is necessary to another for the maintenance of her sense of chastity. Mary Teller in "The White Quail" (1938)[5] demands that her husband poison the cat that intrudes in her immaculate garden, threatening the unspotted bird with which she identifies. Symbolic rather of the woman's sterility, the quail is necessarily somewhat artifical. Yet in actual terms it becomes the pawn of the warring couple, as Mr. Teller shoots it to punish his wife.

It is in an early novel, *To a God Unknown* (1933), that animals appear most directly in their fertility role. While the premise is mystical, the animals here are shown in a pragmatic rather than a spiritual context. As an ordained priest of nature, Joseph Wayne finds the spirit of his father in a tree. But he finds no divine spirit in animals. He does watch his bull breed (one of the few mating animals in American literature)—" 'Mount, you fool! She's ready. Mount now!'"—a viewing which is forbidden by the scriptures. " 'I want calves, . . . Where's the harm in that?' "[6] he explains. Joseph's cattle are his possessions, serving both for vicarious gratification and in their more significant economic role. As the eventual sacrifice, a calf fails to work a miracle. Thomas Wayne, said to have a great kinship with animals, shares his brother's pragmatic spirit. He "liked animals and understood them, and he killed them with no more feeling than they had about killing each other" (19).

While the premise of *To a God Unknown* is nature worship, the approach to animals differs little from that of the other works in its pragmatic materialism. It is more biblical than pagan, as the creatures exist for utilitarian and sacrificial purposes but contain no supernatural spirit of their own. The failure to develop Joseph's conviction of a divinity in nature, according to Howard Levant, is the central flaw of the novel. That the character is a "confused mystic rather than a convinced priest or god profoundly affects the credible presentation of nature worship."[7]

More dominant than the animal in its fertility role in *To a God Unknown* is the creature simply as the object of violence. Joseph's first encounter with wildlife in the West is the huge boar, which "sat on its haunches and tearingly ate the hind quarters of a still-squealing little pig" (5). The man's revulsion rules out both a worshipful approach or an affinity with this low species. He does not shoot only because it occurs to him that this boar may be the father of fifty pigs and perhaps the source of fifty more. But once on his own ranch, Joseph is soon at work with the knife, cutting the Wayne brand in the ears of his calves and performing castrations.

When the fertile cycle gives way to drought, Joseph assumes his priestly role and takes his knife to a calf as sacrifice, yet without the slightest attitude of worship. Joseph does, however, wholeheartedly engage in slaughter as a literal act. His eyes shine with excitement as he holds the calf's head and cuts its throat, the blood reddening the gravel and falling into the bucket. And then comes the distinctive touch of gratification: "It was over too soon," he thinks, the *it* having no referent other than the kill. " 'Poor starved creature, it had so little blood' " (178), he murmurs sadly. And in this apparently empathetic statement is revealed the cunning unbeknown to the character and perhaps even to the author. Beneath words of sympathy lies a man's disappointment that there is so little blood to shed.

In Steinbeck's agrarian world the chopping block is a standard feature of the farmyard. Slaughter, however, is not simply a regular activity—it is a special event of farm life, one in which the thrill of the kill may be openly expressed. A somewhat bizarre revelation of the lust for blood erupts in the story of Raymond Banks in *The Pastures of Heaven* (1932), exploding the myth of pastoral harmony with which this ironic tale begins: "Of all the farms in the Pastures of Heaven the one most admired was that of Raymond Banks. . . . It was a fine thing on a sunny morning to see the great flock of clean, white chickens eating and scratching in the dark green alfalfa, and it was even finer to see the thousand white ducks sailing magnificently about on the pond."[8] Raymond is a jovial man—picked every year as the valley's Santa Claus—who allows young boys to visit his farm and gather up armfuls of furry yellow chicks. But—and this next sentence is eased into the middle of the paragraph about the chicks—"Most of all, though, the boys liked the killing time" (121). With sure, quick hands Raymond slips his spear-shaped blade along the roof of the rooster's beak "into the brain and out again." In one combing motion the feathers are stripped away, and with another snick of the knife the entrails go into a pan. The shrieking boys point to the one moving part that remains. The heart may beat on, Raymond tells them, " 'but the rooster is dead all right' " (121–22).

The story does not end with a show of Raymond's efficiency. It is revealed that he takes his only vacations to witness executions at the state prison, for he "liked the excitement." The whole thing gives him a "fullness of experience" that nothing else in life offers, an emotion he equates with that of the boys who watch him kill chickens, as he "was able to catch a slight spark of their excitement" (123–24). Raymond's life's work betters his voyeuristic vacations— for in it he is the executioner, generally with society's approval and even applause. The man who balks at Raymond's activities is shown to be unduly disturbed, not even a man. In response to this squeamish character, Raymond defends slaughter—" 'it's not nearly as bad as it sounds' " (132).

Slaughter is exciting to most agrarian characters. For Jody Tiflin of *The Red Pony* (1937) "pig killing was fascinating, with the screaming and the blood, but it made Jody's heart beat so fast that it hurt him."[9] This "hurt" is the stimulation he looks for to break the monotony of farm life, both before and after he owns a pony. When Jody's father says he will need him in the morning, the boy tremulously but hopefully asks if it will be to kill a pig. In *The Grapes of Wrath* (1939) the Okies look with nostalgia on "the chopping block where a thousand chickens had been killed,"[10] which they must leave behind—and are most fortunate when they again have something to slaughter. Not only is it a life-sustaining activity but one which demonstrates a man's competence. The ability to make a precise incision is as highly regarded in the farm hand as it is in the biologist or the veterinarian. The Joad brothers "slaughtered quickly and efficiently. Tom struck twice with the blunt head of the ax; and Noah, leaning over the felled pigs, found the great artery with his carving knife and released the pulsing streams of blood" (114). The preparation of rabbits also calls for expertise, a process given in the clinically detached manner that has no place in it for the rabbit's sensations, while at the same time the victim cannot be ignored: "Tom took up a rabbit in this hand. . . . He lifted the skin of the back, slit it, put his fingers in the hole, and tore the skin off. It slipped off like a stocking, slipped off the body to the neck, and off the legs to the paws" (52). The rapid transition from the incision to kill to the cutting of roasted rabbit may well jar the squeamish reader who is also a meat lover.

For George Milton in *Of Mice and Men* (1937), the dream of a rabbit farm revolves on the activity of killing a chicken or rabbit every Sunday. In contrast, Lennie Small is of all Steinbeck's characters the most tender toward animals. And yet, ironically, he too is their killer. Through Lennie's affection for mice and pups, although he unwittingly crushes the life out of them, it might appear that Steinbeck takes a new approach to animals in this work. But the retarded man's attachments are an aberration—a transference of his need for human connection. The tragedy is that Lennie's warm feelings are wasted on animals. The mature man directs his compassion to other human beings—as George cares for Lennie. George's concept of animals, on the other hand, is the standard, materialistic, adult view. He sees the living or the dead mouse as a thing: " 'you've broke it pettin' it. You get another mouse that's fresh and I'll let you keep it a little while,' "[11] he says, after he flings the scrap into the brush. And this attitude applies to other animals. Lennie is far from ignorant in judging his friend's view of the pup. This " 'little son-of-a-bitch wasn't nothing to George' " (94).

A callous attitude toward dogs is reinforced by Slim, who boasts that his bitch " 'slang her pups last night, . . . nine of 'em. I drowned four of 'em right off' " (39). An old dog is shot because it stinks. At the most practical, incidental level, such as the instructions on a can of insect killer— " 'positively kills lice, roaches and other scourges' " (20)—to the method of measuring a man's skill— the man in the Stetson who is "capable of killing a fly on the wheeler's butt with a bull whip without touching the mule" (37)— the disposal of animals is casual. These foreshadowings of the extermination of the human blight occur so regularly as to reflect a core concept rather than a conscious literary reinforcing of the plot. Only a retarded man considers the animal's point of view (while he did kill the pup): " 'Why do you got to get killed?' " (93). And yet only Lennie's killing of animals is taboo—not simply because it suggests a threat to people but because of his desire for physical contact. George is as embarrassed as he is angry that Lennie would carry a mouse in his pocket and crawl into the box with the pups.

In his general description, limited mental capacity, and spontaneous instinctual responses, Lennie is the most animal-like of Steinbeck's major characters. And yet his cravings are altogether human. His desires for affection and approval are more important than his drive for sex. His crime is not rape but murder, resulting from the complex needs of a man, not a beast. And George treats Lennie as anything but an animal. He is, rather, childlike—and in Steinbeck's scheme, only a child places his affections with animals. But even in this case the animals die, with a violence no less terrible because it is touched with a lyrical innocence. By Lennie's own tender account of the mice, " 'I'd pet 'em, and pretty soon they bit my fingers and I pinched their heads a little and then they was dead—because they was so little' " (10).

The single death of an animal treated with great poignance is that of the red pony (in a tale which developed out of a family tragedy, not the death of an animal). Although Jody's colt dies of natural causes, even here human responsibility is involved as the boy, on the assurance of the experienced Billy Buck that it will not rain, allows the pony to stay in the field for the day. It does rain, and the horse gets sick and dies. Jody's suffering over the loss of his pony is the only indulgence of its kind in Steinbeck's work. But as the childlike Lennie misplaces his emotion with animals, so is the boy's involvement with Gabilan an experience of youth that must be outgrown if he is to become a man. The rite of passage which entails an acquaintance with death significantly poses not just any death but that of an animal—for which a sorrow is experienced that indeed may be transcended. Not only is the Steinbeck adult unmoved by the death of animals, but he learns to execute—with skill and satisfaction. Billy, Jody's model of mature responsibility, is disturbed by the pony's death, but primarily because in failing to save it he loses respect. And even the boy's distress has as much to do with the loss of the possession that brought him status as with empathy for the pony. Jody's companions know "instinctively that a man on a horse is spiritually as well as physically bigger than a man on foot" (12).

At birth, Gabilan is a willful colt. With his mane still wet and tangled, he looks at Jody with a "light of disobedience" in his eyes. The pony soon closes his teeth on the boy's hand enough to bruise it and bites him in the pants, proving himself a "bad pony" (17). When things get too peaceful he rears. Excellence in a horse is measured by a resistance to control: "only a mean-souled horse does not resent training" (18); "No matter how good a man is, there's always some horse can pitch him" (19), Billy instructs. Mr. Tiflin echoes the thought: " 'I don't like trick horses. It takes all the —dignity out of a horse to make him do tricks' " (17). The reason Billy agrees to let the colt out for the day is because " 'no animal likes to be cooped up too long' " (21).

Gabilan's freedom is nonetheless short-lived. Like Steinbeck's other creatures, his life is determined—by man and, in this case, by nature. To make the point that animals are naturalistic characters both in being biologically and environmentally determined and in being without spiritual salvation may seem to be a laboring of the obvious. But the fact is that this is the exceptional view in American literature. Free will and even a sense of the spiritual are most dramatically the rule. It is Steinbeck's startling realism to offer what might very well be the commonplace case: human beings are blessed with spirit, and animals are not.

Warren French's examination of naturalism in Steinbeck accurately distinguishes between works that show a determined man and those that develop a more humanistically willed one. French cites all four parts of *The Red Pony* as naturalistic in that the boy does not go on "to exercise conscious control over his destiny."[12] And yet Jody does take a measure of control in training his colt— and it is his decision, however unfortunate, that results in the pony's illness, not sheerly the force of natural law. The fact that he cannot forestall death does not make Jody a naturalistic victim: he learns a painful lesson, but his own life continues under the promising title of the concluding section, "The Leader of the People." It is the limit of Jody's youth to feel more fated than he is. With his new pony and the experience behind him, the conditions for hope exist.

The pony, on the other hand, is most certainly doomed—not simply in a Darwinistic sense as he succumbs to illness as one of the least fit, but as he is owned and controlled by men. His days of health and will are barely touched on as the story turns to the inevitable account of his death struggle, given in that awesomely lucid detail which almost disguises the relish with which Steinbeck describes such scenes. Although Billy's purpose is to save the pony, he poises with the familiar knife to cut the horse's throat: "The blood ran thickly out and up the knife and across Billy's hand and into his shirtsleeve. The sure square hand sawed out a round hole in the flesh, and the breath came bursting out of the whole, throwing a fine spray of blood" (31). As expected, the colt soon dies.

Jody's reaction to his pony's death also takes an expected and credible form as he murderously attacks the buzzard resting on the dead horse's head, one more occasion for gruesome detail. "He held the neck to the ground with one hand while his other found a piece of sharp white quartz. The first blow broke the beak sideways and black blood spurted from the twisted, leatherly mouth corners. He struck again and missed. The red fearless eyes still looked at him, impersonal and unafraid and detached. He struck again and again, until the buzzard lay dead, until its head was a red pulp" (35). Jody's grisly catharsis, however, works out his grief only to the extent that he no longer kills with such passion. Yet he has been and continues to be a boy who picks off animals for entertainment. Ever ready with pieces of quartz in his pocket, he aims at the bird or rabbit that "had stayed sunning itself in the road too long" (7). As the uninitiated boy, he points his gun indiscriminately "at rocks, at birds on the wing, at the big black pig kettle" (8). And the lack of discretion in targets does not alter after the pony's death, an experience that is not balanced by a new sense of life.

After Gabilan dies, the bitter spirit of death predominates. Jody stuffs horny toads, lizards, and grasshoppers in his lunch pail. He brings a thrush down with a broken head, which he cuts off with his pocketknife, then disembowels the bird and takes off its wings. Because "he was bored," he sets a rat trap to torture the favorite ranch dog. The life-death cycle, proposed in such scenes as the mare's dying as her foal lives, is actually weighted heavily to the deathly side in the animal kingdom—not in the number of deaths alone but in the tone associated with animals. Even the breeding of the mare to provide a new pony takes place as a form of destruction: "The stallion spun around and reared. He struck the mare with his front hoof, and while she staggered under the blow, his teeth raked her neck and drew an ooze of blood." Jody's warning, "he'll kill her. Get him away!" (58–59), provides the obvious forewarning. Indeed, in giving birth to the foal conceived on this occasion, the mare does die. Even when Billy first speaks of a second colt, he does so in terms of death—presumably to keep Jody from being disappointed. "Sometimes," he says, you "have to tear the colt to pieces to get it out, or the mare'll die" (61–62). As the colt is about to be born, as Billy had predicted, he proclaims, "It's wrong" (71). And once again he bends over the doomed animal with a knife. A colt is born, but another horse must die a bloody death. Billy "lifted the skin and drove the knife in. He sawed and ripped at the tough belly. The air filled with the sick odor of warm living entrails" (72).

Jody tries "to be glad because of the colt" (73), but it brings no new sense of life. He barely looks at it. Carnage speaks of the central interest in *The Red Pony,* from the casual announcements of death in nature—birds "busy" with worms, a ranch cat carrying a rat—to the more frequent slaying of animals by man. Jody's final project is to kill mice, not as a chore but just as something to do. For a retarded man to squeeze the life out of a mouse because he wants to pet it is unacceptable. But for the average farm boy to kill birds or toads or mice according to whim is a sign of the normal continuity of his life. That Jody lacks his usual enthusiasm in going after the mice indicates a temporary lapse in spirit rather than a change of heart. It is in the choice of prey that this is an unheroic venture, as reflected in his grandfather's comment: "Have the people of this generation come down to hunting mice?"—to which Jody replies, " 'It's just play. The haystack's gone. I'm going to drive out the mice to the dogs. And you can watch, or even beat the hay a little' " (81). Slaying animals was and apparently will continue to be play, and Jody will likely go on to more challenging prey. He will never so mourn the death of an animal again.

The development of the boy Pepe in "Flight" (1938) has been considered an atavistic retreat to mountain wilderness where his final, animalistic inhibitions are released.[13] But no new relationship or likeness to animals develops in his encounter with wildlife. The Steinbeck character does not learn to kill from animals: Pepe flees to the mountain because he has murdered a man with a knife. And his experience there is no Darwinistic struggle in which the boy behaves as one of the beasts. He is, rather, a violent human being who has no apparent motive to kill. Wild animals, on the other hand, are not shown as predators who threaten him. Pepe walks away from a rattlesnake, and a lion turns away from him. Yet he slays a lizard—not for survival but with a casual assertion of power: "when a grey lizard paused in front of him on the parched ground and turned its head sideways he crushed it flat with a stone."[14] The horse that carries the boy up the steep slopes becomes the victim of the bullet meant for him, an attack producing the customary sight of blood. The horse screams and falls, and from a "hole behind the struggling shoulder, a stream of bright crimson blood pumped and stopped and pumped and stopped" (39).

At the metaphorical level animal life in *The Grapes of Wrath* is analogous to that of the migrants who move across the land, "restless as ants, scurrying to find work" (256). The apparent fragility of human beings bared to the elements is that of the least creatures in the kingdom. But any likeness or harmony between man and actual animals is stripped away in his utility of them. And this novel dramatizes the humanity through which human beings transcend the lower beings. Edmund Wilson's establishment of the animalization of Steinbeck's people in this work[15] has since been most convincingly countered.[16]

The varying uses of the insect as metaphor in *The Grapes of Wrath* illustrate the incongruity between the literary and the actual creature. A house is wrenched from its foundation "so that it fell sideways, crushed like a bug" (41), an image playing upon the misfortune of the bug (at the same time it is equated with inanimate matter). Literal insects, on the other hand, are far from the sympathetic victims of machinery, the elements, or man. They are squashed with pleasure by the characters for whom compassion is suggested in the insect metaphor. Nor is it primarily as pests that the lower orders of life are destroyed; they are annihilated in an assertion of power. The bug metaphor is also used for the machine—tractors that come as "great crawlers moving like insects, having the incredible strength of insects" (36), although no such strength is illustrated with actual insects. The analogy is altered from insect as overpowering machine to insect as a paltry vehicle in yet another simile: "the cars of the migrant people crawled out like bugs" (220).

These jalopies teeter on the verge of collapse, but they are powerful weapons when it comes to destroying animals in the road. As Peter Lisca points out, Steinbeck was unsuccessful in using biological metaphors to illustrate or sustain a Christian ethic.[17] The source of that failure lies in Steinbeck's materialistic concept of animals.

As compelling as is man's power over animals, the gratuitous spirit with which it is exerted is even more pronounced. The gesture introducing Tom Joad, before it is revealed that he has murdered a man, is what he does with a grasshopper that lights on the instrument panel of the truck: "Joad reached forward and crushed its hard skull-like head with his fingers, and he let it into the wind stream out the window. Joad chuckled again while he brushed the bits of broken insect from his fingertips" (12–13). While such an incident reveals a brutality in this particular man, it is similar to the gestures of various noncriminal characters. With this same casual relish Jody Tiflin pops a tick with his thumbnail. Billy Buck claps at a moth, only to be bettered by Mr. Tiflin, who "caught the moth and broke it" (84). Even Ma Joad, the life-sustainer of the family, takes an ant scrambling on Granma's neck and "crushed it between thumb and forefinger" (230). The apparent parallel between this destruction of an ant and the turtle's crushing of the ant that goes into its shell is not borne out as a battle for survival. The turtle—by the way, less aggressive than Ma as it simply closes down on what has entered its shell—subsists on the ant. Ma disposes of it as an irritant—and she does so with gusto.

The much discussed turtle of *The Grapes of Wrath* is the one notable survivor in Steinbeck's animal kingdom. More than any other he resembles the stoic, independent animals found elsewhere in American literature. Like most of them, he sets off across the frontier *alone*. The interchapter devoted to this memorable character, given in that rich detail which renders the living animal as it might be seen with the poetic eye, but without entry into the consciousness, stands as one of the most striking in the novel:

> And over the grass at the roadside a land turtle crawled, turning aside for nothing, dragging his high-domed shell over the grass: His hard legs and yellow-nailed feet threshed slowly through the grass, not really walking, but boosting and dragging his shell along. The barley beards slid off his shell, and the clover

burrs fell on him and rolled to the ground. His horny beak was partly open, and his fierce, humorous eyes, under brows like fingernails, stared straight ahead. He came over the grass leaving a beaten trail behind him, and the hill, which was the highway embankment, reared up ahead of him. For a moment he stopped, his head held high. (14–15)

Taken as a symbol, the turtle embodies the enduring qualities of the Okies who travel the same road in a southwestward direction. Like them, he is vulnerable to the elements, the machine, and man, but he is not destroyed. His carrying of the wild oat seeds, however, is accidental: he is not a homesteader. And the analogy breaks down in more significant ways. Tom Joad, who collects a land turtle along that road, cannot be compared to the animal who eats an ant for survival; Joad crushed another's skull in a bar brawl. The ex-convict's repeated observation of the directedness of the turtle marks a discrepancy with the man's misdirected life. The primary quality of the Okies that makes not only for spiritual strength but for physical survival, their brotherhood—sharing, bonding, and the compassion that extends beyond family to other sufferers—is distinctly opposed to the self-reliance of the solitary turtle. As Stuart Burns points out, Steinbeck's intent to show the turtle as a parallel to the Joad family is not accomplished. Unlike the Joads, the turtle survives because of self-interest.[18]

Although the turtle taken by Tom survives as the independent, stoic American animal, like the other lower creatures he too is at the mercy of a human being. As difficult as conditions are for the Joads, none is treated as a pawn in any way comparable to Tom's treatment of the turtle. He plans to take it as a plaything for his brother's children (although he complains of what a meager gift it is). As he first strokes the underside of the turtle, Tom appears to consider it as a sentient being. But as he presses the underside—"It was softer than the back—" his curiosity is more that of one engaged with a mechanical object. "The hard old head came out and tried to look at the pressing finger, and the legs waved wildly. The turtle wetted on Joad's hand and struggled uselessly in the air. Joad turned it back upright and rolled it up in his coat with his shoes" (17–18). Seeing the stirring garment, Casy warns, " 'You'll smother it' " (21). In response, Tom rolls the coat tighter. Despite evidence of its distress, the turtle is no more than a thing to him (and he is not a man without feelings). The turtle escapes twice but is retrieved. When the man finally lets it go, he does so not because of the animal's efforts but because he is tired of carrying it.

A more murderous approach to the turtle occurs on the road as a truck driver aims for it. "His front wheel struck the edge of the shell, flipped the turtle like a tiddly-wink, spun it like a coin, and rolled it off the highway" (16). Such victimization cannot be blamed on the impersonality or even the careless use of machinery. The man swerves to hit the turtle. As a truck driver told Tom when he picked him up just out of prison, guys do "screwy things" (10) on those long drives to pass the time.

In the desert eyes glitter in the dark, but the animals do not come full into the headlights. The scarcity of wildlife is dispiriting not for the lack of life in itself but because there is nothing to hit. Tom's fortune is to meet a rattlesnake, which he runs down, breaks, and leaves squirming in the road, all without a lapse in the conversation. Further on, as Ma chats about what to buy in California, another snake "wriggled across the warm highway. Al zipped over and ran it down and came back to his own lane." Tom tells him he " 'oughtn't to done that,' " for it was only a gopher snake. But Al comes back gaily, " 'I hate 'em, . . . hate all kinds. Give me the stomach-quake' " (403). An attack on the loathed snake, however, is accomplished in the same spirit with which other animals are run over—turtle, dog, or rabbit.

When the family dog is hit, a closeup account of the bloody sight is in order. "The dog helplessly, and with a shriek, cut off in the middle, went under the wheels. The big car slowed for a moment and faces looked back, and then it gathered greater speed and disappeared. And the dog, a blot of blood and tangled, burst intestines, kicked slowly in the road" (141). Young Winfield "gloried in the scene," recounting it in detail. " 'His guts was just strowed all over—all over' " (143), the boy repeats, before he vomits down the side of the truck. In contrast to the child's disturbed reaction is the adult response, uttered by Rose of Sharon's husband Connie: " 'It wasn't nothin' " (141)—a statement that may be taken as a general commentary on the death of animals.

A rabbit goes down cleaner before the Joads' headlights—

with just a "small soft jolt" as it goes under the wheels. " 'We sure squashed him,' said Casy. Tom said, 'Some fellas like to hit 'em. Gives me a little shakes ever' time. Car sounds O.K. Them rings must a broke loose by now. She ain't smokin' so bad.' " And Casy adds, " 'You done a nice job,' " praise that reflects back as much to the job on the jackrabbit as to the job on the car.

Thus animals fall under the dominion of men, who kill them with skill and detachment, out of necessity and for amusement. They are rarely considered to have sensations. While human dignity depends upon ascendance over the creatures, it is very often boredom and gratification in power that lead to the many deaths in Steinbeck's animal kingdom. It serves him well, allowing a freedom to enjoy blood that would not be his in a world limited to man.

Notes

1. Alfred Kazin, *On Native Grounds* (Garden City, N.Y.: Doubleday, 1956), p. 310

2. John Steinbeck and Edward F. Ricketts, *The Log from the Sea of Cortez* (New York: Penguin Books, 1978), pp. 1–2. Subsequent references to this edition will appear in the text.

3. John Steinbeck, *Cannery Row* (New York: Bantam Books, 1959), p. 2. Subsequent references to this edition will appear in the text.

4. John Steinbeck, "The Snake," *The Long Valley* (New York: Bantam Books, 1979), pp. 54–55. Subsequent references to this edition of "The Snake" will appear in the text.

5. John Steinbeck, "The White Quail," *The Long Valley*.

6. John Steinbeck, *To a God Unknown* (New York: Penguin Books, 1978), pp. 22–23. Subsequent references to this edition will appear in the text.

7. Howard Levant, *The Novels of John Steinbeck: A Critical Study* (Columbia, Mo.: University of Missouri Press, 1974), p. 25.

8. John Steinbeck, *The Pastures of Heaven* (New York: Bantam Books, 1962), p. 119. Subsequent references to this edition will appear in the text.

9. John Steinbeck, *The Red Pony* (New York: Bantam Books, 1963), p. 63. Subsequent references to this edition will appear in the text.

10. John Steinbeck, *The Grapes of Wrath* (New York: Penguin Books, 1978), p. 36. Subsequent references to this edition will appear in the text.

11. John Steinbeck, *Of Mice and Men* (New York: Bantam Books, 1963), p. 10. Subsequent references to this edition will appear in the text.

12. Warren French, *John Steinbeck,* 2nd ed., rev. (Boston: Twayne Publishers, 1975), p. 63.

13. See John Antico, "A Reading of Steinbeck's 'Flight,' " *Modern Fiction Studies,* 11, no. 1 (Spring, 1965), 45–53.

14. John Steinbeck, "Flight," *The Long Valley,* p. 41. Subsequent references to this edition of "Flight" will appear in the text.

15. See Edmund Wilson, *The Boys in the Back Room* (San Francisco: Colt Press, 1941).

16. See, for example, George Bluestone, *"The Grapes of Wrath," Novels into Film* (Baltimore: Johns Hopkins Press, 1957).

17. Peter Lisca, "Steinbeck's Image of Man and His Decline as a Writer," *Modern Fiction Studies,* 11, no. 1 (Spring, 1965), 8.

18. Stuart L. Burns, "The Turtle or the Gopher: Another Look at the Ending of *The Grapes of Wrath," Western American Literature,* 9, no. 1 (May, 1974), 53, 55.

Tortured Animals: Richard Wright

Human violence is turned on animals in Richard Wright's world, but never without a sense of their suffering. Identification is with the hunted, not the hunter. The chattel principle of slavery, which equated slaves with livestock, cries for a sympathetic view of any being in bondage—and the assumptions underlying the creation of the free, frontier animal have no place. Houston Baker's point that the frontier was closed to black Americans—"All the pioneers, of course, were white; all the Indians, and even the beasts of the field, were 'dark' "[1]—if it has been disproved in fact, does apply to our literature. Wright's characters, in particular, know only the restraints to freedom. And in his case that makes the drive for it all the more volatile. Like the protagonist in his struggle, the animal is terrible, but not insignificant. White folks "kill us up like flies," a man tells his son.[2] Wright will have no flies. His animals are *big*. While many serve a symbolic function, first they are ever so actual. Indeed, it is the reality of his nightmarish world that strikes terror—not a literary rat.

In Malcolm Cowley's comparison of *The Grapes of Wrath* and *Native Son* (1940), both of which grew out of the radical movement of the thirties and were concerned with the dispossessed, he finds the most striking distinction to be that Steinbeck holds a privileged position in relation to his characters, while Wright was himself a victim.[3] He cannot remove himself from suffering. This distinction is even more pronounced in the treatment of animals, for if Steinbeck looks down with pity on his characters, he is at a much greater remove from the lower forms of life. Wright, on the other hand, recognizes them as fellow sufferers.

It was frequently through the animal figure that the fantasy of power developed in Afro-American folklore. According to Baker, the game of the forest became "the first heroes of black American folklore." The subversive Brer Rabbit is a "shirker of work, a master of disguise, and a cunning figure who wins contests against much larger and stronger animals."[4] Lacking in size, strength, and the natural weapons such as teeth and claws, he overcomes by wit. The hunter, representative of a privileged class, is made ridiculous. From the point of view of those who have been treated as prey, the hunt is evil. Zora Neale Hurston relates the story of the nigger who was taken hunting by his master and posted to shoot the deer. When it came tearing by, that nigger "didn't make a move to shoot de deer," claiming he had seen nothing—just a white man with a pack of chairs on his head.[5] When a hunter levels his gun to shoot at a pond of 3,000 ducks, the lake freezes and the ducks fly away. Better still, the prey controls the predator—a catfish pulls the fisherman into the lake. A boll weevil asks to drive a car. The least creature is entitled to power, and he demands it. Devoid of feet or claws, even the snake is considered a victim, who complains to God that everything steps on him: " 'Ah ain't got no kind of protection at all.' " Accordingly, God apologizes and gives him poison to put in his mouth.[6]

Such myths of power for the lower creatures speak the antithesis of the dark reality of Wright's world. "All my life," he says, "shaped me for the realism, the naturalism of the modern novel,"[7] a world not of the triumphant but of the entrapped. While the metaphor of man as beast is a standard feature of literary naturalism, that image for this Afro-American turns on the fact that black people were literally treated as such. The stereotype of the brute Negro is grounded in the belief that he is subhuman, a rationale used to justify slavery. Charles Carroll's *The Negro a Beast* (1900), for example, reasons that "to conceive the design of enslaving an

individual we must presuppose that he is free; the first act of en-
slavement is to deprive him of his liberty. This the Negro never
had since the creation of man. The Negro is an ape."[8]

In addition to giving us characters whose experience is closer
to that of trapped animals than the more literarily contrived versions of man as beast, such as those of Norris and O'Neill, Wright
is unique in including actual animals in the naturalistic framework
of the urban, as well as the rural, jungle. And if the animal remains
the purely naturalistic subject, while human reason may take a man
from a deterministic to an existential outlook, that creature exempt
from a knowledge of certain doom may exert a force more Faustian
than deterministic in spirit.

More often than they are victims of inexorable forces, Wright's
animals serve as scapegoats for man. *Black Boy* (1945) reveals such
a viewpoint in depicting Wright's youth. His abuse of animals,
which is more than the mere foreshadowing of a violent future, is
a crime in a purer sense than most others he and his older counter-
parts commit. Even murder carries a justification of its own. But
to hurt an innocent creature cannot be justified: this the young
Richard knows. He recalls the "disdain that filled me as I tortured
a delicate, blue-pink crawfish that huddled fearfully in the mudsill
of a rusty tin can" (14). An awareness of his cruelty in this incident
announces a life of self-loathing to come.

Black boy abuses but at the same time identifies with the victimized animal, while the romantic one is remote. Birds, as they
represent a world of freedom, are the vain specters of a privileged
class. What Richard sees is the "petty pride of sparrows wallowing
and flouncing in the red dust of country roads." The "solitary ant
carrying a burden upon a mysterious journey" (14) brings a yearning for identification, but the boy finds nothing in common with
the purposeful insect. Little emotion is associated with the successful creature. On the other hand, Wright's emotive imagination
flourishes where there is pain—"a hog stabbed through the heart,
dipped into boiling water, scraped, split open, gutted, and strung
up gaping and bloody"—a chicken leaping "blindly after its neck
had been snapped by a quick twist" (15) of his father's wrist. That
black boy comprehends these agonies makes his infliction of them
all the more diabolical.

Richard's hatred of his father leads to an incident more telling of the boy's doomed nature than setting the curtains on fire, which is something of an accident. In response to his father's outburst against the meowing of a stray cat—" 'Kill that damn thing!' "— the boy hangs the kitten for spite. And the cat must suffer too. Richard jerks it off the ground with a noose; it "gasped, slobbered, spun, doubled, clawed the air frantically; finally its mouth gaped and its pink-white tongue shot out stiffly" (17–18).

That this spiteful act achieves a certain victory bears out the grim pattern of reversals summed up by Roger Rosenblatt: "Characters in black fiction behave savagely in order to be considered civilized, . . . murder in order to create."[9] But if black boy finds a new power over his father in killing the cat, at the same time he relinquishes the sanctity of his soul fostered by his mother. It is her teaching he turns from in this rite of passage in which he makes his pact with evil. And his sin is burned into him as the lapse of his humanity is ritualized in the funeral of the cat. " 'You owe a debt you can never pay,' " Richard's mother charges, sending him into the night to bury the kitten.

> "I'm scared!"
> "And wasn't that kitten scared when you put that rope around its neck?" she asked.
> "But it was only a kitten," I explained.
> "But it was alive," she said. "Can you make it live again?" . . .
> I closed my eyes tightly, my hand clinging to hers.
> "Dear God, our Father, forgive me, for I knew not what I was doing. . . ."
> "Dear God, our Father, forgive me, for I knew not what I was doing," I repeated.
> "And spare my poor life, even though I did not spare the life of the kitten. . . ."
> "And spare my poor life, even though I did not spare the life of the kitten," I repeated. (19–20)

The fond association of child and pet is beyond the scope of Wright's people, viewed as the prerogative of the privileged class alone. For a time Richard cares for a poodle given him as a bribe by an "uncle" courting his aunt. But in a spasm of hunger the boy is driven to sell it for a dollar, prevented only by pride from accepting the ninety-seven cents offered by a white girl. Then a week later the dog is crushed under the wheels of a coal wagon.

Dogs are usually the possessions of the white man, often his vicious emissaries. But their ferocity may be understood as the result of conditioning, while the cool enmity of their masters is beyond comprehension. As a water boy in a brickyard, Richard is bitten by the boss's dog who haunts the clay aisles, snapping and growling. But, unlike its owner, the dog may be attacked. And it "had been wounded many times, for the black workers were always hurling bricks at it" (179).

The black protagonist's alliance with the suffering animal—and his alienation from the white man, the perpetrator of suffering—is never more explicit than in Wright's last published work, *The Long Dream*. Attracted to the "lonely yelping" of a dog whose back has been broken by a car, Fishbelly calls to him "tenderly, involuntarily." Unable to leave the big "squirming and gasping" dog to a slow death, the boy kills him with a broken whiskey bottle "so he won't suffer" any more. The dog's "passion of pain" is equated to the lynching of a black man. Then as Fishbelly goes on down the road and finds a white man trapped under his car—calling for help from the "nigger" and claiming he tried not to hit the dog—the boy walks away.[10]

The most poignant incident in which an animal catches the fire meant for man is the accidental killing of the mule in "The Man Who Was Almost a Man" (1961). Dave Saunders believes that if only he could shoot someone, he would become a man. But with his newly acquired gun he goes to the field with the mule Jenny and carelessly blows a hole through her instead. The association of neuter mule with an emasculated people, those other beasts of burden, is borne out in Dave's impotence in directing violence to an enemy. His blunder is self-destructive not only in the sense that the mule represents him—"They treat me like a mule, n then they beat me"[11]—but as he destroys a companion. And Dave's own sense of a genuine wrong is reinforced by the mule's white owner. " 'Ah didn' go t kill the mule, Mistah Hawkins!" Dave pleads. " 'But you killed her!' " (19), Hawkins answers.

The dying mule is given that dignity specifically associated with the unsightly victim in pain. "Trembling, walling her big eyes," Jenny stands with blood pouring from a hole in her side. The scene of suffering focuses on the animal's eyes—which Wright features oftener than human eyes. With "sleepy, dreamy eyes," the mule kneels to the ground, "her front knees slopping in blood. . . . For a long time she held her neck erect; then her head sank, slowly. Her ribs swelled with a mighty heave and she went over" (17).

In "Big Boy Leaves Home" (1936) the protagonist has killed a white man in self-defense. Big Boy is hardened to violence as Dave was not—and he is equated to a more dangerous and despicable animal, the snake he batters to death so he might take its place in the kiln. Thrust together in a hole out of town, the two dark creatures find no escape in this grim parody of a pastoral retreat. Like Big Boy, the snake is a pariah, fighting for the dubious privilege of inhabiting a hole. Both are objects of a loathing based on appearance. Rather than using the symbolic animal simply to reinforce the plight of his character, which it neatly does, Wright also shows the liabilities of the symbolic process for man and for beast. The fact that the most despised creature is equated to Wright's desperate character is not, however, the worst comparison that might be made. For if these black fighters are destructive, there is a sympathetic basis for their behavior. It is better to be compared to a black snake than to a white man.

Without an attempt to enter the snake's consciousness, Wright does bring its struggle close enough to force the thought that even a snake may experience agony in death. Big Boy beats it with a stick until it lies still; "then he stomped it with his heel, grinding its head into the dirt,"[12] an attack aimed not only at the fangs but at the center of consciousness. While the snake is first an enemy in its own right, it also serves for Big Boy's fantasy of how he would drive his white pursuers into the ground.

The lynchers' bloodhound is specifically the intermediary victim between white and black man. Big Boy may not get his hands on those murderous men, but he strangles their dog, a most palpable monster. The dog's paws scrape overhead as the boy crouches in the hole. Then the hot scent of dog breath is on his face, and the dog's nails bite into his arm. The dog's green eyes are before him.

Two desperate characters meet, and Big Boy does not know "whether he had lunged or the dog had lunged—they were together, rolling in the water" (50) until the boy feels the dog's body heave as the life goes out of it. After strangling it, Big Boy "held the dog, held it long after the last footsetp had died out, long after the rain had stopped" (51).

In a nonheroic mode Saul Saunders in "The Man Who Killed a Shadow" (1949) finds temporary relief from the ghosts that haunt him (the white woman's scream that sounds a man's death sentence) by becoming an exterminator of roaches, mice, and rats. Plagued by a lifelong sense of unreality, "he liked seeing concrete evidence of his work and the dead bodies of rats were no shadows. They were real."[13] While the poisoning of pests is not shown as an abusive act, destroying them does substitute for an attack on a representative of the white shadow world. (Saul is eventually provoked to kill a white woman.) That the work of exterminator is Saul's only means of "killing with the sanction of society" (160) makes a mocking reminder that the black man is excluded from more glorified adventures such as the hunt. Killing animals may be a compensation, but it offers no romantic possibilities for a man like Saul.

The rat is that all too palpable inhabitant of a nightmarish world. What is a mental space for Dostoevsky's underground man is turned to foul substance in "The Man Who Lived Underground" (1944), where the fugitive takes to the sewer, face to face with the filthy rodent. As this rat illuminates the depths of Fred Daniels's life, the man's descent to that lower world is also a revelation of the conditions experienced by a rat. Although seen only momentarily, this resident of the sewer is impressive by his size and the capacity to survive—"a huge rat, wet with slime, blinking beady eyes and baring tiny fangs."[14] The corpse of a baby that floats by and the undertaker's establishment above the sewer are the more obvious hints of the death that awaits the man who cannot adapt. Death to any animal is paralleled in the butcher shop, where "halves and quarters of hogs and lambs and steers" hang from "metal hooks on the low ceiling, red meat encased in folds of cold white fat" (37). The butcher whacking a hunk of steer with a cleaver, while reminiscent of a Bigger Thomas, is rather a hard-faced member of the ruling class—not a being driven by the desperation that leads the black man, and the animal, to violence.

Although the rat in *Native Son* is killed in the first scene of the novel, he screams his way into the rank of most memorable animals in American literature. Here is the rare case of the animal himself trapped in a naturalistic scheme, where he must fight not simply the struggle of a biological Darwinism but the more elusive threats of a society, which include the scientist's maze. Yet what might seem to be the purely naturalistic subject, one who is both hunted and trapped, the rat puts up a heroic struggle. Ironically, while the naturalistic protagonist is characterized by a sexual drive which is his downfall, that urge plays no part in the doom of this animal. The absence of the mating instinct—missing in most animals in American literature out of a puritanical restraint or, more significantly, a drive for freedom—here suggests a different set of reasons. Like Wright's other animals, the driven rat is not allowed the luxury to pursue his needs—neither the place nor the time, much less the opportunity to propagate his own kind.

The symbolic significance of this rat unfolds to perfection, as big, black, trapped Bigger Thomas desperately tries to escape in a maze of rooftops and alleyways. But before the full parallels are drawn, the rat lives and dies in as complete a dramatic scene as any in the novel. For him to be forced on the reader at a bloodcurdling proximity not only makes a brilliant beginning for this shattering book about a man, but it gives a chilling sense of what it might be like to be a rat.

This rat did not exist in the first version of the novel. "How 'Bigger' Was Born" explains as well how the rat made his way into the story. Wright had been having difficulty with the opening scene when one night, after several drinks, it came to him that Chicago was overrun with rats. At first he rejected the idea of having Bigger fight with a rat for fear the creature would "hog" the scene—which he very nearly does. But the rat would not go away, so Wright let him "walk in."[15] Liquor might have taken the novelist's imagination toward fantasy, but instead it brought him to the more palpable horror that is the backbone of his art. And the rat scene is flawless—marred neither by the exaggerated gore of the beheading of Mary Dalton nor by the dry waste of abstract argument that follows.

The rat rips onto the stage introduced by the personal pronoun: " 'There he is again, Bigger!' " his mother screams, as a sleepy scene is "galvanized into violent action"[16] by this antihero from a lower order. The dread name *rat* is not immediately uttered, and as it is withheld, the mighty rodent makes his way as an individual. Four adults freeze at the sight of him. The women stay "tense and motionless" (8), dull by comparison, while Bigger and Buddy are forced to defend against this terrifying and terrified attacker—a "huge black rat" that leaps at Bigger's trouser leg and snags "it in his teeth, hanging on." It takes "all the strength" (9) of Bigger's body to kick him loose. Hurled across the room, the rat takes on the impersonal pronoun, which then alternates with the personal, as the forces working on him would reduce him to matter but his savage endurance earns back his individual stature. Slamming the wall, "instantly, it rolled over and leaped again" (9). The scourge of urban man, surviving on his garbage, the rat yet maintains the perverse dignity of life against the odds. He is *the* life that sets this mighty novel in motion—leaping, sailing, rolling, landing, scurrying, rearing, pawing the air, skidding, scuttling, searching, running, quivering, and squealing.

> The rat's belly pulsed with fear. Bigger advanced a step and the rat emitted a long thin song of defiance, its black beady eyes glittering, its tiny forefeet pawing the air restlessly. Bigger swung the skillet; it skidded over the floor, missing the rat, and clattered to a stop against a wall.
>
> "Goddamn!"
>
> . . . The rat scuttled across the floor and stopped again at the box and searched quickly for the hole; then it reared once more and bared long yellow fangs, piping shrilly, belly quivering. (9–10)

Wright's genius for dramatizing fear works as well with animals as with men. This rat is damn scared. Only after his desperation and his drive are established is the single detail of ugliness given—the bared yellow fangs. His hideousness may indeed be assumed. But that it is a first fact only makes the awfulness of his situation more convincing. Loathing automatically follows the ugly creature. He is trapped and beaten. But he is also dignified as a mighty underdog.

After Bigger has killed the rat, he beats the head with a shoe, cursing " 'You sonofabitch,' " a tribute to the rat's demonic stature. " 'Lord, Lord have mercy,' " Bigger's mother sobs, a prayer in behalf of her violent son—and a last rite over the fallen beast. Buddy and Bigger stare at the dead rat with fearful respect: " 'That sonofabitch could cut your throat.' " " 'He's over a foot long' " (10). Bigger wraps the rat in a newspaper and *puts* the bundle in the trash, not as one would drop a load of garbage. The blood spot left on the floor—indeed, the sign of things to come for Bigger—is first the reminder that here a life was lost.

The rat that Bigger identifies with all too well overwhelms the images of those vapid creatures of a distant, more romantic world. Birds in flight may be envied (although Bigger is instead transfixed by the airplane), but up close they appear as dismal representatives of a world denied—the "slate-colored pigeon" that vainly struts, "its fat neck bobbing with regal pride" (23). The rat's natural enemy, the cat, is distanced as is the entire sphere that includes pets. And the feline's self-containment is antithetical to Bigger's desperate and ill-controlled nature. The white cat that trails Mrs. Dalton, overly obvious in its symbolism of a sterile, blind existence, is necessarily artificial. But it is an actual cat, and Bigger's attempt to kill the cat puts it in the scapegoat predicament between white and black worlds.

As the specter of conscience, the Dalton cat derives much from Poe's black cat, a connection examined by Michel Fabre.[17] After his crime Bigger is followed by "two green burning pools—pools of accusation and guilt" (90). But as the cat does reflect Bigger's conscience, its escape suggests a release of guilt, a beginning in the evolution of the trapped figure of naturalism to the existential man proud of his crime.

Wright's use of the cat, however, differs from Poe's in substantial ways (other than the neat reversal of the color scheme). While Bigger's hostility reaches to his core, he shows no particular antipathy toward the cat. Even when it jumps on his shoulder during the investigation of the house, he registers no murderous impulse; his curse is only that it might leave him alone. When the cat watches him stuff the body in the furnace, he considers killing it and makes "a move." But when it bounds away, Bigger does not chase it, reminding himself that, after all, a cat cannot talk. As it bounds past him, Bigger hears its "long wail of fear" (90)—a sensation he shares with animals but not with their white owners. No fear is attributed to Mary Dalton. When Bigger smothers her, she simply stops moving under the pillow. The sense of suffering in Wright's world—indeed, emotion itself—extends to animals but rarely to white people.

In fleeing from his crime, Bigger takes on both the frenetic role of trapped rat and the simian designation that links him to the actual condition of an animal in pursuit. He is captured with the cry, "Kill that black ape!" (253). The *Chicago Tribune* maintains that, "all in all, he seems a beast utterly untouched by the softening influences of modern civilization" (260). The shocking parallels in a news account of Robert Nixon, a black man accused of murdering a fireman's wife, which appeared in the same newspaper (May 1938) *after* the conception of Bigger Thomas, eerily reinforce Wright's fictional picture. Nixon is described as a "jungle beast," "just like an ape," with "hunched shoulders and long sinewy arms that dangle almost to his knees."[18]

As Edward Margolies sees it, Wright "utilized the image of the primitive in order to destroy it."[19] Indeed, he does reveal that image to be the monstrous creation of a society. The prosecuting attorney at Bigger's trial emphasizes that the noncriminal man "stepped forward from the kingdom of the beast" (373). But even if Wright's men could rise above the beasts they are equated with, to transcend them entirely would be to achieve the sterile superiority of the white man. While compassion is all but void in Bigger, a rare sensitivity does, in fact, work downward—only downward—on the scale of being. It is animals, not people, that come to mind in his thought that he must "meet his end like any other living thing upon the earth" (256).

Whereas *Native Son*'s rodent shows a mighty struggle, rats and other specimens used for scientific study are subdued in "The Man Who Went to Chicago" (1961). Nowhere does Wright make a more direct, sympathetic case for the animal caged in a white man's world than in this story based on the author's experience as an orderly in a medical research institute. Placed by the relief system in one of the wealthiest hospitals in Chicago, Richard is assigned to clean the cages of dogs, cats, rabbits, and rats—a typical association of the black man with the unsavory side of animal life—a side he not only sees but is forced to share. "Four of us Negroes worked there and we occupied an underworld position"[20] as though "close kin to the animals we tended." They are "separated by a vast psychological distance from the significant processes of the rest of the hospital" (204). The exclusion from scientific information keeps the orderlies nearly as ignorant of the experiments done on the animals as they are. Richard inquires "if the dogs being treated for diabetes were getting well; if the rats and mice in which cancer had been induced showed any signs of responding to treatment" (194). But the doctors "laughed at what they felt was our childlike interest in the fate of animals" (201).

The sufferings of these subjects of science are reflected in the futile gesture, the muted cry. A "rabbit leaped restlessly in its pen. A rat scampered around in its steel prison." "The lonely piping of guinea pigs floated unheeded about us" (198–99). Richard's most painful task is to assist in "slitting the vocal cords of a fresh batch of dogs from the city pound"—devocalized so as not to disturb the patients. "I held each dog as the doctor injected Nembutal into its veins to make it unconscious; then I held the dog's jaws open as the doctor inserted the scalpel and severed the vocal cords. Later, when the dogs came to, they would lift their heads to the ceiling and gape in a soundless wail. The sight became lodged in my imagination as a symbol of silent suffering" (195).

Still, the sympathizer, if accidentally, is the victimizer. In a fight the orderlies knock the cages over and release the sickly specimens to the destructive chaos of an unaccustomed freedom. "Rats and mice and dogs and rabbits moved over the floor in wild panic. . . . Here and there an animal had been crushed beneath a cage" (200). The orderlies haphazardly refill the cages—"we did not know a tubercular mouse from a cancerous mouse" (201)—replacing the dead with healthy specimens. And the coverup works, as one proud doctor calls for "My rats, please," injecting them with the mysterious fluid as usual, while another requests "A-Z rabbit number 14" (203) and takes it to the operating room without noticing anything wrong. But while the doctors' callousness is central to the suffering of animals in this story, its sad irony is that even though the black men empathize, their misdirected violence is also responsible for the creatures' suffering and death.

Wright's great empathy for the tortured animal makes for the most moving passages of *Pagan Spain* (1957)—those describing the bullfight. Like Ernest Hemingway, Wright understands it as a ritual for the overcoming of fear. But his version is distinguished in that he feels nothing for the matador, only for the bull. To fully experience the bullfight, a bullfighter explains, the spectator must make two identifications at once, "jumping from the bull to the matador."[21] *Pagan Spain* never makes that second identification—neither in the expression of desire to kill a bull nor in the triumph experienced in a public display of courage. The crowds press forward with " '*Bravo hombre . . .!*' " but Wright does not join in. "I watched the bull," he says (126–27).

First and last, Wright concentrates on the bull—who, like the other animals featured, is an uncomely victim. To make his violation an aesthetic event would be a lie. The bull is forced in the ring with "nostrils quivering, his open mouth flinging foam, his throat emitting a bellow" (114). Drawn at close range, the face shows an "almost hoglike distension of the wet and inflated and dripping nostrils, that defiant and careless lack of control of the anal passage, that continuous throbbing of the thin, trembling flanks, that open-mouthed panting that was so rapid that it resembled a prolonged shivering" (115). Mighty as the bull is, he alone is vulnerable. While he is the life force of this pageant, his energy is by definition restless, out of control. And his controllers conspire to reduce him not with weapons alone but with taunts and tricks in what to men is a mere "bloody game" (113).

The thundering pace of the black beast (and the description returns to the word *black*) is soon checked by the work of the picador, whose steel-tipped tool resembles an "enormous fish hook" that shreds the flesh and tendons of the charging animal. The panting bull stands alone, "heaving his vast black shoulders and feeling the steel slashing his flesh" (120). He careens, bellows, whirls in agony. Again and again the steel tips sink in the "shaking flesh" (121), "the tormented and bloody mound of wounds on the bull's back" (126). At last he sags, "his eyes on his tormentor," in the inevitable outcome of this gory game.

> The bull now advanced a few feet more on tottering legs, then his back legs folded and his hind part sank to the sand, his forelegs bent at the knees. And you saw the split second when death gripped him, for his head nodded violently and dropped forward, still. A heave shook his body as he gave up his breath and his eyes went blank. He slid slowly forward, resting on his stomach in the sand, his legs stretching straight out. He rolled over on his back; his four legs, already stiffening in death, shot up into the air. (127)

Opposed to the black, uncontrolled bull is the gaudily cos-tumed, cold matador. He is not introduced until Wright has won us to the bull, and then with little ado: "The matador was Cha-maco" (121) (followed by another sentence about the bull). What someone else might see as the discipline of emotions is presented here as the absence of them. The key to the matador's art is said to be immobility, but that translates to an icy form of control. He is not shown in his fear, and he is not wounded, although the discus-sions after the fight center on those subjects. Rather, he is a manip-ulator working for the benefit of the crowd. "This beast had to be educated quickly, so that he could serve human ends, human pur-poses" (116). The matador *checks, conditions, plays,* and *coaxes* the bull, assisted by the banderillo, who teases and laughs at him. Then, plunging the darts into the "gaping, bloody wound," the man leaps aside, "escaping to safety" (120). There is no chance of escape for the bull. After the bullfight Wright sees a photo of Chamaco that gives him "the creeps" (128). He meets the young man and learns that he was afraid in the bull ring. But that is not the way Wright saw it.

The account of bullfighting concludes with a return to the bull—to a village bullfight which is altogether repulsive. When the bull is killed, the people rush to his testicles and begin "kicking them, stamping them, spitting at them, grinding them under their heels," with an "excited look of sadism." Their need to destroy his "sexual machine" shows the entire, sick ritual as an outpouring of "hate and frustration" (142–43), one more vicious case where a symbol is made of a living being—the bull as the "hallucinatory image of the lust to kill" (115).

If Wright's characters themselves rise to negative destinies through violence, they do so only in their attack on the objects of hate. They must defend themselves against a rat or a snake, when they would destroy a truer enemy. That the bull the matador swears to kill is "deeply loved; no mistake must be made about that" (115) presents a paradox that reaches beyond the most diabolical acts of Wright's protagonists.

They do not set out to kill what they love—and they find no glory in hurting innocent animals. They have shared too much with them to make a game of that kind of torture.

Notes

1. Houston A. Baker, Jr., *Long Black Song: Essays in Black American Literature and Culture* (Charlottesville: University Press of Virginia, 1972), p. 7.

2. Richard Wright, "Fire and Cloud," *Uncle Tom's Children* (New York: Harper & Row, 1965), p. 171.

3. Malcolm Cowley, "The Case of Bigger Thomas," *New Republic,* 102 (Mar. 18, 1940), 382.

4. Baker, pp. 11–12.

5. Zora Neale Hurston, *Mules and Men* (New York: Harper & Row, 1970), p. 103.

6. Ibid., p. 131.

7. Richard Wright, *Black Boy* (New York: Harper & Row, 1966), p. 274. Subsequent references to this edition are cited in the text.

8. Charles Carroll, *The Negro a Beast* (Miami: Mnemosyne Publishing Co., 1969), p. 289.

9. Roger Rosenblatt, *Black Fiction* (Cambridge, Mass.: Harvard University Press, 1974), p. 19.

10. Richard Wright, *The Long Dream* (New York: Ace, 1958), pp. 120–21, 123.

11. Richard Wright, "The Man Who Was Almost a Man," *Eight Men* (New York: World, 1969), p. 20. Subsequent references to this edition of the story will be cited in the text.

12. Richard Wright, "Big Boy Leaves Home," *Uncle Tom's Children,* p. 42. Subsequent references to this edition of the story will be cited in the text.

13. Richard Wright, "The Man Who Killed a Shadow," *Eight Men,* p. 160. Subsequent references to this edition of the story will be cited in the text.

14. Richard Wright, "The Man Who Lived Underground," *Eight Men,* p. 24. Subsequent references to this edition of the story will be cited in the text.

15. Richard Wright, "How 'Bigger' Was Born," *Saturday Review of Literature,* 22, no. 6 (June 1, 1940), 19.

16. Richard Wright, *Native Son* (New York: Harper & Row, 1966), p. 8. Subsequent references to this edition will be cited in the text.

17. Michel Fabre, "Black Cat and White Cat: Richard Wright's Debt to Edgar Allan Poe," *Poe Studies,* 4, no. 1 (June, 1971), 17–19.

18. June 5, 1938, quoted in Dan McCall, *The Example of Richard Wright* (New York: Harcourt, Brace & World, 1969), p. 5.

19. Edward L. Margolies, "A Critical Analysis of the Works of Richard Wright" (Dissertation, New York University, 1964), p. 25.

20. Richard Wright, "The Man Who Went to Chicago," *Eight Men,* p. 192. Subsequent references to this edition of the story will be cited in the text.

21. Richard Wright, *Pagan Spain, Richard Wright Reader,* ed. Ellen Wright and Michel Fabre (New York: Harper & Row, 1978), p. 110. Subsequent references to this edition will be cited in the text.

CHAPTER 8

"My kingdom for a horse."
—Shakespeare

Animal Crazy:
William Faulkner

A bear looms deep in Yoknapatawpha County. But most animals in Faulkner's world share the society of man—as aids, possessions, and objects of passion. They provide an escape from women, usually a purifying release from the sexual bondage that dooms men, not a symbolic or an actual version of the erotic. The distinguishing mark of these animals is a flaw, a handicap. They are incorrigible and enduring, and may inspire the most generous affections. But they also uncork fatal doses of greed and foolhardiness, which are turned with equal artistry to the pathetic or to the comic denouement. Either way, out there beyond reason, the Faulkner male plunges to his destiny over a horse.

As the bear comes first to mind of Faulkner's animals, the hunt was a primary ritual in his life, an activity that pleased him to the end. As Francis Utley puts it, "many Northern boys know a hobby called hunting; most Southern boys know hunting as a way of life."[1] When asked just months before his death what delighted him most, Faulkner said it was fox hunting.[2] That he preferred his hunting companions to his literary peers is known to the world. Appropriately, the morning his Nobel Prize was announced the author was deer hunting in Mississippi.

The hunt turned to fiction, however, becomes a strangely confused moral issue: killing animals does not easily fit into Faulkner's artistic scheme. He personally may have experienced the classic paradox of the hunt—the satisfaction of killing what one loves. According to his brother John, Bill was "a tenderhearted someone, with a very real feeling for those creatures he killed for food." As a child when he killed his beagle hound while aiming at a rabbit, he did not go hunting again for years. But he later got his buck and was ritualistically smeared with its blood. Faulkner also killed a bear.[3] The satisfaction of slaying animals, however, is not passed along in the fiction. Far from being a pleasant pastime, neither is it the ennobling initiation to manhood one might expect in "The Bear" (1942). Following the motions of a hunt, the annual quest for Old Ben is rather a pilgrimage in which *seeing* the great animal is the climax, not conquering him. The young Ike McCaslin senses that the hunters go "not to hunt bear and deer but to keep yearly rendezvous with the bear which they did not even intend to kill."[4] (In the earlier, simpler version of "The Bear" [1935] this theme remains intact as Old Ben is left unharmed.)

In Wiley Umphlett's study of the sporting myth in American literature, in which he equates fishing, hunting, bullfighting, and boxing as rituals for obtaining immortality, he includes Faulkner with those whose protagonists are driven to "kill or defeat that which they instinctively love." He thus maintains that "The Bear" is written from an ironic point of view as it reflects compassion for the defeated.[5] Umphlett is correct in seeing that "The Bear" does not fit into his definition, but the discrepancy is not due to irony. Umphlett's version of the myth generally does not apply to Faulkner. His men are more likely to benefit from the strengths of animals than to try to destroy them. The whole, extraordinary point of Ike's meeting the bear is that he leaves his gun behind and faces the beast without the urge to kill. Boon Hogganbeck, on the other hand, after killing the bear reverts to a maniacal obsession with the squirrels he plans to kill next: " 'Don't touch a one of them! They're mine!' " (331).

Yet reverence for life is not a convincing center of this strangely confused tale either. Ike apparently upholds a superior morality in his regard for the life of the bear. (And this is not merely the case of the totem animal that cannot be killed, because twice Ike meets the bear with a gun but does not shoot.) But Old Ben is the only prey whose life Ike sanctifies. His "kindergarten" was rabbits and squirrels (meaning he killed them). He advanced to shooting a buck, and he has slain another bear. By what standard, then, is Old Ben's life to be spared—because he is the biggest and the most powerful prey? William Van O'Connor raises the pertinent question of "how respectful one should be of a bear or any other creature that wantonly would crush one's head or rip off one's limbs."[6] Respect for the bear is beautifully drawn, but the story does not support the reverential ideology it suggests. Nor does any hunt.

Other stories of *Go Down, Moses* (1942), as well as the fourth section of "The Bear" with its examination of racial issues, substantiate the hunt as an *immoral* activity. Slavery is a form of the hunt. In "Was," which opens the volume, the Negro is the quarry. Faulkner says that in the heat of running, the slave would have received the same respect as the bear or the deer.[7] What, then, does that say of the hunter? And "Delta Autumn" shows Ike shrunken from his hour of nonviolence to a narrowed existence as a hunter, with one pathetic boast: "he still shot almost as well as he ever had, still killed almost as much of the game he saw as he ever killed."[8]

The lush spirit of affirmation that does mark "The Bear" as a turning point from the pessimism of Faulkner's earlier works comes neither from the challenge of the hunt nor from a countering theme of reverence for life. The work's richness springs from a profuse affection not simply for wilderness, generally—vegetation or an expanse of land—but for particular animals, both wild ones and those that accompany the hunters.

First is the legendary bear who, as O'Connor says, "almost begs to be treated as a symbol."[9] The mythic bear, which has been the primary focus of literary criticism, is, as one critic says, a figure as "ambiguous as Moby Dick."[10] Embodiment of (rather than symbol of) the wilderness, he stands as the totem animal, mysteriously related to both god and man, carrying the seeds of both salvation and destruction. But as Irving Howe reminds us, while "The Bear" is "a story that can hardly be grasped if taken in narrowly realistic terms," it "cannot be grasped at all if those terms are dismissed. . . . the bear, like the white whale, is a 'real' animal, not a specter of allegory, and in this case an animal with fur and four legs." The enriching but finally inferior fourth section, continues Howe, cannot equal the image of that bear in the forest. "Perhaps it is the point and purpose of the story to show that nothing can."[11]

Old Ben was modeled on a bear known to Faulkner—Old Reel Foot, who had lost two toes from his left front paw.[12] That flaw becomes the fictional bear's first identifying feature, his badge of suffering. The "print of the enormous warped two-toed foot" is also the initial evidence that an actual bear walks the woods. When Ike sees the footprint, "for the first time he realised that the bear which had run in his listening and loomed in his dreams since before he could remember . . . was a mortal animal" (200–201). Similarly, the imperfection of a big wood tick inside the bear's hind leg, in the earlier version of the story, establishes the credibility— the vulnerability, even—of the mighty creature. Far from detracting from his stature, the bear's flaws are his most illuminating features.

Ike's first awesome sight of the bear inspires the boy for the years until he meets him again. In a simple sentence, buried in a labyrinthine paragraph exquisitely evocative of the tangle of legend, the living bear appears: "Then he saw the bear. It did not emerge, appear: it was just there, immobile, fixed in the green and windless noon's hot dappling, not as big as he had dreamed it but as big as he had expected, bigger, dimensionless against the dappled obscurity, looking at him" (209).

In seeing the bear, Ike experiences one of reality's rewards— that the tangible may be better than the dream. The most marked discrepancies between the mythic bear and the real one, in this first view, are that he is more serene and more graceful than imagined. In place of the hunter's urge to kill, Ike feels a bond with this other being, one who makes eye contact, as many of Faulkner's animals do (and the stale-water eyes of a Flem Snopes do not). Myth is not dispensed with for Ike but fuses with the tangible for the most remarkable bear of all: "It was quite familiar, until he remembered: this was the way he had used to dream about it" (211). Thus, for him to become a hunter again, as he does in the years to come when there is no longer an inspiring mythic prey, indicates a loss of the reverence for the physical world, which for Ike climaxes when he sees the bear.

Power and size are to be expected in the animal hero, and Old Ben, the "head bear" (198), is secure in both. But in accord with a passivist motif, his ferocity is downplayed: the bear did not kill the farm animals he was blamed of slaying (an accusation that rather affirms his potential, however). Old Ben looms as a "shaggy tremendous shape," though "not malevolent but just big, too big for the dogs which tried to bay it, for the horses which tried to ride it down, for the men and the bullets they fired into it; too big for the very country which was its constricting scope" (193). In battle it continues "rising and rising as though it would never stop" (241) until it is erect, a giant before it falls.

Still, Faulkner is no worshipper of size. The bear's most valued quality is "fierce pride of liberty and freedom" (295). Old Ben is that classic American animal: a male, "solitary, indomitable, and alone." That he is "widowered" and childless grants him past experience—and present freedom. Being apart from family ties, he is "absolved of mortality" (194). His liberty—his independence—is the envy of men, who are not strong enough to stand alone. "No man is ever free and probably could not bear it if he were" (281). Thus Old Ben reigns as the single king of the wilderness.

But if the creature of myth sets the quest in motion, the familiar dog Lion who meets him in the yearly hunt is equally impressive. Only he can stop Old Ben. With the bear and Sam Fathers, this mongrel is "taintless and incorruptible" (191). Like conventionally heroic beasts, Lion is big, fierce, and independent. But he and the other dogs exemplify what the king of the forest rarely needs—courage. "Lion inferred not only courage" but "endurance, the will and desire to endure beyond all imaginable limits of flesh" (237). As with the bear, he is modeled on an animal of the author's acquaintance (one which he admits to making more heroic in the fictional version). Lion is that naked mystery, a complete individualist who did not love anybody.[13]

Above all, Lion will not be tamed. Sam Fathers maintains, " 'I don't want him tame' " (217): only as he is will Lion go against the bear. So Sam locks the ninety-pound dog in a crib for two weeks without food. And it is in the doomed gesture that Lion is most himself. Each morning the animal "hurled itself tirelessly against the door and dropped back and leaped again. It never made any sound and there was nothing frenzied in the act but only a cold and grim indomitable determination" (217). At the end of the two weeks the "tremendous" dog remains, lying on its belly, "its head up, the yellow eyes blinking sleepily at nothing: the indomitable and un-broken spirit" (219). Even Major De Spain's loathing generates a tribute: " 'I'd rather have Old Ben himself in my pack than that brute' " (217).

Ike repeatedly states that he should hate and fear Lion, but in the gun-blue dog whose eyes reflect a "cold and almost impersonal malignance" (218) obstinancy is as intriguing as majesty. He cannot hate this dog. And Boon's single passion is love for his mighty mongrel. Boon sleeps with the dog. It is devotion to Lion that provokes the attack on the bear, not the hunter's ambition for a trophy. With Lion clinging to the bear's throat and Old Ben raking at Lion's belly with his paws, Boon runs, flings himself astride the bear, and, with his "arm under the bear's throat where Lion clung" (214), plunges his knife.

The death of Lion, the central issue of an earlier story incorporated here, is a more moving event than the death of the bear. Old Ben is man's enemy, after all, and Lion is an ally that will be dearly missed. Farmers and hunters fill the yard to see the bear but then "go on to the front where Lion lay. . . . the great blue dog would open his eyes, not as if he were listening to them but as though to look at the woods for a moment before closing his eyes again, to remember the woods or to see that they were still there. He died at sundown" (248).

Also crucial to the hunt are the "patient and steaming mules" (195) that make the long trip into the wilderness possible. They, too, must be brave. It is the characteristically flawed animal, the "one-eyed mule which would not spook at the smell of blood, of wild animals" (200), not even at the smell of bear, that carries Boon to Old Ben. The debt to mules here calls to mind the moving paean to them in *Sartoris*:

> Some Homer of the cotton fields should sing the saga of the mule and of his place in the South. He it was, more than any other one creature or thing, who, steadfast to the land when all else faltered before the hopeless juggernaut of circumstance, impervious to conditions that broke men's hearts because of his

venomous and patient preoccupation with the immediate present, won the prone South from beneath the iron heel of Reconstruction and taught it pride again through humility, and courage through adversity overcome; . . . Father and mother he does not resemble, sons and daughters he will never have; . . . Outcast and pariah, he has neither friend, wife, mistress, nor sweetheart; celibate, he is unscarred.[14]

Great regard is also shown for the smaller dogs. These intermediaries between man and his prey are first to encounter the bear—and to suffer the wounds as evidence. The "passive and still trembling bitch" returns with a "tattered ear and raked shoulder. . . . Just like folks," she has put off being brave, yet "knowing all the time that sooner or later she would have to be brave once so she could keep on calling herself a dog" (199). Though the dogs charge as a group and give off a general murmur, their distinct voices allow Ike to call the five dogs his cousin owns from the others. Social enough to take up their rooms in the house—the dogs are already in the kitchen when the hunters return—they are never fully tamed. Courage in them, as in other animals, is equated with wildness.

The smallest dog, known in local parlance as a *fyce,* exhibits the most outrageous bravery. Indeed, the handicap of diminished size is more comic than tragic. But the nerve of this under-underdog is as remarkable a virtue as any in "The Bear." Even the two hounds seem to take a "kind of desperate and despairing courage from the fyce" (211). The grandeur of the wilderness may have vanished with Old Ben, but Faulkner applauds the fyce as the antithesis of the bear, one who has coped with the environment. " 'All's against him is his size. But I never knew a fyce yet that realized that he wasn't as big as anything else he ever saw, even a bear.' "[15]

As Boon develops courage in behalf of Lion, Ike finds his resolve in rescuing his little dog "not much bigger than a rat and possessing that sort of courage which had long since stopped being bravery and had become foolhardiness" (211). The fyce frantically charges the prey, and in overtaking the shrill, "pinwheeling" dog, Ike looks up to find himself directly under the bear.

That it is not the slaying of the animal but its living presence which inspires is evident even in such hunting stories as "The Old People." The deer as quarry appears as a flesh-and-blood miracle out of the void: "At first there was nothing. . . . Then the buck was there."[16] This nonmythicized though extraordinary creature, balancing antlers like a rocking chair on his head, suspends motion as serenely as the bear, with the grace that belies slaughter. It turns, "not fleeing, not even running, just moving with that winged and effortless ease with which deer move" (184). The thought of killing this lovely animal is dispensed with at the beginning of the story (which goes on to show the living deer). "The boy did not remember that shot at all." And the deer lies "not looking at all dead" (163–64).

To Vardaman Bundren, in *As I Lay Dying* (1930), a fish is alive as long as it is not cut into pieces. Sliding out of the boy's hands, it is lively enough. Even "caked over with dust where it is wet, the eye coated over, humped under the dirt,"[17] the fish appears capable of movement. Faulkner's corpses, in fact, seldom rest. As the spirit of a dead mother continues to operate, so does that of the fish. But as it is compensation for a lost mother, to the child the fish is symbolic in only the most refreshingly literal manner. The jagged, bleeding pieces of the nonfish dramatize for Vardaman his mother's slow manner of dying. But one is equally struck with the boy's satisfaction in the fish he hauls in his arms, nearly as big as he is, simply as something to hold. (On the other hand, a live fish may appear lifeless. On the verge of suicide, Quentin Compson recalls a trout that "hung, delicate and motionless among the wavering shadows," a fish that is, by the way, a member of the community; the boys "knew the fish. He was a neighborhood character"[18]—as Quentin is no more.)

The childlike Benjy Compson, in his sensual response to the world (and in confusing the senses), accords unthought-of powers to animals: he can "hear the crickets watching" (173). The association of Benjy with low-status creatures is a reflection not only of his retarded condition but of an openness that negates social standards. Luster reminds him, " 'You aint got no spotted pony to ride' " (32). Uncle Maury's " 'Keep him in the yard, now' " (25) reflects on Benjy as a barnyard animal. But from Benjy's innocent point of view, the barnyard is not repulsive. Simply, "the pig pen smelled like pigs" (54), and, unconventionally, he is struck by the energy of *cows*—*"jumping out of the barn"* (40) and running up the hill. Of all Faulkner's characters, Benjy is the most openly appreciative of the whole spectrum of animals, seeing the simplest phenomena with the refreshing eye of the primitive.

Removed to the cold end of the country is Quentin, alien to that warm earth of his home. At a rational pole away from Benjy, he reasons himself to suicide. An emissary of life beckons at the window—the sparrow that slants "across the sunlight, onto the window ledge, and cocked his head at me. His eye was round and bright. First he'd watch me with one eye, then flick!" (98). Neither ethereal nor deromanticized, the bird levels at Quentin with the charge of life—which he can no longer meet.

Although Jason is rooted in the South, he never experiences a warm link with the living. Animals, like people, are things to him— sparrows "rattling away in the trees" (268). With animals, more readily than with people, he may apply a price. Jason's first comment when he enters a livery stable is to ask whether the hack had been paid for yet. He broods at length on the cost of eliminating pigeons: "it would take a millionaire to afford to shoot them at five cents a shot. If they'd just put a little poison out there in the square, they'd get rid of them in a day." If a merchant can't keep his stock from running around the square, thinks Quentin, he'd better try to deal in something "that don't eat, like plows or onions" (265).

The Sound and the Fury (1929) concludes with Jason beating a horse. He "sawed Queenie about and doubled the reins back and slashed her across the hips. He cut her again and again, into a plunging gallop" (336). But this serene sufferer responds with a comforting rhythm. "Her feet began to clop-clop steadily again, and at once Ben hushed." In spite of all, a sense of enduring life is echoed in one of Faulkner's favorite sounds: hoofbeats.

When asked what he liked best in life Faulkner replied, " 'Silence and horses. And trees.' " As to whether he preferred horses to people he quipped, " 'I like intelligent animals. Horses are intelligent, and so are dogs. Not as intelligent as rats.' " When it came to the more sophisticated pleasures, " 'If I could ride into a theatre on horseback, I would go.' "[19] Faulkner owned several horses and once gave up a lucrative script-writing job in Hollywood to take his mare back to Mississippi to deliver her foal on home ground. He maintained that he wrote the pornographic, commercially successful *Sanctuary* (1931) for money to buy a horse. Of his passion for horses he said, " 'I think I inherited it. My father was a horseman. Well, my first memories are of horses, of being on ponies in front of greens. . . . I believe I learned from horses to have sympathy for creatures not as wise, as smart, as man, to have pity for things that are physically weak.' "[20] But it is not the weakness of horses but men's weakness for horses that gives them their crucial place in Faulkner's fiction. A hunting companion reports that most of the stories the author told in camp were about horses.[21]

The magical image of man on horseback, easily the most perfect association of human and animal in art, is in Faulkner's work not the lone figure on the horizon central to the myth of the American West but the image in the community. The horse is transportation—for errands in town as well as for a major journey or battle—and status, every bit as much as the automobile came to be. A particular mule, horse, or buggy determines immediate rank and whereabouts. It carries a man to the woman he courts, but it also provides the escape into a nonsexual, masculine world. It is the cow that is erotic. Horses also provide that opium of entertainment, the horse race. All in all, the coveted creatures are the supreme objects of commerce, and in the scramble to possess them, extremes of ingenuity, con-artistry, and human folly are unleashed. The horse trade makes for some of the most hilarious—and pathetic—of Faulkner's stories, as even the sanest folks go bananas over a horse.

The love of a horse untainted by adult shenanigans is that of Jewel Bundren. The boy's intensified bond with the horse as his mother lies dying is, indeed, a response to grief—a healthy one. To assume, as André Bleikasten does in his book-length study of the novel, for example, that Jewel's love of the horse is "obviously a defense mechanism indicative of the incestuous nature of Jewel's love for his mother"[22] offers no more than one of criticism's favorite clichés, one which in this case reveals an ignorance of horse love. When Faulkner was asked, " 'Did Jewel buy that horse as a substitute for his mother?' " his answer was, " 'He bought that horse because he wanted that horse.' " Jewel is the toughest one in the family, the author says—and the one whose reaction to Addie

Bundren's death makes the most sense. Jewel " 'behaved better than he thought he would in sacrificing the only thing he loved for someone's good.' "[23] Vardaman's observation that Jewel's mother is a horse is accurate only as the animal is a primary focus of affection. But the boy would have cared for that horse regardless of his mother's death.

Jewel is introduced as one who strides with "rigid gravity" (4), his face wooden. The horse that elevates him, "his body in midair shaped to the horse" (12), allows a sort of conquering of the gravity that pulls his mother into the ground. The life Jewel finds in the horse—motion, freedom, and ownership—are satisfactions not to be matched in a mother. He worked nights clearing a neighbor's land for money to buy that horse; in doing so, he wins independence from the family and a companion. More than a means of escape, the horse is a fellow sufferer, "trembling, its eye rolling wild and baby-blue in its long pink face, its breathing stertorous like groaning" (135). With him Jewel may live out his suffering, expressed in such images as the two descending the hill in a "series of spine-jolting jumps" (12). When the horse kicks, Jewel kicks back, even strikes it across the head. As he rides, the boy digs his heels in, "shutting off the horse's wind with one hand, with the other patting the horse's neck in short strokes myriad and caressing, cursing the horse with obscene ferocity" (12).

In a novel in which a major theme is the insidiousness or at least the inefficacy of words—they go "straight up in a thin line, quick and harmless" while "doing goes along the earth" (165)—the nonverbal bond is markedly pure. At the same time, Jewel is free to express paradoxical emotions without the requirements of reason or diplomacy, without retribution. Through expurgation in the presence of his horse, Jewel is freed. Lifted off the ground, he "sees his whole body earth-free, horizontal, whipping snake-limber, until he finds the horse's nostrils and touches earth again" (12). A coffin topples and the rest of the family slide. Jewel "sits lightly, poised, upright" (102)—balanced on his horse.

Anse Bundren, at the unfeeling end of the family, is never more heartless than when he takes Jewel's horse and trades it for a pair of mules. Truly Anse is not Jewel's father, and his distance from the feeling boy is appallingly evident as he leaves Jewel in "that swole-up way, watching the road like he was half a mind to take out after Anse and get the horse back" (177). (Jewel later delivers the horse to be sold himself, and walks back.) But more than he is out to hurt Jewel, Anse is the stranger who misses the intrigue of owning a horse altogether—telling Jewel not to ride it alongside the coffin "out of respect for his dead ma" (99)—a sure sign of a voided man.

As the horse steadies Jewel, to the family it provides a balance in the haphazard funeral journey not matched even by mules. Jewel asks if Tull will use his mule to try out the bridge, but he refuses. " 'Jewel's going to use his horse,' " Darl protests. " 'Why wont you risk your mule, Vernon?' " But he cares only for his animal: " 'My mule aint going into that water' " (120). The mules that do serve the Bundrens, whose coffin careens in the swirling waters, lose their footing. "The head of one mule appears, its eyes wide; it looks back at us for an instant, making a sound almost human." Like frail humans, the stoic mules are undone by water, "their legs stiffly extended as when they had lost contact with the earth" (142). It is the "wild drowning horse" that recovers, "throwing its head up" (147) and going for shore, with one of the Bundrens hanging for life to the saddle.

If *As I Lay Dying* gives the noblest version of man and horse, *The Unvanquished* (1938) provides the most romantic account, in the image of war hero on horseback, Colonel Sartoris, etched splendidly against the sky. In the confusion of the Civil War, Confederate and Union riders form similarly exquisite silhouettes on the moonlit night that belies war. "The whole rim of the world was full of horses running along the sky,"[24] hooves crashing on the bridge's floor. Bayard Sartoris's keenest sensations are tuned to horses. Thick in the memory, they "seemed to cease galloping and to float, hang suspended rather in a dimension without time" (58). The attempt to stop time—Quentin Compson's destruction of the hands of a clock, for example—is met better with horses than with any Faulkner subject, for it is not so much a particular horse that captivates as horses in general—as they have been and will be. Perhaps even more important, passion for horses does not run dry.

Bayard's adoration of his father is for the man on his horse. The colonel is home when the stallion enters the gate; first, and most lengthily, is the description of the horse—"the big gaunt horse almost the color of smoke, lighter in color than the dust which had gathered and caked on his wet hide where they had crossed at the ford three miles away, coming up the drive at a steady gait which was not a walk and not a run, as if he had held it all the way from Tennessee—because there was a need to encompass earth . . ." (17). One with this steed rather than master of it, the colonel arrives with no more than " 'Well, boys' " before he looks to the primary matter (a priority happily accepted by all), Jupiter: " 'Curry him. . . . Give him a good feed, but don't turn him into the pasture. Let him stay in the lot.' " Then, "as if Jupiter were a child" (17), the colonel slaps the horse on the flank.

Dethroned from his horse, the colonel is comically shrunken. "He was not big, yet somehow he looked even smaller on the horse than off of him, because Jupiter was big and when you thought of father you thought of him as being big too" (17). Repeatedly, his shortness is emphasized: as illustration, the colonel's sabre bumps the steps as he walks. Faulkner himself, at five feet five and a half inches, with a grandfather, a father, and a younger brother who were six-footers, was sensitive to his own diminutive stature. In order to qualify for the army, he tried to grow by eating huge quantities of bananas, but was rejected as being under the regulation weight and height.[25] One more reason to love a horse is because it can make a man tall.

That soldiers come by horseback only emphasizes the folly of killing one's fellow men. All share the connection with horses, the nonpartisan victims of war. This association, which is central to an antiwar sentiment in this novel, is also the focus of satire. Bayard and his friend Ringo roll a musket out of the closet, aim wildly at approaching soldiers (no matter whose), and shoot, instead, a horse. Now there *is* cause for war. While Bayard's Granny tremblingly protects the boys for fear they have killed a man, to the regiment the death of their prize horse is a worse catastrophe. " 'Dead? Hell, yes! Broke his back and we had to shoot him! . . . The best horse in the whole army! The whole regiment betting on him for next Sunday—' " (31–32). A sergeant reports to his colonel that " 'I heard the general say myself that if he had enough horses, he wouldn't always care whether there was anybody to ride them or not' " (32).

The endearing Colonel Sartoris " 'didn't fight; he just stole horses' " (49). Following the family tradition, Bayard confesses that he "borrowed" the horse he rides. And Granny wangles a deal to equal the best of them, in altering an order for the army to restore 110 Mississippi mules to 122. The lieutenant forced to make up the difference with horses is so pained by his duty "he looked like he was fixing to cry" (93).

The dependence on the horse in battle—and his dark destiny— is rendered with gothic splendor in the image of one enervated corpse that rides "shining up from out of the yelling faces and went down slow again, exactly like a fish feeding, with, hanging over his rump by one stirrup, a man in a black uniform, and then I realized that the uniform was blue, only it was wet." The soldier's death, whatever his affiliation, is second to that of his steed. It is the mutual concern for horses, rather than for men, that establishes the brotherhood of soldiers from North and South: "A Yankee patrol helped Ringo and me cut the drowned horses out of the harness" (86–87). When Cousin Drusilla—that rare Faulkner woman who is "manly" enough to ride a horse—is trapped in a backyard full of Yankees, she holds the pistol to her horse's head, warning that since she cannot shoot all the soldiers, she will use her one shot for the horse. They turn and go. Consensus comes with that subject responsible in so great a part for *The Unvanquished*'s action, ro- mance, and delight—aptly credited in the novel's last word, *horses*.

A darker version of hero on horseback is Thomas Sutpen, who rides into town "with a horse and two pistols and a name which nobody ever heard before, knew for certain was his own any more than the horse was his own or even the pistols."[26] If he had walked, he would never have ruled. Sutpen's special facility is that he con- trives "somehow to swagger even on a horse" (16). This cold, amoral equestrian, so far in spirit from the roguish Colonel Sarto- ris, does share with him the heroic stature of those who know how to ride. (And, as it is later revealed, Sutpen rode a black stallion second in command to Colonel Sartoris.)

Despite the shifting point of view of several generations, Sutpen is consistently enhanced by an account of his horse. Mr. Compson saw him on a "big hard-ridden roan horse, man and beast looking as though they had been created out of thin air" (32). Later the town learns that "the strong spent horse," Sutpen's clothes, and a saddle bag were all he possessed. Every morning he went directly from his hotel, "fed and saddled the horse and rode away before daylight" (33).

Many a man's fate is traced by horses or mules in *Absalom, Absalom!* (1936). The biblical Absalom, in fact, rides to his death as his mule rips under the boughs of a tree and Absalom is strangled. At his Spartan best, Sutpen keeps a "masculine solitude" (39), accompanied only by his stallion, Negro servants, and dogs. During this pristine period at Sutpen's Hundred there is "no woman to object if he should elect to have his dogs in to sleep on the pallet bed with him" (40). Years later Sutpen's degeneration is registered as he appears on the "gaunt and jaded horse on which he did not seem to sit but rather seemed to project himself ahead like a mirage" (159). His son Henry locates Charles Bon by the horse he rides, and the half-brothers duel, their "two gaunt horses" (133) announcing a shabby inferiority to their father. Down another rung in status, Wash Jones leaves a saddleless mule to announce that Bon is dead.

Hatred of Sutpen, who sees people in terms of breeding (although he does not care for them as he does for animals), reaches its climax in the last revelation of his well-known preference for horses over human beings, even his own flesh and blood. Entering the stall only hours after his mulatto granddaughter has been born, Sutpen praises his horse Penelope, who foaled that morning—" 'A damned fine colt.' " His question as to the child's gender follows: " 'Horse or mare?' " To his mistress he says, " 'Well, Milly; too bad you're not a mare too. Then I could give you a decent stall in the stable' " (285–86). Milly's father, Wash Jones, will take no more. *"It was that colt. It aint me or mine either. It wasn't even his own that got him out of bed"* (288). With this knowledge Wash kills Sutpen. But if Sutpen's esteem of the horse over the human being is the most explicit case, it is far from the only instance of such a preference for the Faulkner male.

Joe Christmas walks. And no man in this South is so alone and devoid of status as this dark figure of *Light in August* (1932). Hoofbeats do not gladden this novel, however the Reverend Gail Hightower might hear in Tennyson's poetry the "fine galloping language"[27] of a better world and affirm "how right the ancients were in making the horse an attribute and symbol of warriors and kings" (66). Lena Grove, abandoned by the father of the child she carries, goes afoot as well, relieved only by occasional stints in a stranger's buggy. Up one step in status is the surrogate father, Byron Bunch, who around midnight every Saturday "saddles the mule again and rides back to Jefferson at a steady, allnight jog" (42).

That Joe Christmas might learn "the responsibility of possessing, owning, ownership" (142), his adopted father McEachern gives him, if not a horse, at least a cow. But Christmas sells the heifer; he misses not only the prestige of ownership but the bond with animals that motivates others. When he takes McEachern's "spent old horse," whose suffering mocks his own, "its head down, trembling, its breathing almost like a human voice" (183), he beats the failing animal until the stick breaks. Then Christmas runs "as completely out of the life of the horse as if it had never existed" (184)—pariah in a tale whose sadness is unbroken and where horses play but little part.

The book bursting with horses is *The Hamlet* (1940). Stories from the twenties and thirties—most notably "Fool about a Horse" and "Spotted Horses"—are united in this masterpiece of the horse-trade, completed at the ripe end of Faulkner's most fertile period. His labyrinthine style is never more utilitarian than here, as it allows the horse dealer's sleight of hand to go undetected amidst the vines of language. Destinies rise and fall according to the horse in Frenchman's Bend, where a man is readily characterized and located by his mule or horse, each an individualized citizen in the community. Narrator Ratliff maintains he knows "everyone, man mule and dog, within fifty miles."[28] The "chief man" of the country, Will Varner, goes by "the old fat white horse," whose appearance, chapters later, announces that Will is no longer a buggy man: "he's back to the horse again" (159). Will's son Jody is likewise identified by the roan saddle horse that waits for him at the gallery posts.

Horse power in Frenchman's Bend is documented early on in the account of Ab Snopes's fall, a stunning comical chronicle of failure. " 'Ab was a horse-trader then,' " Ratliff relates of better days. But " 'the horse-trading give out on him and left him just a farmer. He aint naturally mean. He's just soured' " (27). Eliminated from horse-trading by Pat Stamper, Ab " 'just went plumb curdled' " (30).

In his mock-objective tone Ratliff relates that Ab formed a horse-and-mule partnership " 'in good faith and honor, not aiming to harm nobody blue or gray but just keeping his mind fixed on profit and horses' " (29). But in Yoknapatawpha, this "science and pastime" (35) is the way to madness. Ab's wife bitterly proclaims: " 'Horsetrader! Setting there bragging and lying to a passel of shiftless men . . .' " (32). When Ab and Ratliff (who admits he, too, is a "fool about a horse" [31]) set out with Mis Snopes's cream separator money, they " 'wasn't even thinking about horse-trading.' " But they " 'was thinking about horse all right' " (33). And as the day's saga unfolds, the horse itself carries evidence of foresight of a trade in the form of a technique so unthinkingly cruel as to indicate Ab's oblivion to wrongdoing where a horse is concerned. He had rubbed saltpeter into the horse's gums to make it drink and fill out the gaunt ribs, cut it with barbed wire, and worked a fish hook into the hide for more spirit. Yet Ab follows the occupation of horse-trading " 'not for profit but for honor' " (36).

The first step in his public humiliation is Ab's exchange of a horse and a mule for a pair of mules—which operate as a team, all right: just out of Pat Stamper's sight, they stop in unison. Ab marches through town, willing to pay to get his team back. But Stamper claims he no longer has Ab's horse, just a fat one nobody would want. Ab must have it, though, and makes the foredoomed move toward the cream separator. His new acquisition is "a little bigger than the one he traded Stamper" and "hog fat" (41). But on the way home if that black horse doesn't melt down to brown— and shrink with a swish to the same lean beast Ab left home with that morning. The next day he finds a bicycle pump inserted under its hide to blow it up. Ab has had it. The next time Ratliff sees him, years later, he is a "stiff, harsh, undersized figure behind a plow drawn by two mules" (49).

If horses are a masculine province, Ike Snopes, who neither in mind nor body (with female thighs) developed as a man, is attached to a cow. His affair is the only love story in *The Hamlet*.

Faulkner's elevation of a crude barnyard incident to a richly lyrical (if mock-epic) episode is evidence of that ease with which he depicts love of animals—here, that rarely adored female animal: "blond, dew-pearled, standing in the parted water of the ford, blowing into the water the thick, warm, heavy, milk-laden breath" (168). That Faulkner's men and women are incapable of a generous romantic attachment is all the more evident for the existence of Ike's union of charitable and erotic love. He is the abnormal male who does not find love a threat to freedom, joyfully assuming himself and his mate "somewhere in immediate time, already married" (167). They eat from the same basket, and "they lie down together" (189).

As Boon and Ike found courage to defend the dogs they loved, Ike surpasses himself for his lady love, charging into a burning barn where he hears "the steady terrified bellowing of the cow" (174). The masculine horse materializes "furiously out of the smoke, monstrous and distorted, wild-eyed and with tossing mane, bearing down on him" (174–75). But Ike runs into and through the fire, tumbling "beneath the struggling and bellowing cow," where he receives "the violent relaxing of her fear-constricted bowels" (176). Yet manure dampens his love no more than terror did. Patiently Ike follows the cow into the ditch, crying "lest he alarm her," then steps "onto the receptive solid" (177) where he touches her. With the willow branch that a more manly figure would use to whip his horse, Ike washes the cow's legs.

The cow's stridently masculine owner, Jack Houston, takes the more conventional view of the sexual female animal: " 'Git on home, you damn whore!' " (178). He allows Ike's activities in his barn to be a sideshow for neighbors, but with them decides on a cure for Ike's sodomy: he must be fed the meat of the animal he loves. To replace Ike's cow, they give him a wooden one to play with.

Houston's destiny, too, is determined by an animal—twice. His wife is killed by the stallion he bought "as if for a wedding present to her" (218), and he is killed by Mink Snopes in a dispute over the pasturing of Mink's cow. Rather than a sanction of the marriage—that "immemorial trap" (208), essence of "true slavery" (210)—the stallion is the representative of "that polygamous and bitless masculinity which he had relinquished" (218) when he married. Although Houston assumes a form of mourning his wife's death—he shoots the stallion and remains sullen for years—he becomes the enviable rich man who rides again with horse and hound to return to no woman. Mink is one who must step aside for this powerful team, until the day Houston charges him a dollar too much for boarding his cow and Mink murders him.

That human paragon of bovine sexuality, Eula Varner, not moving of her own volition, is hauled into the world by horseback. The masculine, energetic horse towers in contrast above her: " 'God damn it, cant you try to get up without making it look like the horse is twenty feet tall?' " (101), her brother demands. And—the horse delivers Eula's many suitors. The school teacher Labove, so fatally drawn to her, comes from the university forty miles away on the promise of " 'a horse that can make the trip in eight hours' " (106). He may not "ride a horse for fun" (116) (although this does not distinguish him from other characters as much as it might, as *fun* is too light a word for experience with horses), but no one rides with greater necessity.

The courting of Eula Varner may be charted by the horses parked at her door. By the third summer of her flowering "the trace-galled mules had given way to the trotting horses and buggies" (132), at one time four buggies, "to be exact," in almost constant rotation. *The* buggy is that of the prosperous Hoake McCarron. The deflowering of Eula in that buggy is not accounted for by any interaction of the couple but by the lyrical description of the mare relaxing at streamside: "the mare's feet like slow silk in the dust as a horse moves when the reins are wrapped about the upright whip in its dashboard socket, . . . nuzzling and blowing among the broken reflections of stars, raising its dripping muzzle and maybe drinking again or maybe just blowing into the water as a thirst-quenched horse will. There would be no voice, no touch of rein to make it move on; anyway, it would be standing there too long, too long, too long" (137).

McCarron's rivals, whose "spiritless plow-animals would not stand ground" (138), have not been able to ambush him until Eula is in the buggy and the mare stops to drink. Even McCarron's alibi for the wounded arm relies on the horse, as he tells Eula's father he hurt himself trying to catch his mare. " 'Serve you right for keeping a mare like that in a woodshed' " (140), Varner comes back. Their conversation may reflect on Eula, but it follows the comfortable male topic of horses.

As Eula's popularity was marked by the horses lined up at her place, her fall is marked by their absence: "the day came for the delicate buggies and the fast bright horses and mares to be seen no more along the Varner fence" (141). Eula is pregnant. The man with the fastest buggy took her virginity, and now the head horse dealer marries her. Eula is secured on a "glittering buggy powdered only lightly over with dust, drawn by a bright mare or horse in brass-studded harness, driven by the man who owned them both" (132)—Flem Snopes.

He came to town by mule and two months later was running a blacksmith's shop. This slime, this super con-artist, rides to power not by the fiery obsession with horses that ravages more passionate men but by taking advantage of that weakness in others. The notion that Flem's connection with ponies is compensation for his sterility shows an ignorance of the mania for horses and also misses the point of Flem's ingenious manipulations. The infamous spotted ponies he brings from Texas are never even determined to be his. But he is the overall director of the horse show of Frenchman's Bend. Ironically, while Flem uses horses more skillfully than anyone else (keeping a noticeable distance from them), his spotted ponies are the freest of Faulkner's animals. And that, of course, is the joke on those who succumb to the auction: they buy horses they can't catch.

Flem's Texas associate begins with Eck Snopes, the man in town wisest to horse folly, but one whose resistance hints of his fallibility: " 'What need I got for a horse I would need a bear-trap to catch?' " (293). So he is offered the first horse for nothing—if he will just start the bidding. Sensible though he may be, Eck is a normal Faulkner male. He starts at a dollar, ups it to two, and is promptly the owner of a second horse. At that moment the most vulnerable citizen arrives—Henry Armstid, chaperoned by the wooden wife, futile against the horse fever that draws Henry from their paintless wagon with the five dollars she earned for her children by weaving. When the Texan tells Armstid to go ahead and take his horse, however, he can't get near it. " 'Who'll help me catch my horse?' " (298).

As T. Y. Greet points out, the horse need not be a symbol of abnormal sexuality here, as some critics insist, but rather a masculine prerogative threatened by marriage or subjugation of any sort. The horse in itself is the source of a passion that sets up a conflict between man and wife.[29] Indeed, the lust to possess the ponies is its own disease, " 'that Texas sickness' that spotted corruption of frantic and uncatchable horses" (327).

Only the women are untouched, unimpressed by the horses. When a horse clatters into Mrs. Littlejohn's boarding house, she levels with " 'Get out of here, you son of a bitch' " (308), breaking her washboard over its face. On the ponies trample, ripping into Vernon Tull's mule-drawn cart. Mrs. Tull takes legal action against their possessor, but, since no owner can be determined, reparation is made in the form of one of the delinquent ponies—to one of the last people who would want it, Mrs. Tull.

The ponies are pre-eminently *gaudy*. Although the motley hide is not precisely a flaw, "wild mismatched eyes" with the "blue-and-brown eyeballs rolling alertly in their gaudy faces" (283) are an aberration. Something has gone awry. Yet chaos is the natural outcome of freedom, wildness. Faulkner says of the range-bred ponies brought to the auctions of his youth (and at the age of ten he bought one for $4.75), they were wild beasts, totally undomesticated.[30] Their trail of ruin is, however, to be distinguished from that of the predatory animal: the horses destroy as a reaction to being civilized. But their energy is essentially an incorruptible, natural force.

> The earth became thunderous; dust arose, out of which the animals began to burst like flushed quail and into which, with that apparently unflagging faith in his own invulnerability, the Texan rushed. For an instant the watchers could see them in the dust—the pony backed into the angle of the fence and the stable, the man facing it, reaching toward his hip. Then the beast rushed at him in a sort of fatal and hopeless desperation and he struck it between the eyes with the pistol butt and felled it and leaped onto its prone head. The pony recovered almost at once and

pawed itself to its knees and heaved at its prisoned head and
fought itself up, dragging the man with it; for an instant in the
dust the watchers saw the man free of the earth and in violent
lateral motion like a rag attached to the horse's head. (292)

If *The Hamlet* is the chronicle of human failure, it is also the
testament of the horses' triumph. The famous words of Faulkner's
Nobel Prize address, uttered in behalf of the human spirit, apply to
these characters too. The spotted ponies do not "merely endure."
They prevail.[31]

The other volumes of the trilogy are not alive with horseflesh
as is the far superior *Hamlet*. Tales of the spotted ponies are retold.
But the heat of the action is past, and a cynical view prevails. What
was hinted at about Houston in the earlier volume is confirmed: he
"was not only rich enough to own a blooded stallion capable of
killing his wife, but arrogant and intolerant enough to defy all
decency, after shooting the horse that killed her, to turn right around
and buy another stallion exactly like it, maybe in case he did get
married again."[32] The peak of the horse trade has given way to the
cruel game of planting mules on the railroad tracks for the sixty
dollars the company gives for each one hit by a train.

Faulkner's great period of writing was over. But that the horse
was ever alive to him as a subject is never more pronounced than
in the generally unsuccessful *A Fable* (1954). This essentially sterile
allegory of a Christ-like corporal in France in World War I comes
to life only with the insertion of a horse story (published separately
as "Notes on a Horsethief"). Philip Rice uneasily senses that "it
may seem that Faulkner makes love for horse more vivid than love
for man."[33] And so he does. Faulkner says *A Fable*'s horse is proof
that " 'the Cockney hostler was still capable of love for something.' "[34]

Although the horse story supports the Christ allegory in its
spirit of sacrificial love, it is not in the animal tale that this novel is
a fable. The three-legged racehorse stands only for his own incredible self. The most bizarrely handicapped of all Faulkner's animals,
this crippled creature " 'never knowed nothing but just to run out
in front of all the other horses in a race.' "[35] While the attachment
to horses is "no mere rapport but an affinity, not from understand-

ing to understanding but from heart to heart," it is recognizable as a variation on the obsession that has nothing to do with altruism. The groom is "not merely included in the sale of the horse, he was compelled into it. And not by the buyer nor even the seller, but by the sold: the chattel: the horse itself" (146). For this underdog, three men and a boy become fugitives from five agencies, one the federal government—not for the sake of Christian virtues but for the horse's freedom, so he can run races and they can watch.

Only in following the sacrificial theme of *A Fable* to its ultimate conclusion does the horse story take a jarring turn. The groom kills the horse in what seems a highly unlikely act. But an impassioned argument follows that the animal was killed to be spared the fate of becoming a stud horse. What in the Christ allegory calls for this sacrifice? Rather, it is motivated by the horror of losing the male prerogative to be free—and that includes freedom from mating. The groom stole the horse so it could run, " 'keep on running, keep on losing races at least, . . . because it was a giant and didn't need even three legs to run them on but only one with a hoof at the end to qualify as a horse. While they would have taken it back to the Kentucky farm and shut it up in a whorehouse where it wouldn't need any legs at all, . . . because any man can be a father" (155–56).

A fitting finale to his career is Faulkner's cheering recapitulation to the horse fever of youth, *The Reivers* (1962), his tempest. As it follows an idealistic quest in a naturalistic world, Olga Vickery also compares it to *Don Quixote*.[36] The works do share the same undauntable spirit. But in the source of the quest they are a world apart: Cervantes dreams of the perfect woman—Faulkner of the perfect horse.

Lucius Priest "borrows" his grandfather's automobile, and with his pals Boon Hogganbeck and Ned McCaslin trades it for a sardine-loving "racehorse" that won't move. In a tour de force against the most enticing product of encroaching industrialization, Faulkner sticks the car in the mud where only mules are able to drag it out. They are "not only unalien but in fact curiously appropriate, being themselves biological dead ends and hence already obsolete before they were born; the automobile: the expensive useless mechanical toy rated in power and strength by the dozens of horses."[37]

Paradoxically, the obsolete endures and the beasts of burden in their traces are the purveyors of freedom: "breaking the automobile free of the mud" (89). Beyond desire, ambition, second only to the rat in intelligence (the horse is fifth and last), a mule is too smart "to break its heart for glory running around the rim of a mile-long saucer" (121). And it is " 'neat and nimble, raising barely half as much dust as a horse would' " (246).

Still, such logic does not budge the heart. The boys must have their horse. Their political freedom itself ensures the pursuit of such sweet bondage—"inalienable constitutional right of free will and private enterprise" (215), which allows for a private horse race between two local horses. Private enterprise, however, turns up a stolen horse, one that has never won a race and won't try unless it is drugged. But love alters not when alteration finds. Lightning has "every quality you could want in fact except eagerness, his brain not having found out yet that this was a race" (238). He resists solitude out in front of him, and the thoroughbred Acheron beats him badly twice. But in a third race the underdog Lightning strikes. Lucius has the happiest day of his life, and they win back the car for grandpa. Such is the triumph of Faulkner's supreme subject of enjoyment and enduring life.

Faulkner's bear is awesome. Dogs are courageous companions. Mules are honored. But the man is in love with the horse.

Notes

1. Francis Lee Utley, "Pride and Humility: The Cultural Roots of Ike McCaslin," *Bear, Man, and God: Eight Approaches to William Faulkner's "The Bear,"* ed. Francis Lee Utley, Lynn Z. Bloom, and Arthur F. Kinney (New York: Random House, 1971), p. 167.

2. *Faulkner at West Point,* ed. Joseph L. Fant III and Robert Ashley (New York: Random House, 1964), p. 64.

3. John F. Faulkner, "My Brother Bill," *Bear, Man, and God,* pp. 94, 97.

4. William Faulkner, "The Bear," *Go Down, Moses* (New York:

Vintage Books, 1973), p. 194. Subsequent references to this edition of "The Bear" will appear in the text.

5. Wiley Lee Umphlett, *The Sporting Myth and the American Experience: Studies in Contemporary Fiction* (Lewisburg, Pa.: Bucknell University Press, 1975), pp. 80, 67.

6. William Van O'Connor, "The Wilderness Theme in Faulkner's 'The Bear,' " *William Faulkner: Three Decades of Criticism,* ed. Frederick J. Hoffman and Olga W. Vickery (New York: Harcourt, Brace & World, 1963), p. 326.

7. *Faulkner in the University: Class Conferences at the University of Virginia 1957–1958,* ed. Frederick L. Gwynn and Joseph L. Blotner (Charlottesville: University of Virginia Press, 1959), p. 45.

8. William Faulkner, "Delta Autumn," *Go Down, Moses,* p. 336.

9. O'Connor, p. 326.

10. Utley, p. 184.

11. Irving Howe, *William Faulkner: A Critical Study,* 2d ed., rev. (New York: Vintage Books, 1952), pp. 255, 259.

12. Joseph Blotner, *Faulkner: A Biography* (New York: Random House, 1974), I, 177.

13. *Faulkner in the University,* p. 59.

14. William Faulkner, *Sartoris* (New York: Harcourt, Brace, 1929), p. 278.

15. *Faulkner in the University,* p. 37.

16. William Faulkner, "Old People," *Go Down, Moses,* p. 163. Subsequent references to this edition of "Old People" will appear in the text.

17. William Faulkner, *As I Lay Dying* (New York: Vintage Books, 1930), p. 29. Subsequent references to this edition will appear in the text.

18. William Faulkner, *The Sound and the Fury* (New York: Vintage Books, 1929), p. 136. Subsequent references to this edition will appear in the text.

19. *Lion in the Garden: Interviews with William Faulkner 1926–1962,* ed. James B. Merriwether and Michael Millgate (New York: Random House, 1968), pp. 64, 282–83.

20. Ibid., pp. 92, 139.

21. Jerrold Brite, "A True-Blue Hunter," *William Faulkner of*

Oxford, ed. James W. Webb and A. Wigfall Green (New Orleans: Louisiana State University Press, 1965), p. 160.

22. André Bleikasten, *Faulkner's As I Lay Dying,* trans. Roger Little (Bloomington: Indiana University Press, 1973), p. 93.

23. *Faulkner in the University,* pp. 109–10.

24. William Faulkner, *The Unvanquished* (New York: New American Library, 1959), p. 54. Subsequent references to this edition will appear in the text.

25. Blotner, pp. 187, 196.

26. William Faulkner, *Absalom, Absalom!* (New York: Modern Library, 1936), pp. 14–15. Subsequent references to this edition will appear in the text.

27. William Faulkner, *Light in August* (New York: Modern Library, 1932), p. 278. Subsequent references to this edition will appear in the text.

28. William Faulkner, *The Hamlet* (New York: Random House, 1940), p. 13. Subsequent references to this edition will appear in the text.

29. T. Y. Greet, "The Theme and Structure of Faulkner's *The Hamlet,*" *William Faulkner: Three Decades of Criticism,* p. 343.

30. *Faulkner in the University,* pp. 29–30.

31. William Faulkner, "The Stockholm Address," quoted in *William Faulkner: Three Decades of Criticism,* p. 348.

32. William Faulkner, *The Mansion* (New York: Vintage Books, 1965), p. 7.

33. Philip Rice, "Faulkner's Crucifixion," *William Faulkner: Three Decades of Criticism,* p. 376.

34. *Faulkner in the University,* p. 63.

35. William Faulkner, *A Fable* (New York: New American Library, 1968), p. 185. Subsequent references to this edition will appear in the text.

36. Olga W. Vickery, *The Novels of William Faulkner* (Baton Rouge and New Orleans: Louisiana State University Press, 1964), p. 228.

37. William Faulkner, *The Reivers: A Reminiscence* (New York: Vintage Books, 1962), p. 87. Subsequent references to this edition will appear in the text.

CHAPTER 9

The Integrity of Animals: Ernest Hemingway

Ernest Hemingway loved places and he loved animals. "The country was always better than the people,"[1] he says of Africa. And the whir of wings moved him more than love of country. The might of bull and buffalo count for much—but no more than the stoicism of the trout. Above all is a clean, disciplined form. "Do you know the sin it would be to ruffle the arrangement of the feathers on a hawk's neck if they would never be replaced as they were?"[2]

Yet the excellent animal must be slain. Hemingway is *the* writer purely given to the hunt, and he alone meets the paradox of killing what one reveres, head-on. *Death in the Afternoon (*1932) begins with the admission that "from a modern moral point of view, that is, a Christian point of view, the whole bullfight is indefensible; there is certainly much cruelty, there is always danger, either sought or unlooked for, and there is always death, and I should not try to defend it now, only to tell honestly the things I have found true about it" (1). Even the seasoned fisherman doubts the morality of killing the fish as a livelihood, for he considers him a brother. In the words of Isak Dinesen, Hemingway maintains that " 'all real hunters are in love with the animals they hunt.' "[3] But it is equally true that a "great killer must love to kill." Accomplished cleanly, killing brings an "aesthetic pleasure and pride . . . the feeling of rebellion against death" (232–33).

The hunt is therapy—ritual—art. "I spend a hell of a lot of time killing animals and fish so I won't kill myself," Hemingway told his friend A. E. Hotchner.[4] The rules that give it an ethical as well as an aesthetic value were those the author learned as a youth: do not waste, kill cleanly and humanely, and use no mechanized devices. Malcolm Cowley argues, citing examples of horses gored in the bull ring and mules with broken legs drowning in shallow water, that "in no other writer can you find so many suffering animals."[5] His observation misses the point, however, that wounding is precisely Hemingway's wrong.

The heroic death is another matter. Here his prey are not so much victims as they are fighters, almost as if they shared their creator's desire to meet death directly. Philip Young's application of Freud's pleasure principle to Hemingway[6] is also inescapably appropriate in understanding the instinct he attributes to animals—that the goal of life is death. The bull charges full force at the matador, the wounded buffalo heads at the hunter, and with his own force the fish drives the hook deep in his mouth and pulls until he is dead. "We speak of killing a trout with a rod. It is the effort made by the trout that kills it" (67). Even the cockfight, as Hemingway sees it, is based in part on the will of the animal. "Some people put the arm on fighting cocks as cruel. But what the hell else does a fighting cock like to do?"[7]

Only the Spanish bullfight offered the opportunity to study death directly. The classic guide to bullfighting that resulted, *Death in the Afternoon,* invites the reader to hold back a judgment of bullfighting until he has seen a bullfight. Hemingway himself expected it to be simply barbarous and cruel and to gain only in the observation of definite action. Instead, he found a classic drama in the death of the bull. The killing of the horses brought no feeling of horror: they were pathetic, rather comic characters who moved in "stiff old-maidish fashion" around the ring. The exposed viscera, the "opposite of clouds of glory," alternately disgusted and amused the crowd. Above all, the aged horses have lost the integrity of their form. They are "so unlike horses; in some ways they are like birds, any of the awkward birds." In death, with "the canvas covering the body to make a sort of wing, they are more like birds than ever" (6–7).

The bull's mighty form does endure. His identity remains distinct even in the ear or tail taken in tribute. The practice of dismembering the bull is a means not of destroying his essence but of possessing it. One notorious bull who had killed sixteen people and maimed sixty others in local bull baitings was pursued by the brother of a victim to the slaughterhouse where the boy killed him, dug out his eyes, and roasted and ate the bull's testicles. The prize bull is immortalized in death, and his head takes its place on the wall, his title engraved below.

A first determinant of the prize bull is size. In preparing for the bullfight the matador's representative investigates the bull's exact measurements—height, weight, length and width of horns. But at the same time a more subtle measure of the opponent's integrity may be determined; when "talkers to bulls" taunt them before the fight, it is said that a noble one will pay no attention to a drunk. Size, which must be matched by speed and "suavity" in the charge for which the bull is bred (69), is as significant for the wounds the animal may accept as for the injury he inflicts. Bulls of the past could take as many as seventy pics—in modern times, only seven (183). The bullfighter hopes for a bull who is not too big or too strong but above all one with good vision, which is especially important in Hemingway's world, where a first measure of truth is a clean edge. A good bullfight always takes place in the sun.

For the bull, the fight is admittedly unfair. "The bullfight is not a sport in the Anglo-Saxon sense of the word, that is, it is not an equal contest or an attempt at an equal contest between a bull and a man. Rather it is a tragedy; the death of the bull" (16). But if it is not a fair fight, neither is it merely a defensive one for the bull, whose attack is not simply a means of survival but an exercise of power. "The bull is a wild animal whose greatest pleasure is combat and which will accept combat offered to it in any form" (113). He will charge anything—lions, tigers, trains—growing braver under punishment. "All of bullfighting is founded on the bravery of the bull, his simplicity and his lack of experience" (145). The premise of modern bullfighting is that the bull has never been in the ring before—that it is the first meeting of this wild animal and a dismounted man. To Hemingway, the true fighting bull is "the finest of all animals to watch in action and repose" (109).

The perfection of the bull's charge is in its absolute directness. At the end of each charge he will turn by himself and come again, "straight as though he were on rails" (160). Harry Levin aligns this image with Hemingway's style: a holding of the "purity of his line by moving in one direction, ignoring sidetracks and avoiding structural complications."[8] The incredible quietness of the bull's charge is not what one would expect of the beast: he gallops softly, turning on his four feet almost like a cat. The calmer the bull is in the corrals, the greater the chance that he will be brave in the ring. A completely brave bull will never open his mouth. Even with the sword in him, he keeps his mouth shut to hold the blood inside.

The final sword thrust is for the artist Hemingway, as for the Spanish *aficionado,* "the moment of truth." Only when the sword goes all the way in are bull and matador brought into the perfectly balanced image. The popularized version of this union as erotic metaphor is established by Waldo Frank, for one, who calls it a " 'searching symbol of the sexual act.' "[9] Hemingway saw such "erectile writing" as "nonsense" (53)—the very thing, blurring actual experience, which was the basis of his literary rebellion.

His account of the bull's death reads: "the beauty of the moment of killing is that flash when man and bull form one figure as the sword goes all the way in, the man leaning after it, death uniting the two figures in the emotional aesthetic and artistic climax of the fight" (247). As Carlos Baker observes, it is easy to see how these sentences might have been written in an erotic manner. "Knowing truth from falsehood, however, Hemingway does not confuse the torero with a woman, the uniting of the two figures with the sexual act, or the thrust of the blade with the thrust of anything else."[10]

The only references to the bulls' sexual virility in *Death in the Afternoon* are in answer to the old lady's question about their "love life," to which the author replies that it is "tremendous. . . . The little calves are born in the winter months." Bulls turned loose with cows may fight them or have nothing to do with them, but if the bull services too many, he will eventually weaken and become impotent. Bulls "destined for the ring are never let run with the cows at all" (120–21).

Jack Conrad's study of bullfighting makes the case that the bull, who no longer serves his original function as a fertility symbol, in modern times works as the embodiment of power to a proud people who are coerced by church, state, and their own authoritarian fathers. The modern Spaniard may enjoy killing bulls because of his resentment of authority.[11] Hemingway clearly takes the bull for his power, but without the resentment—with an empathy, in fact, that the Spaniard does not share.

The bullfight turned to fiction injects passion into the war-torn continent of *The Sun Also Rises* (1929). " 'Nobody ever lives their life all the way except bull-fighters.' "[12] Pedro Romero is that fully alive man—not in the company of his lover Brett Ashley but in contest with the bull, where he holds his "purity of line through the maximum of exposure" (168). As Jake observes, Romero "loved the bulls" (216); he tells Brett they are his " 'best friends.' " " 'You kill your friends?' " she comes back bitterly. " 'Always, . . . so they don't kill me' " (186). And in that death is the perfect intimacy: for an instant, "he and the bull were one" (218).

For Whom the Bell Tolls (1940) is threaded with images of the bullfight, which is held as a standard of glory, despite the novel's premise of brotherly love. Even a man's failures in the bull ring give him a special status. One weary fighter finds strength in the memory of killing a bull as a youth. All year he waited for that time when the bull would come into the town square, attacking with that "head-lowering, horn-reaching, quick cat-gallop that stopped your heart dead when it started." The youth had pulled such a bull away from a fallen man, had bit the bull's ear, and had plunged the knife into his neck until he was dead. The boy was then "as proud as a man could be."[13]

Perhaps the most moving account of any bull is the closeup in "The Undefeated" (1929)—a battler as valiant as the aging matador, Manuel. We feel the bull skid into the wall. From the matador's place we see the chip in one of the horns, the wet muzzle, the light circles about the eyes. From there the "pumping flow of blood" shines "smooth against the black of the bull's shoulder."[14]

The bull looks at Manuel. The matador sees nothing but his opponent, who even on top of him is not hatefully portrayed. He *bumps* Manuel's back, bumps his face in the sand. But only this bull shares the essential struggle. The crowd, and especially the reporters, are merely critics. The bull is the solid reality—hard as bone, so well does he resist the sword that buckles and shoots into the crowd. Manuel hangs to the bull's horn but is thrown clear. When at last the matador finds his mark, the bull goes down stoically, if not elegantly, rolling slowly on his side. Suddenly his four feet are in the air, and his thick tongue is out.

After Spain, Africa offered the contest with wild animals. There Hemingway said he was "altogether happy." It was the place "to really live. Not just let my life pass."[15] The experiment to see if a nonfictional book about the country and the animals of Tanganyika could compete with a work of the imagination does not dramatize the hunt as the fiction does. But it offers finely detailed animals and a sharpening of Hemingway's views about them.

Organized by quarry, *Green Hills of Africa* (1935) moves through the obscene to the noble, as the native gunbearer M'Cola classifies them. The mark of the rhino, fatally flawed by poor eyesight, is his trail of dung, the baboons their bloody tracks. Most obscene is the hermaphroditic hyena, "stinking, foul, with jaws that crack the bones that the lion leaves" (38). In addition to the filth of natural functions are the unsightly heads of animals left by the hunter. Although decapitation may not violate the rules of the hunt, it is aesthetically impure, whereas the straight shot leaves the animal intact. Rising on the scale are the noble lion, leopard, water buffalo, and the exquisitely clean kudu bull.

The obscene animals are comical to the African, but that humor does not take with Hemingway. M'Cola jokes as he shoots at a flock of guineas, and another hunter laughs a "bird-shooting laugh" while he cuts off the birds' heads. The African hunters find the hyena the most comical of all, a view Hemingway assumes— "highly humorous was the hyena" (37)—but with a lack of comic spirit. No animal is taken lightly. Even the rabbit, the least disciplined of creatures, "zig-zagging wildly," is attributed with that universal suffering—fear. "I held him and could feel the thumping of his heart through the soft, warm, furry body" (220). The hyena eating his own entrails is horribly exposed, not funny as he is said to be, circling madly, "snapping and tearing at himself." He too senses—races against—"the little nickelled death inside him" (37).

But if Hemingway does not share a lighthearted view of animals, the cultivated Kandisky cannot comprehend why any man would shoot a kudu. At the book's end Hemingway answers: "I did not mind killing anything, any animal, if I killed it cleanly, they all had to die . . ." (272). And it is the swiftly executed death of the kudu, noted for his cleanliness, that climaxes the ten-day hunt (not that of the traditional king, the lion, who goes down anticlimactically near its beginning).

Throughout most of the book the kudu is kept at a distance, topping the horizon with his marvelous horns. The "heart-shaped, fresh tracks" lead to the clearing where he stands, "heavy-necked, gray, and handsome, the horns spiralled against the sun" (5). The clean-edged, indestructible weapons are a perfect form. It is as much the quest for such form as the contest of the hunt that defines "Pursuit as Happiness," the final chapter of *Green Hills of Africa*. Here the kudu at close range, perfected in death, is even lovelier than he was at a distance:

> It was a huge, beautiful kudu bull, stone-dead, on his side, his horns in great dark spirals, widespread, and unbelievable as he lay dead five yards from where we stood when I had just that instant shot. I looked at him, big, long-legged, a smooth gray with the white stripes and the great, curling, sweeping horns, brown as walnut meats, and ivory pointed, at the big ears and the great, lovely heavy-maned neck the white chevron between his eyes and the white of his muzzle and I stooped over and touched him to try to believe it. He was lying on the side where the bullet had gone in and there was not a mark on him and he smelled sweet and lovely like the breath of cattle and the odor of thyme after rain. (231)

"The Snows of Kilimanjaro" (1936), the African experience turned to fiction, also contrasts the obscene and the noble animal. A hyena and "huge, filthy" buzzards with "their naked heads sunk in the hunched feathers"[16] reflect the impure state of the unfulfilled author dying of gangrene. In contrast to these tainted beings is the leopard preserved at the top of Mount Kilimanjaro, one who aspired to the heights and whose integrity is literally intact, in epigraph, from the diseased breath of the story. Interpretations of this reference range from Alfred Engstrom's allusion to Dante's leopard, the symbol of worldly pleasure and lechery,[17] to Oliver Evans's view of life-in-death.[18] The latter interpretation is easily the more persuasive when one considers Hemingway's approach to animals generally: those who die nobly remain intact.

The hunt climaxes in the breathtaking "Short Happy Life of Francis Macomber" (1936). The irony of its title lies not in a false sense of happiness—for Macomber's growth into courage is one of the most exhilarating episodes in all Hemingway—but in its source: joy comes not through the ease of the affluent or marriage to a beautiful woman, which only tears a man down, but in bravery against the wild animal.

The king of beasts gets full play here: "the lion looked huge, silhouetted on the rise of the bank in the gray morning light, his shoulders heavy, his barrel of a body bulking smoothly." The intrusion into his consciousness, if not altogether credible, intends to convey sympathetically what it feels like for a lion to be shot. "He felt the blow as it hit his lower ribs and ripped on through, blood sudden hot and frothy in his mouth."[19] The following scene projects hostility in the wounded lion whose eyes are "narrowed with hate" (19), a breakdown of detachment which too obviously reflects the other contest in this richly dramatic tale—the battle of the Macombers.

But if this is not Hemingway's most disciplined portrait of an animal, neither is it a careless lapse. A critical aspect of Macomber's education is for him to learn that the animal feels. The rendering of the lion's consciousness is specifically the author's, not Macomber's: he had "not thought how the lion felt as he got out of the car" (15). If an exaggerated projection of the lion's sensations lacks viability, it does insist on the hunter's sensitivity to the animal's experience. Only then does the rule against abandoning the wounded prey become meaningful. The job must be finished not only because the beast is dangerous but to relieve his suffering. An ethical and an aesthetic code demand that he be granted a swift and dignified death.

Played against Macomber is his wife Margot, the classic American "bitch" as designated by the British guide Wilson. As her husband develops courage, and consequently independence, her hostility deepens. But it is not altogether the loss of power that makes a monster of her. Margot Macomber is never a participant of the hunt, which is *the* means of ennoblement and in this case of happiness itself. Relegated to the position of voyeur, she sees all too well the effects of courage and is understandably envious. Margot too takes aim, but her only shot makes a murderer of her.

A vital contact with animals is dramatized only with men in Hemingway's fiction. The few occasions where women make the connection reveal rather a neurotic dependence on the less spectacular creatures—nothing resembling the hunter's ennobling reliance on his prey. The American wife of "Cat in the Rain" (1925), wishing her husband's attention, seeks solace in a kitten left out in a storm. But for her affection she makes an imbecilic apology: " 'I don't know why I wanted it so much. I wanted that poor kitty. It isn't any fun to be a poor kitty out in the rain.' "[20] Hemingway personally liked cats and had a special house built for the fifty-two he kept at Finca Vigia near Havana.[21] But they do not fit the combative, heroic scheme of his fiction.

"A Canary for One" (1927) features another unnamed American woman, whose own lack of a center is evidenced by an obsession with a caged bird she cannot even appreciate. He "sings very beautifully," but she is deaf; and she keeps a cloth over the cage. Apparently to mimic her, the bird is awkwardly self-oriented rather than self-contained, as Hemingway's other animals are: the canary "dropped his bill and pecked into his feathers."[22] The confinement of the bird is paralleled with the woman's attempt to capture an American husband for her daughter. To make up for driving her daughter's foreign suitor away, the mother offers her the canary. This too obvious manipulation of the animal to illuminate the female character lacks Hemingway's usual discipline as well as his customary vividness with animals.

A somewhat sentimentalized treatment is given the horses in "My Old Man" (1923). Reminiscent of Sherwood Anderson's "I Want To Know Why" (which Hemingway never read), it is the story of young Joe Butler's introduction to human corruptibility, played against the integrity of the racehorse. The jockey's failure of ethics is predictable. But a sharper sense of wrong comes with injustice to the horses. The grace of Kzar, who moves quietly and carefully, is violated by the jockey who holds him back. The crowd senses where the wrong lies: " 'Poor Kzar! Poor Kzar.' "[23]

A second horse, Gilford, is as smoothly elegant in the steeplechase, but the jockey, again the boy's father, is paid to keep him back. There's a pileup, Butler dies, and Gilford is shot. The jockey's practice, in dramatic contrast with the effort of the valiant horse, is exposed to his son. "I couldn't help feeling that if my old man was dead maybe they didn't need to have shot Gilford" (204), the boy observes. But in the familiar, fatal framework the animal is killed. "My Old Man" is, once again, the case of competition between man and animal, as even a jockey fights his horse, and of the death of the heroic animal.

The horse is again the object of love—and of death—in *For Whom the Bell Tolls*. As Robert Lewis points out, "horses are at once the wealth of and the source of danger" to the community, appearing throughout the novel.[24] For the horse-thieving Pablo, horses are the pleasure of his life. The sadness of Anselmo's old age is that he is without them. They also bring the enemy. As heroic death is the guerrilla fighter's highest fate, the horse too dies nobly—an individualized death inflicted by man. Wounded and splattering his bright blood on the snow, El Sordo's horse makes it to the top of the crest. There El Sordo shoots him "quickly, expertly, and tenderly" (307), letting him fall to plug a gap between two rocks.

Lewis sees this incident as a sacrifice symbolic of the act of creation.[25] This insight, in part, applies to Hemingway's animals generally: killing them is life-giving for bullfighter, hunter, and fisherman (as it was for Hemingway). But, overwhelmingly, the spirit of the kill is *proud,* not sacrificial. The supreme act of creation held out in *For Whom the Bell Tolls* is not the necessary execution of a horse but the exuberant triumph of the bullfighter.

The animal most perfectly suited for the Hemingway contest is the fish. The subterranean influence, the taut fishing line between competitors, and the clean compact form retained in death are finely attuned to the man and the artist. Malcolm Cowley compares Hemingway's work to a deep cool brook which on second reading reveals "shadows in the pool that you hadn't noticed before"[26] (shadows which in the literal case are fish). Hemingway's advice to the writer also turns on fishing, not only as analogy but as subject matter. If you get excited by something such as a fish on the line, he says, try to remember exactly what you saw that produced the emotion, "whether it was the rising of the line from the water and the way it tightened like a fiddle string until drops started from it" or the way the fish "smashed and threw water when he jumped."[27]

Fishing was "certainly the best thing in the world"—from Hemingway's third birthday when he caught the biggest fish.[28] But far from the soothing pastime it is for some anglers, for him it is always a competitive, strenuous endeavor. His fishermen seek peace of mind, but that comes only after struggle, if at all. According to Cowley, the fishing trip in Hemingway's fiction works as "an incantation, a spell to banish evil spirits."[29] Leslie Fiedler likens it to a prayer.[30] In any case, it is an ordering in each of its stages: catching and killing the fish, cleaning them, and lining them up with their heads pointing the same way.

The fishing expedition in *The Sun Also Rises* is neither a conventional pastoral retreat nor a companionable escape for men. It characteristically involves a therapeutic violence, a poisonous competition, and a pleasure in the fish. The usually gentle Jake Barnes brings a trout up "fighting and bending the rod almost double, out of the boiling water at the foot of the falls"; then he "banged his head against the timber so that he quivered out straight" (119). Jake catches an even six. They are firm and hard from the cold water—complete. The only thing to mar his pleasure is learning a companion's fish are bigger than his. Jake's satisfaction comes in his solitude, as he packs his trout neatly between layers of fern.

Nick Adams similarly orders his scarred life. The fishing trip, in fact, is a considerable link in the seemingly unrelated tales about him. At different ages, at home or overseas, he turns to fishing for the same steadying effect. Nick resembles his father, who was as sound on hunting as he was "unsound on sex, for instance, and Nick was glad it had been that way."[31] Not only does fishing allow a control not possible with a woman, but it is the source of something even rarer—a satisfaction that endures. "The End of Something" (1925) shows the death of one romance so definitively as to suggest the inevitable decline of any love affair. Majorie's presence on the fishing trip, a contaminant of the pure sport (which must be undertaken alone), is generalized to be a thoroughly debilitating effect on Nick. He appears incapable of human love, but he is ever alive to fishing. Looking away from the girl, Nick concentrates on a trout feeding at the bottom of the stream, "taking line out of the reel in a rush and making the reel sing with the click on."[32]

In "Now I Lay Me" (1927) the memory of fishing comforts the insomniac soldier Nick, who rehearses the process in the form of a nightly prayer, with considerable detail given to the killing of the bait. Another ordering image is the memory of snakes and other specimens his father had preserved in alcohol. Nick is finally relaxed by the sound of silk-worms that were "not frightened by any noise we made and ate on steadily." Just when Nick has calmed himself, a fellow soldier breaks the peace by telling him he ought to get married. That thought "killed off trout-fishing and interfered with my prayers. Finally, though, I went back to trout-fishing, because I found that I could remember all the streams and there was always something new about them." The girls of his memory all blurred and became the same.[33]

The superb employment of fishing in "Big Two-Hearted River" (1925) renders the disturbed psyche of the protagonist and speaks as well for the fearful sensations of fish. "Nick looked down into the clear, brown water, colored from the pebbly bottom, and watched the trout keeping themselves steady in the current with wavering fins."[34] The burned-over country, by contrast, is not only the more obvious symbolic representation of the ravages of war—or whatever else has occurred in Nick's past—but it is inaccurate as a metaphor for Nick. He is not wasted like the landscape but unnervingly sensitive. His mechanical motions, like the more violent ones, are an attempt at steadiness—the most sought-after quality in man and animal. Like Nick, the trout maintains a precarious suspension. Neither relaxed nor buoyed by his element, he is frighteningly submerged, tightening as he faces the current.

The blackened grasshoppers also maintain a perilous position. The crusty insects have resisted fire, and they stay stiff when they land, "as though they were dead" (222); Nick must crush many of them for bait. Holding one so that his feet wave in the air, Nick threads him with the slim hook "under his chin, down through his thorax and into the last segments of his abdomen" (224). With the apparent detachment of the entomologist, Nick is anything but the dispassionate man. He knows the panic in those waving legs. And the only resolution is death. In putting a match to a mosquito, he produces a "satisfactory hiss in the flame" (218).

Tension is eased as the trout take the life-and-death leap for insects that bares them to the alien element and to the fisherman. Nick returns the first small fish, holding on for a last "smooth, cool underwater feeling." Out of water, too, the fish is held with special care: the hand must be wet so as not to "disturb the delicate mucus that covered him. If a trout is touched with a dry hand, a white fungus attacks the unprotected spot." Those who break the rule destroy the clean form, leaving the fish "furry with white fungus, drifted against a rock, or floating belly up in some pool" (225). Properly cared for, the dead fish are perfect. Nick whacks a trout against a log and breaks the necks of the other fish the same way, arranging them side by side. "They were fine trout" (231).

The mighty inhabitants of the Gulf Stream offer the spectacular contest—as demanding as a ten-round fight. *Islands in the Stream* (1970) shows even an intensely creative life on land to be slow compared to the encounter with a single fish. Sea urchins on the sand tempt one toward the waves, and in the light green water the dark shapes lure a man out. The drama of Thomas Hudson's reunion with his three sons revolves on the struggle with the big fish. The boys go for a swim, and the fin of a huge hammerhead cuts the horizon. But even in his paternal horror Hudson sees this enemy with an admiring eye. "The biggest hammerhead he had ever seen rose white-bellied out of the sea and began to plane over the water crazily, on his back, throwing water like an aquaplane." And a mate's remark, " 'Thank God they show on the surface when they hook up,' "[35] echoes not only relief but gratitude.

David Hudson's life is more dear for the threat to it, and he is prepared for the other fish of his destiny, a swordfish that breaks open the sea, "rising, shining dark blue and silver, seeming to come endlessly out of the water, unbelievable as his length and bulk rose out of the sea into the air" (115). As if fashioned by nature for the author's own purposes, the fish comes with sword—a sword as long as the boy. "If David catches this fish," Hudson thinks, "he'll have something inside him for all his life and it will make everything else easier" (124).

But at the last moment of the hoist the big blue fish slips off the line and shrinks into the sea. Even so, in his back-bending struggle with this opponent, the boy develops that affection so suspect when it applies to people—and so generously acknowledged in the case of animals: in contest with the swordfish, David "began to love him more than anything on earth.' "

> "If you'd have caught him," Andrew [his brother] said, "you'd have been probably the most famous young boy in the world."
>
> . . .
>
> "What about the fish? Wouldn't he be famous?" David asked. . . .
> "He'd be the most famous of all," Andrew said. "He'd be immortal." (133–34)

And so is the supreme fish, the marlin of *The Old Man and the Sea* (1952). He is big, he is beautiful, and he is *steady*. Here is the classic solitary male, whose masculinity is no more "tested by erotic love"[36] than is Santiago's. The marlin's character rests in an independent and stoic will. He takes the bait "like a male and he pulls like a male and his fight has no panic in it." (A female marlin Santiago once caught put up a "wild, panic-stricken, despairing fight that soon exhausted her."[37]) In transforming the account of the fisherman who returned hysterical with his spare carcass that was the source of Hemingway's tale, he gives his fisherman grace under pressure. The marlin too is disciplined, just as the novel, with the concentration of a short story but the space for a 1,500-pound fish, holds its classically tight line.

Discussions of the biblical allusions in *The Old Man and the Sea* turn on the likeness of Santiago (Spanish for Saint James) to the New Testament fisherman apostle or even to Christ.[38] Joseph Waldmeir maintains, to the contrary, that the religious references provide a framework for a religion of man.[39] But while Waldmeir's case is the stronger, even his persuasion is misleading. Man is not the focus of Santiago's regard. "Never have I seen a greater, or more beautiful, or a calmer or more noble thing than you" (102), he says of the *marlin*. Fondness for the boy is peripheral. And the boy's affection was inspired by fishing: "The old man had taught the boy to fish and the boy loved him" (10). Santiago's real life is in his violent contest with the creatures of the sea.

A parallel drawn between Coleridge's ancient mariner and Santiago only heightens the fundamental distinction between a Christian, nonviolent concern for one's fellow beings—which extends to animals—and a combative one. The comparison also reveals a totally unlike approach to the animals themselves. Baker maintains that the mariners develop a similar compassion and that the killing of the albatross and the marlin are in "no way comparable," as one is wanton and the other "professional and necessary."[40] But if fishing for Santiago were only a trade—and he says he killed the fish for pride, not need—in Baker's distinction is the very point that sets the cases apart: shooting the albatross *is* a sin, and the dead bird the odious reminder of sin. Although Santiago doubts the morality of his killing the fish, that act is nonetheless the triumph of the man's life. And the marlin is a beautiful trophy.

The great size of the marlin is a tangible measure of Santiago's skill, even in the remains that are of no material value. The long white spine measures "eighteen feet from nose to tail" (135). Size, however, has less to do with length than with weight, which in the case of fish is translated to gravitational pull. The drama of fishing, set off with the gentlest pressure on the hand, may hint of the spectacular in the plain phrase: the old man feels "something hard and unbelievably heavy" (47) on his line. From the first tentative tug he is able to determine that "one hundred fathoms down a marlin was eating the sardines" (45). Weight also translates to depth, as the line uncoils downward. Contrarily, a bird is pitiably light, separated from the earth, moving "wildly and ineffectually" (37). The flight of a fish exhilarates no more in his release from the sea than in the gravitational plunge back into it. With the hairbreadth suggestion of suicide, fish head down, at the same time defying the myth that they will die if they go too deep.

At last the marlin makes his hero's entrance out of that sea:

> The line rose slowly and steadily and then the surface of the ocean bulged ahead of the boat and the fish came out. He came out unendingly and water poured from his sides. He was bright in the sun and his head and back were dark purple and in the sun the stripes on his sides showed wide and a light lavender.

His sword was as long as a baseball bat and tapered like a rapier
and he rose his full length from the water and then re-entered
it, smoothly, like a diver and the old man saw the great scythe-
blade of his tail go under and the line commenced to race out.
(69)

The chiseled line climaxing with weaponry, the mighty balancing tail, and the clean dive proclaim this warrior the king. He
climaxes a book of color. Out of a wealth of blue, reflecting the
red sifting plankton, where weeds are phosphorescent yellow, fish
turn in the light to give off the rainbow. The golden dolphin becomes green; silver tuna show blue and gold when they are reeled
in. The marlin comes in the royal hue, from the purple crown to
the stripes of lavender that the fastest fish wear, stripes that do not
fade in death.

Man would be equal to this splendid fish. Pulling at his end of
the line, Santiago is balanced against the marlin in contest. They
share the same punishment of hunger and of the unknown. The
fish pulls the boat, then the boat pulls the fish. When Santiago
brings the marlin alongside his craft, at last, they sail together,
"lashed side by side" (109). And when the shark strikes, the man
feels "as though he himself were hit" (113).

Even so, to Santiago the fish is superior. "Man is not much
beside the great birds and beasts" (75). The marlin may not be
intelligent enough to know his own strength, but mind is not ranked
first: the marlin is "more noble and more able" (70) than the fisherman. "I wish I was the fish," Santiago thinks, "with everything
he has against only my will and my intelligence" (71). No one is
worthy to eat this fish because of his great dignity. Santiago's
allegiance is to him. "I'll stay with you until I am dead" (58). "Fish
. . . I love you and respect you very much" (60).

The first great irony of *The Old Man and the Sea* is that although the man calls the fish "brother," he "must kill him" (65).
How far Santiago is from the apostle James in this. His fish are little
more than metaphors, while the modern man recognizes feeling in
his prey. Santiago weighs his own pain against "the fish's agony"
(103), which is not fully justified in the fisherman's trade. A special
affection only complicates the problem: "If you love him, it is not

a sin to kill him. Or is it more?" (116). A prayer to the Virgin for the "death of this fish. Wonderful though he is" (72) further intensifies the irony. Peace of mind comes not in the resolution of the dilemma but in spite of it: Santiago accepts his inexplicable satisfaction in killing what he loves. He reconciles his part in the contest with the thought that the fish could win. "I do not care who kills who" (102).

If the marlin must die, he is never more magnificent than in his death, which not only sharpens the paradoxical thrust of the tale but reflects on the role of Hemingway's other animals. The "fish came alive, with his death in him, and rose high out of the water showing all his great length and width and all his power and his beauty" (104). Only now may he be fully viewed, measured, touched. The stripes are "wider than a man's hand" (106–7). "The old man looked at the fish constantly to make sure it was true" (110).

To be chewed away by sharks is the violation to the marlin, not his death. Only at this point, not when he dies, does Santiago find he can no longer talk to the fish because he had been "ruined too badly" (127). But the awful irony of his destruction yields to paradox for the marlin as well as for the man. In spite of defeat, indeed because of it, a new level of integrity is attained. Santiago is never nobler than in his loss. And the marlin, although apparently destroyed, as a skeleton is whole.

In form—the direct charge of the bull, a cleaned trout, the backbone of a marlin—Hemingway found his truth. And through death the respected and loved animal is preserved. To further understand why the beloved prey must die, we need to look as well to the heroic ideal that once made it an honor to meet death boldly. Only then does it become clear just what measure of immortality Hemingway bestows on his excellent creatures—and the dramatic part they play in their destiny.

Notes

1. Ernest Hemingway, *Green Hills of Africa* (New York: Charles Scribner's Sons, 1935), p. 73.

2. Ernest Hemingway, *Death in the Afternoon* (New York: Charles Scribner's Sons, 1932), p. 159. Subsequent references to this edition will appear in the text.

3. Quoted in Scott Donaldson, *By Force of Will: The Life and Art of Ernest Hemingway* (New York: Viking Press, 1977), p. 77.

4. A. E. Hotchner, *Papa Hemingway: A Personal Memoir* (New York: Random House, 1966), p. 139.

5. Malcolm Cowley, "Nightmare and Ritual in Hemingway," Introduction to *The Portable Hemingway,* in *Hemingway: A Collection of Critical Essays,* ed. Robert P. Weeks (Englewood Cliffs, N.J.: Prentice-Hall, 1962), p. 41.

6. Philip Young, *Ernest Hemingway: A Reconsideration* (New York: Harcourt, Brace & World, 1966), p. 166.

7. Hotchner, p. 8.

8. Harry Levin, "Observations on the Style of Ernest Hemingway," *Hemingway: A Collection of Critical Essays,* p. 80.

9. Quoted in Carlos Baker, *Hemingway: The Writer as Artist* (Princeton, N.J.: Princeton University Press, 1963), p. 152.

10. Ibid.

11. Jack Randolph Conrad, *The Horn and the Sword: The History of the Bull as Symbol of Power and Fertility* (London: Macgibbon & Kee, 1959), p. 185.

12. Ernest Hemingway, *The Sun Also Rises* (New York: Charles Scribner's Sons, 1926), p. 10. Subsequent references to this edition will appear in the text.

13. Ernest Hemingway, *For Whom the Bell Tolls* (New York: Charles Scribner's Sons, 1940), pp. 364–65. Subsequent references to this edition will appear in the text.

14. Ernest Hemingway, "The Undefeated," *The Short Stories of Ernest Hemingway* (New York: Charles Scribner's Sons, 1953), p. 251.

15. *Green Hills of Africa,* pp. 6, 285. Subsequent references to this edition will appear in the text.

16. Ernest Hemingway, "The Snows of Kilimanjaro," *Short Stories of Ernest Hemingway,* p. 53.

17. Alfred Engstrom, "Dante, Flaubert, and 'The Snows of Kilimanjaro,' " *Modern Language Notes,* 65 (1950), 203–5.

18. Oliver Evans, " 'The Snows of Kilimanjaro': A Revaluation," *PMLA*, 76 (Dec., 1961), 602–7.

19. Ernest Hemingway, "The Short Happy Life of Francis Macomber," *Short Stories of Ernest Hemingway*, pp. 14–15. Subsequent references to this edition of "The Short Happy Life . . ." will appear in the text.

20. Ernest Hemingway, "Cat in the Rain," *Short Stories of Ernest Hemingway*, p. 169.

21. Lillian Ross, *Portrait of Hemingway* (New York: Simon and Schuster, 1961), p. 23.

22. Ernest Hemingway, "A Canary for One," *Short Stories of Ernest Hemingway*, pp. 337, 339.

23. Ernest Hemingway, "My Old Man," *Short Stories of Ernest Hemingway*, p. 200. Subsequent references to this edition of "My Old Man" will appear in the text.

24. Robert W. Lewis, Jr., *Hemingway on Love* (Austin and London: University of Texas Press, 1965), p. 161.

25. Ibid., p. 165.

26. Cowley, p. 40.

27. Ernest Hemingway, "Monologue to the Maestro: A High Seas Letter," to *Esquire*, Oct., 1935, in *By-Line: Ernest Hemingway*, ed. William White (New York: Bantam Books, 1968), p. 190.

28. Donaldson, pp. 69, 72.

29. Cowley, p. 48.

30. Leslie Fiedler, *Love and Death in the American Novel* (New York: Dell, 1966), p. 356.

31. Ernest Hemingway, "Fathers and Sons," *Short Stories of Ernest Hemingway*, p. 490.

32. Ernest Hemingway, "The End of Something," *Short Stories of Ernest Hemingway*, p. 109.

33. Ernest Hemingway, "Now I Lay Me," *Short Stories of Ernest Hemingway*, pp. 367, 371.

34. Ernest Hemingway, "Big Two-Hearted River Part I" and "Big Two-Hearted River Part II," *Short Stories of Ernest Hemingway*, p. 209. Subsequent references to this edition of these stories will appear in the text.

35. Ernest Hemingway, *Islands in the Stream* (New York: Ban-

tam Books, 1978), p. 81. Subsequent references to this edition will appear in the text.

36. Bickford Sylvester, "Hemingway's Extended Vision: *The Old Man and the Sea*" (Dissertation, University of Washington, 1966), p. 83.

37. Ernest Hemingway, *The Old Man and the Sea* (New York: Charles Scribner's Sons, 1952), p. 54. Subsequent references to this edition will appear in the text.

38. See Melvin Backman, "Hemingway: The Matador and the Crucified," *Hemingway and His Critics: An International Anthology,* ed. Carlos Baker (New York: Hill and Wang, 1961); Clinton S. Burhans, Jr., "*The Old Man and the Sea:* Hemingway's Tragic Vision of Man," *American Literature,* 31 (Jan., 1960); and Carlos Baker, "Hemingway's Ancient Mariner," *Hemingway: The Writer As Artist.*

39. Joseph Waldmeir, "*Confiteor Hominem:* Ernest Hemingway's Religion of Man," *Papers of the Michigan Academy of Science, Arts, and Letters,* vol. 42 (Ann Arbor, Mich.: University of Michigan Press, 1957).

40. Baker, p. 82.

Conclusion

A tantalizing view is at play in American literature that animals are better than people. Herman Melville mourns the displacement of human grandeur—but he also triumphs with his whale. Emily Dickinson and Marianne Moore breathe most easily with their out-door acquaintances. And Mark Twain declares man to be the lower animal. Jack London's strongest characters are dogs; William Faulk-ner's ponies prevail; and Ernest Hemingway's purest hero is a fish.

Even obvious limitations are seen as advantages. Without lan-guage, animals do not tease or prevaricate or bore. Without ego, they bear no pride. And without conscience, they escape the Puri-tan curse. As literary subjects, wild animals, in particular, fall to the genres (with the exception of the atypical *Moby-Dick*) appropri-ate for the brief appearance: the lyric poem, the short story or novella, or the episode within a novel. But rather than being set apart from the literary mainstream in this, they enter our premier forms. Without supernatural powers, animals stir a reverence in the otherworldly and profane author alike. They are not valued pri-marily as the handiwork of God, although He may be acknowl-edged, or as the mystic embodiment of the spirits. Instead, they count mightily for themselves.

The desire to capture moves artist and hunter alike. Still, the hunt does not predominate quite as one might expect in a national literature inspired by the frontier. Hunting and fishing take place only with moral reservations. America's first literary hero is a deer-slayer—but even he is uneasy defending what is his vocation. "They can't accuse me of killing an animal when there is no occasion for the meat or the skin. I may be a slayer, it's true, but I'm no slaugh-terer."[1] Melville makes one chase so perverse it calls into question the validity of all others. The satirist contrarily mocks the hunter into oblivion. The protagonists of the Far North do not hunt, and Steinbeck's people are rather biologists and farmers. An ethical confusion constrains Faulkner's version of the kill, while Wright shows the terror of the hunted. Only Hemingway goes all the way with the hunt, and even he finds it morally indefensible.

The abundance of our literary inheritance is in the free, willful, and often joy-inspiring animal. Moby Dick lives, and who but a twisted soul would have it otherwise? A poet abandons her subject death for a singing bird. A growling traveler abroad can be brought to smile whenever he sees a stray dog (which is, by the way, *god* spelled backward). Buck's buoyant determination is never matched by the human hero, and a rare peace of mind is found in a spare desert rat. The happiest a boy—or a man—can be is to own an untameable horse, or to contest a mighty fish.

The passion for liberty that may be played out with animals is a freedom from the obligations of human connections. As with the human protagonist in American literature, mating is a liability. But unlike man, the animal on his own is not alienated or lonely or aimless. Motion is direct, purposeful. A bird migrates—he doesn't waste time in the air. A pony goes express, while a dog leads his pack to a single goal, food. Upturned off his path, a solitary turtle flips back and keeps to Route 66, and a good fighting bull goes as straight as though he were on rails. By the same rule, a rat's lack of direction terrifies, and frenzied horses comically disrupt a town.

Free of otherworldly concerns, most of these animals adhere to this world. A bird comes home to the ground, and a turtle hugs it like a lid. Coyote and cat are enhanced by the grey dust of the West. An elephant sleeps peacefully in the dirt that becomes part of his hide. Buck's unobtrusive coat, and White Fang's too, are made to match the ground. A swordfish, rising as blue as the sea, dives gloriously back to it. Only the fearful blacks—a rat, a snake—preclude light and find no home.

Theirs is not a conventional but a shocking beauty. Exotic shades complete the spectrum of the earth's, not heaven's, hues—the hummingbird's blood-red spot at the throat, the gold belt of the bee. To the south a basilisk sets a limb alive with his green-blue flame, and a marlin in purple explodes from the sea. Trout glitter with their own rainbow. And a single whale holds all the hues—a white tainted by way of metaphor, divinely pearl-like in life.

The shape is whole. The biggest animal on earth is smooth, the organs kept inside. A bird's suit fits without a seam, and a bee is round with honey. A pangolin rolls himself into a ball, tough as asphalt. And a fish stripped of his flesh is still intact.

Never have so many animals played such roles. They give American literature a cast like no other on earth, born as they are of regard and love.

Note

1. James Fenimore Cooper, *The Deerslayer* (New York: Collier Books, 1962), p. 54.

Index

A Note on the Author

Mary Allen was born and received her early education in Provo, Utah, and earned a Ph.D. from the University of Maryland in 1973. She has taught at Brigham Young and Howard universities and is presently a lecturer at Northern Virginia Community College and George Mason University. She has published several articles on American writers, as well as a book on women in major American fiction of the 1960s, *The Necessary Blankness* (University of Illinois Press, 1976).